MISSISSIPPI
Its People and Culture

MISSISSIPPI
Its People and Culture

by

David G. Sansing

University of Mississippi

General Editor: W. E. Rosenfelt

Publishers

T.S. DENISON & COMPANY, INC.

Minneapolis

T.S. DENISON & COMPANY, INC.

Standard Book Number: 513-01695-3
Printed in the United States of America
Copyright © 1981 by T.S. Denison & Co., Inc.
Minneapolis, Minn.

Introduction

Mississippi may seem quite large, but it is really only a small part of the world we live in. It is one of the fifty states that make up the United States which is located on the continent of North America. The continent of North America is but one of several continents that make up our global world. The portion of the globe called Mississippi is really very small indeed. If all the land area of the world would suddenly disappear, leaving only Mississippi, it would appear as a tiny speck in a vast ocean.

History and You

The United States of America is called a democracy because the people rule themselves. That is what the word democracy means—rule by the people. The process by which the people govern themselves is called a federal system. That means the power to rule is divided between the federal government located in Washington, D.C., and the state governments located in each of the fifty different capitals. All Americans are citizens both of the United States and of the individual states in which they live. The students reading and studying this history book are both Americans and Mississippians. Your ideals, your traditions, and your cultural heritage have been shaped by the broad sweep of American history. But you have also been greatly influenced by the history of your state and of the locality in which you were born and in which you are growing up. This is especially true for Southerners and Mississippians, perhaps more so than for Americans in general. The great waves of European immigrants who came to the United States in the nineteenth century did not come to the South. Most of those first generation Americans settled in the North and Mid-West. Therefore, Mississippi's customs and traditions were not influenced to any significant degree by the cultural infusion of these ethnic groups.

Also, the industrial and technological developments that gave rise to large cities and transformed America from an agricultural to an urban nation had less impact upon Mississippi than on other parts of the country. Mississippi traditions and customs and even speech patterns remained more constant and over the years Mississippi developed a dislike for change, especially when the pressure to do so came from outside forces. Mississippi was not completely out of the mainstream of American progress. It merely changed less drastically, more slowly, and with less disruption to its traditional values and lifestyles. Both the pace and extent of change in Mississippi have always caused controversy, but especially during the last forty years. Some Mississippians advocated broader changes and are impatient even with what has already come about. Others have opposed or at least have been reluctant to accept most of the changes that have occurred since World War II (1941–1945).

Many Mississippians are proud, even boastful about being a Mississippian. Some are not so proud and may even be ashamed of being a Mississippian. What does it mean to be a Mississippian? Is it really different from being a Nebraskan, a Californian, or even a Tennessean? Is there a composite character that distinguishes Mississippians from other Southerners and other Americans? How about you? Are you proud or ashamed of being a Mississippian? Your answer to this question is basically determined by what you know and understand about your past and the history of your state. It will be interesting for you to record your feelings about being a Mississippian now and then compare those feelings to the way you feel after studying your state's history and development.

The Legacy of History

The normal course of history is something like a Sunday afternoon drive along a winding country road. Most of the ride is usually boring with not very much interesting scenery. Suddenly, a sharp turn is encountered which causes the driver to make a quick turn and the car might jolt or swerve. After making the turn, the driver and the passengers settle back in the routine of the drive until the next curve appears. In studying history, those times of excitement and crisis are much more interesting to both the participants and to students who study

6

those events. But the long routine stretches in-between the times of excitement are just as important to an understanding of our past. So, let us retrace the winding road of history that has brought us to the present.

Dedication

To Elizabeth, David, Beth, and Perry, who sustained me in the long months during which this book came together. With deep affection I dedicate this book to them.

David G. Sansing

Contents

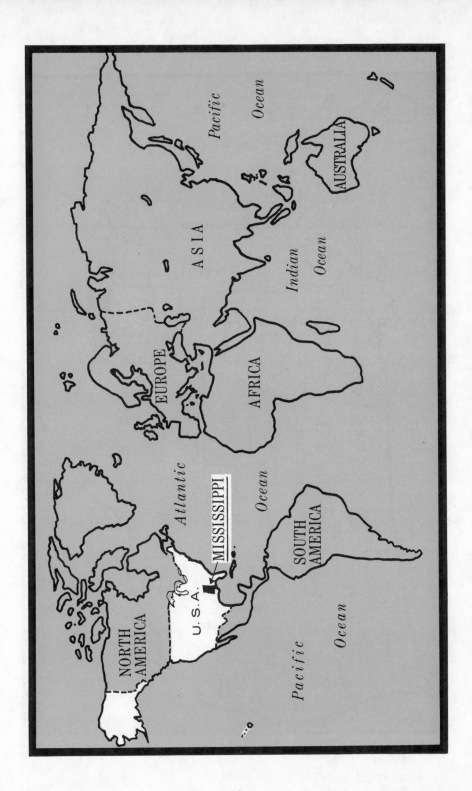

14

CHAPTER I

The Land

A famous Southern historian U. B. Phillips, began his book entitled **Life and Labor in the Old South** by suggesting, "Let us begin by discussing the weather, for that has been the chief agency in making the South distinctive." This historian did not mean to exclude all the other forces that make history. He only wanted to emphasize how important mild temperatures, high rainfall, and fertile soil were in Mississippi's past. From its very beginning Mississippi seemed destined to be an agricultural state. The growing season in Mississippi ranges from 210 days in the northern part to as many as 270 days along the Gulf Coast. An average rainfall of about 57 inches a year and mild temperatures produce nearly ideal conditions for farming. Contrary to what is often believed about Mississippi's "long, hot summers" the average July temperature is only 81°. Winter in Mississippi is also mild with the average temperature being 48°.

Soil Regions

In addition to a very favorable climate, Mississippi has some of the richest and most fertile soil in America. During the early years of statehood, a great land rush brought thousands of settlers from the Atlantic states into Mississippi. These settlers brought with them the customs and traditions of the colonial South, especially those traditions concerning the ownership of land. During the colonial period of American history, land owners enjoyed higher social status and exercised more political power than those who did not own land. In some colonies only land owners could vote or hold public office. Throughout the antebellum period these traditions were very important in Mississippi. The antebellum period of Mississippi history is the period from its establishment as a territory in 1798 to the Civil War in 1861.

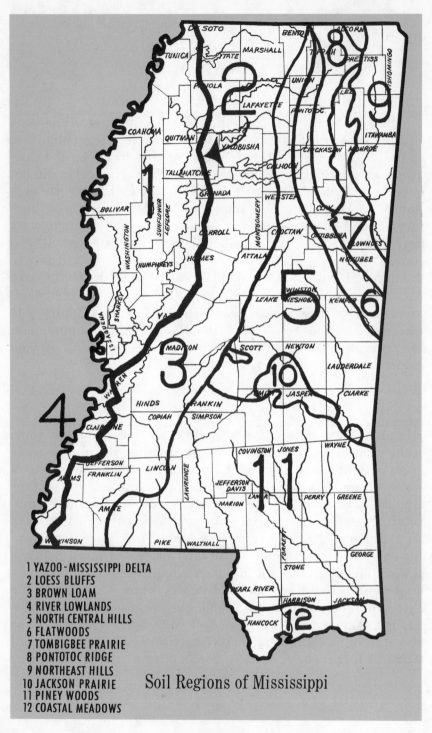

1 YAZOO-MISSISSIPPI DELTA
2 LOESS BLUFFS
3 BROWN LOAM
4 RIVER LOWLANDS
5 NORTH CENTRAL HILLS
6 FLATWOODS
7 TOMBIGBEE PRAIRIE
8 PONTOTOC RIDGE
9 NORTHEAST HILLS
10 JACKSON PRAIRIE
11 PINEY WOODS
12 COASTAL MEADOWS

Soil Regions of Mississippi

Old Jacinto Courthouse in Tishomingo County.

Northeast Hills

In the extreme northeast corner of the state there is a hill section known as the Tennessee Hills or Northeast Hills. The average elevation of these hills is 650 feet above sea level. The highest point is 806 feet. During the antebellum period, farms in this region were located in the bottom lands along creeks and rivers. These hill farmers had more in common with the mountaineers in East Tennessee than they had with most other Mississippians. They were small farmers and very few of them owned any slaves. For example, in Tishomingo County there were only 4,981 slaves in 1860, but there were 24,149 white people. When Mississippi seceded from the Union in 1861, many people in this region opposed secession and some even joined the Union Army.

After the Civil War the phrase "Northeast Hills" was used to describe a political section of the state rather than a soil region.

17

"Northeast Hills" referred to the predominantly white counties in north Mississippi. During the 1880's the small farmers in the hill counties became dissatisfied with the state's political leaders who were mostly from the Delta or the counties along the Mississippi River which had large black majorities. Eventually, the predominantly white counties in the Piney Woods and coastal section joined with north Mississippi to take control of the state government. This takeover is called the "Revolt of the Rednecks" and culminated with the election of Governor James K. Vardaman in 1903. The term "redneck" refers to white farmers who usually owned only a few acres and did the plowing and other field work themselves. Exposure to the southern sun for long hours had given these white people a deeply tanned, rustcolored neck which was also rough and leathery. Sometimes they were called leathernecks, but most often "rednecks." James K. Vardaman and later Theodore G. Bilbo were proud to be identified with the small white farmers and often wore red neckties to symbolize their connection with them. The revolt of these small white farmers will be discussed in more detail later. But for now, let us resume the discussion of the various soil regions in Mississippi.

Tombigbee Prairie

To the west of the Northeast Hills is a strip of highly fertile soil 20 to 25 miles wide extending from Alabama into Mississippi up to the Tennessee border. It is called the Tombigbee Prairie and sometimes the Alabama black belt. It is characterized by a gently rolling terrain averaging 200 to 300 feet above sea level with rich, dark soil. Parts of Kemper, Noxubee, Lowndes, Oktibbeha, and Chickasaw Counties lie within the prairie. In the antebellum period there were large plantations in these counties. Many examples of Old South architecture appeared throughout this region, especially in such towns as Columbus, Macon, Aberdeen, and Starkville. Although located in northeast Mississippi, this region had much in common with the Delta and the river counties in the western part of the state. When political campaigns involved social and economic issues, the prairie counties usually voted with the western part of the state.

Pontotoc Ridge

Extending southward from the Tennessee line through Tippah, Union, Pontotoc, Chickasaw, and ending in Clay County, is a land formation called the Pontotoc Ridge. At its highest point, the ridge is approximately 600 feet above sea level. Flanked on the east by the prairie and on the west by the flatwoods, the Pontotoc Ridge can be seen clearly during the fall of the year when foliage has disappeared. The red clay and sandy loam that form the soil along the ridge was fertile during the state's early history. It was along the Pontotoc Ridge that the Chickasaw Indians grew their corn. After this tribe moved to the Indian territory out west, white farmers plowed the same furrows—but where the Indians had planted mostly corn, the whites planted mostly cotton.

After the Civil War, the Pontotoc Ridge lost much of its fertility, and the small farmers were forced to become sharecroppers. They farmed another man's land for a share of the crop instead of fixed wages.

The Flatwoods

To the west of the Pontotoc Ridge is a long narrow strip of land, 6 to 12 miles wide, that extends from the northwestern corner of Tippah County on a southeast line through Kemper County and finally into Alabama. The gray soil of this region, called the Flatwoods, is infertile and because of its poor drainage it is not conducive to cultivation. Although the section can sustain several varieties of upland hardwood, it is considered one of the least productive soil regions in the state.

The North Central Hills

A very large and prominent region, the North Central Hills, lies to the west of the Flatwoods and extends from the Tennessee border southwestward into Rankin County and southeastward into Clarke County. The region includes a variety of soil types. Sands, clays, and loams, varying in color from dark red to light orange, can be found throughout the North Central Hills. This area is sometimes called the sand-clay hills or the red-clay hills.

Because of its elevation, ranging from 400 to 600 feet, this region is also known as the North Central Plateau. Over the years rivers and streams have cut broad and deep gullies through the region because the sandy-loam soil is especially susceptible to erosion. The river bottoms of silt and loam, which may be found throughout the region, are highly fertile and have been the scene of productive farms.

The Petrified Forest near Flora is one of the largest in America.

Jackson Prairie

In the southern part of the North Central Hills is an intermittent soil formation known as the Jackson Prairie. This area, which is similar to the Tombigbee Prairie, extends from Wayne County through Clarke, Jasper, Newton, Scott, Rankin, and Madison Counties. This prairie not only sustains highly productive farms, but also contains quantities of limestone and the type of clay from which cement is produced.

Piney Woods

South of the Jackson Prairie and Central hills is a vast expanse of woodlands called the Piney Woods. This region, also

20

Pulp wood operations in the Piney Woods.

known as the Longleaf Pine Belt, was a spectacular forest of virgin longleaf pine when the white men first came to Mississippi. Although most of the region lies 300 to 800 feet above sea level, the loamy soil in the river bottoms makes profitable agriculture possible. During the territorial period, the small farmers in the Piney Woods developed a strong resentment toward the wealthy merchants and large planters around Natchez. A mounting antagonism between the backwoodsmen in the Piney forest and the urban areas along the Mississippi River led the residents of the Piney Woods to consider seceding from Mississippi on at least two occasions during the territorial period. The reform ideas of President Andrew Jackson (1829–1837) were especially popular in this area, and in the secession crisis of 1861 there was strong opposition. Many residents of the Piney Woods wanted to stay in the Union.

During the antebellum period there was a thriving cattle industry in the Piney Woods and many people in this area farmed only to supplement their herding. While their cattle grazed in the forests, the herdsmen grew small patches of vegetables. It usually appeared to travelers that these vegetable patches were their only means of livelihood. These quaint folk who were observed by many travelers were mistakenly classified as poor whites—idle, lazy, and unproductive. However, this was not a true picture of these people who made their living raising cattle and sheep and who once a year drove their livestock to Mobile or Pascagoula.

Over the years the term "Piney Woods" like the term Northeast Hills was used more often in reference to the social and political customs of a particular section rather than a soil region. After the Civil War, the Piney Woods united with the Northeast Hills in support of "redneck" leaders.

Coastal Meadows

Extending 15 to 20 miles inland from the Gulf Coast is a region called the Coastal Meadows. Although the surface is generally flat, the yellow-gray soil is very sandy and not highly fertile. Throughout most of the nineteenth century this area was sparsely settled. After World War II, however, the Gulf Coast became the state's major tourist attraction and one of the most heavily industrialized sections of the state. The rapid increase in population along the coast also made it one of the most important political divisions in Mississippi during the post-war years. Because of its beautiful beaches and its tourist attractions, the Gulf Coast is called the "Mississippi Riviera."

Shrimpboats along the Mississippi Gulf Coast.

Brown Loam Region

To the west of the North Central Hills and Piney Woods, extending from Tennessee to Louisiana, is a highly fertile soil belt called the Brown Loam Region. The history of this region could serve as a case study of soil abuse. In the antebellum era the Brown Loam Region attracted land-hungry planters in great numbers and was the scene of many large and prosperous plantations. Because of its large slave population, this region was also called the "Black Belt." After the Civil War, the Brown Loam Region suffered from a high concentration of farm tenancy or sharecropping. Years of abuse and misuse depleted the soil and it was badly eroded. However, sound conservation practices and good land management have restored most of the region's productivity and it is again the scene of prosperous agriculture.

Loess Bluffs

Along the western rim of the Brown Loam Region are the Loess Bluffs, or hills, separating the Brown Loam from the flat Delta and river lowlands. These bluffs, formed by prehistoric dust storms sweeping across the flood plain, are 5 to 15 miles wide and extend the length of the state from Tennessee to Louisiana. The loess soil is highly fertile but very susceptible to erosion.

Delta

West of the Loess Bluffs and north of the Walnut Hills at Vicksburg is the Yazoo-Mississippi Delta which includes some of the most fertile soil in the world. The Delta is a wedge of land about 200 miles long and 85 miles wide. The rich, dark, alluvial silt is thirty-five feet deep in some parts of the Delta. Along the small meandering streams, the soil contains some clay, but it can be made productive if worked properly. In the Delta's swampy backwaters where the land drains poorly the soil contains a much greater clay content. This soil is black and sticky and is often referred to as "buckshot" or "Mississippi Mud."

Although there were some plantations located in the Delta before the Civil War, the Delta planters did not achieve the prestige and prominence enjoyed by their counterparts in the Old Natchez District. Before the Civil War the lack of an effective flood control system prevented the Delta from being more heavily populated. Levee construction during the 1870's and 1880's reduced the dangers from annual flooding, and the Delta population grew rapidly. Like the Piney Woods and the Northeast Hills, the term Delta has become more than a geographic term. It also describes a political and socioeconomic region with a lifestyle and culture somewhat different from other sections of Mississippi.

River Lowlands

South of Vicksburg, extending to the Louisiana line along the Mississippi River, is a highly fertile region called the River Lowlands. Like the Delta, the soil in this region is composed largely of silt and loam. From the time of the early French settlements among the Natchez Indians, this area along the Misssissippi was known as the Natchez District. Over the years the terms River Lowlands and Natchez District were used almost interchangeably to describe both the soil region and the geographic area. During the antebellum era the Natchez District was the wealthiest section in the state. The large and highly profitable cotton plantations produced several very wealthy families. It was also in this area that the heaviest concentration of slave population was located. With its gracious mansions and plantation heritage, Natchez has become a symbol of the "Old South."

Timber Resources

Even though this discussion of soil regions has emphasized the importance of agricultural resources, most of Mississippi's land is not used for that purpose. In fact more Mississippi land is devoted to forestry than to agriculture, shopping centers, football fields, houses, pastures, and all other land uses combined. Approximately 17 million acres, or 55.8%, of the state's total land area is in timber.

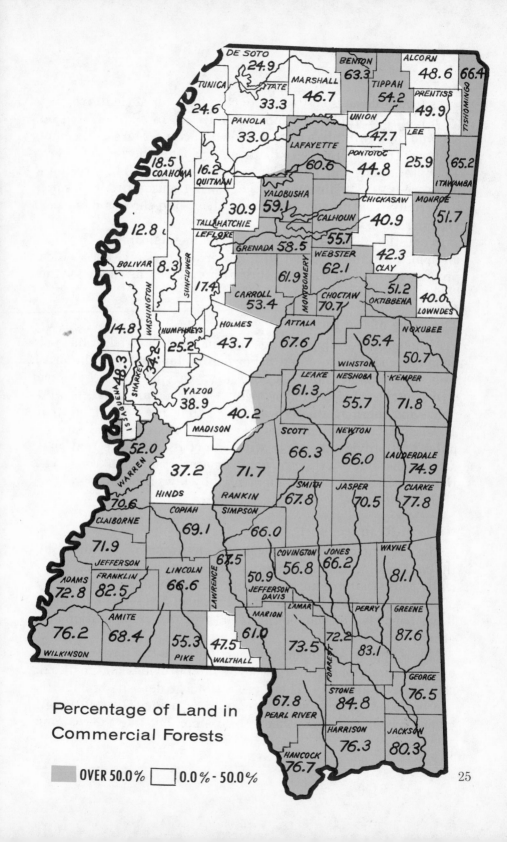

DE SOTO 24.9

TUNICA 24.6

STATE 33.3

MARSHALL 46.7

BENTON 63.3

TIPPAH 54.2

ALCORN 48.6

TISHOMINGO 66.4

PRENTISS 49.9

PANOLA 33.0

UNION 47.7

LAFAYETTE 60.6

PONTOTOC 44.8

LEE 25.9

ITAWAMBA 65.2

COAHOMA 18.5

QUITMAN 16.2

YALOBUSHA 59.1

CHICKASAW 40.9

MONROE 51.7

TALLAHATCHIE 30.9

CALHOUN 55.7

LEFLORE

GRENADA 58.5

WEBSTER 62.1

CLAY 42.3

BOLIVAR 12.8

SUNFLOWER 8.3

17.4

CARROLL 53.4

MONTGOMERY 61.9

CHOCTAW 70.7

OKTIBBEHA 51.2

LOWNDES 40.0

WASHINGTON 14.8

HUMPHREYS 25.2

HOLMES 43.7

ATTALA 67.6

NOXUBEE 65.4

50.7

SHARKEY 4.2

YAZOO 38.9

WINSTON

LEAKE 61.3

NESHOBA 55.7

KEMPER 71.8

ISSAQUENA 48.3

MADISON 40.2

SCOTT 66.3

NEWTON 66.0

LAUDERDALE 74.9

WARREN 52.0

HINDS 37.2

RANKIN 71.7

SMITH 67.8

JASPER 70.5

CLARKE 77.8

CLAIBORNE 70.6

COPIAH 69.1

SIMPSON 66.0

JEFFERSON 71.9

LINCOLN 66.6

LAWRENCE 67.5

COVINGTON 56.8

JONES 66.2

WAYNE 81.1

ADAMS 72.8

FRANKLIN 82.5

JEFFERSON DAVIS 50.9

LAMAR

PERRY 72.2

GREENE 87.6

AMITE 68.4

76.2

PIKE 55.3

WALTHALL 47.5

MARION 61.0

73.5

FORREST 83.1

WILKINSON

STONE 84.8

GEORGE 76.5

PEARL RIVER 67.8

HARRISON 76.3

JACKSON 80.3

HANCOCK 76.7

Percentage of Land in Commercial Forests

OVER 50.0%   0.0% - 50.0%

25

As favorable as the Mississippi climate is for agriculture, it is even more favorable for timber production. In addition to good soil and high rainfall, a critical growth factor for forests is temperature. Trees will not grow during prolonged periods of below 43° Fahrenheit. But since Mississippi's average January temperature is 48.7° Fahrenheit, the growing season in Mississippi is virtually continuous and yields about one cord or more per year per acre.

In addition to several varieties of commercial timber, the Mississippi woodlands abound with flowering trees and flora which produce a lush and fragrant springtime as well as shade for the "long, hot summers."

The Face of the Land

Although Mississippi's landscape has been scarred, it has not been defaced. Hunters and fishermen no longer enjoy the pristine environment that was here fifty years ago, but there are still stretches of woodlands which abound in many kinds of wild game and there are many waterways that are still unpolluted. Mississippi watersheds and reservoirs consist of 493 square miles and provide the state with one of its major recreational attractions. But to preserve what remains, traditional conservation practices must be supplemented by laws prohibiting abuse of the land and waterways.

Natural Resources

The present controversy over the environment is caused by the nation's increasing consumption of natural resources, especially those that are not renewable. For example, when a barrel of oil is burned, it is irreplaceable. In contrast, a forest even after it has been cleared, can be renewed through a reforestation program.

Mississippi is an important contributor to the nation's never ending search for natural resources and provides oil, gas, coal, sand, gravel and clay. There are also large deposits of bauxite, the basic ore from which aluminum is made. Over fifty salt domes are located in southern Mississippi, but like the coal and

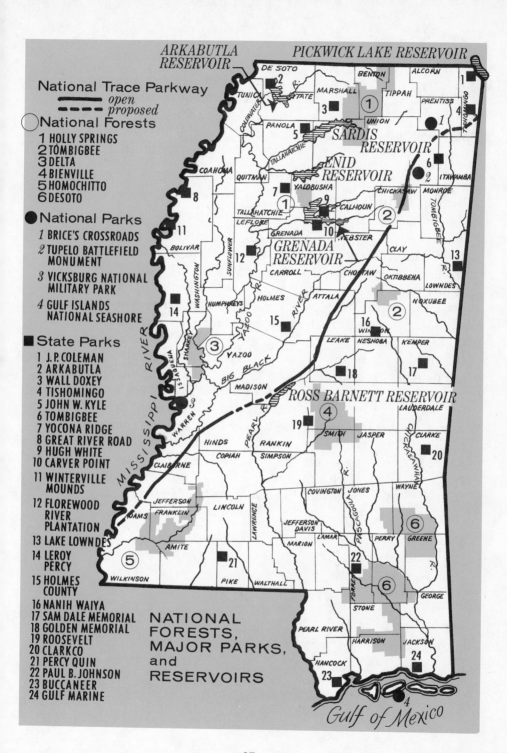

National Trace Parkway
— open
-- proposed

○ National Forests
1 HOLLY SPRINGS
2 TOMBIGBEE
3 DELTA
4 BIENVILLE
5 HOMOCHITTO
6 DESOTO

● National Parks
1 BRICE'S CROSSROADS
2 TUPELO BATTLEFIELD MONUMENT
3 VICKSBURG NATIONAL MILITARY PARK
4 GULF ISLANDS NATIONAL SEASHORE

■ State Parks
1 J.P. COLEMAN
2 ARKABUTLA
3 WALL DOXEY
4 TISHOMINGO
5 JOHN W. KYLE
6 TOMBIGBEE
7 YOCONA RIDGE
8 GREAT RIVER ROAD
9 HUGH WHITE
10 CARVER POINT
11 WINTERVILLE MOUNDS
12 FLOREWOOD RIVER PLANTATION
13 LAKE LOWNDES
14 LEROY PERCY
15 HOLMES COUNTY
16 NANIH WAIYA
17 SAM DALE MEMORIAL
18 GOLDEN MEMORIAL
19 ROOSEVELT
20 CLARKCO
21 PERCY QUIN
22 PAUL B. JOHNSON
23 BUCCANEER
24 GULF MARINE

NATIONAL FORESTS, MAJOR PARKS, and RESERVOIRS

bauxite, the salt has not been mined to any significant degree. Eventually, industrial demands for natural resources will force the processing and utilization of these raw materials. In anticipation of the increasing demand for coal, the Mississippi legislature recently enacted a law regulating the strip mining of coal in the state.

Best of Both Worlds

Mississippi still has its open woodlands, clear streams, creeks and rivers. But it also has urban centers like Corinth, Tupelo-Lee County, Meridian, Natchez, Hattiesburg-Laurel, Vicksburg, Greenville, Southhaven, Jackson, and the Gulf Coast. Few states have had the opportunity that Mississippi has in pre-planning its future economic development. However, if Mississippi leaves that growth to happenstance it will repeat the mistakes of its sister states. We must somehow find a way to meet the needs of a technological society without unduly disturbing the delicate balance of nature. If we lived as simply and as close to nature as did Mississippi's first inhabitants there would be no problem at all. But our world is vastly different from theirs. Although it is interesting to study the culture and lifestyle of the Indians who lived in the Southern woodlands over a thousand years ago, there are probably very few of us who would voluntarily trade the comfort and convenience we now enjoy and return to those days when man lived in a state of nature.

A. KEY TERMS—Explain the following terms. If necessary, use a dictionary or encyclopedia.

1. climate
2. traditions
3. social status
4. political power
5. antebellum period
6. geographic section
7. soil region
8. rednecks
9. architecture
10. prairie
11. fertility
12. drainage
13. petrified
14. silt
15. pulpwood
16. limestone
17. agriculture
18. urban area
19. rural area
20. reform ideas
21. secession crisis
22. tourist
23. planters
24. "Black Belt"
25. sharecropping
26. bluffs
27. erosion
28. loam
29. "Old South"
30. timber production
31. conservation
32. natural resources
33. reforestation
34. environment

B. MATCHING EXERCISE:

1. U. B. Phillips
2. antebellum
3. "rednecks"
4. "Revolt of the Rednecks"
5. Tombigbee Prairie
6. Pontotoc Ridge
7. Flatwoods
8. North Central Hills
9. Piney Woods
10. Coastal Meadows
11. Brown Loam Region
12. Loess Bluffs
13. Delta
14. River Lowlands

a. James Vardaman
b. least productive soil region
c. scene of cattle herds
d. before the Civil War
e. "Mississippi Riviera"
f. Alabama black belt
g. *Life and Labor in the Old South*
h. red clay hills
i. white, small farmers
j. where Chickasaws grew corn
k. caused by dust storms
l. state's most fertile soil
m. Old South heritage
n. case study of soil abuse

C. WRITING EXERCISE:

1. Suppose you have a pen-pal in a country in Africa or Europe. With particular emphasis upon the locality in which you live, write a letter to your foreign friend describing the weather, physical characteristics and natural resources of Mississippi.

2. If your pen-pal were to visit you for a week, what would you like to show your friend? With the aid of a map, plan a week-long tour that would allow your visitor to see the most interesting and important sights in Mississippi. Explain why you would include these points of interest on your tour.
3. Is there a prominent landmark, an unusual physical structure, or any other important natural formation in your community? If there is, write a brief report about it and if possible, take pictures to illustrate your report.

CHAPTER II

Indians of Mississippi

When Christopher Columbus landed in the Bahama Islands in 1492, he believed he had arrived at the shores of India. Therefore, he called the natives of those islands "Indians." Other European explorers continued to use the word Indian to identify the native inhabitants in both North and South America. Not much is known about who they were, where they came from, or how they got here. It is believed that the native Americans migrated from Asia across the Bering Straits down through Alaska, Canada, the United States and eventually South America.

Scattered across the southeastern United States were hundreds of tribes of remarkably diverse and rich cultures. The population of the Southern Woodland Indians was approximately 1,700,000 at the time of European exploration. Four major language families—Algonkian, Iroquoian, Siouan, and Muskhogean—were found among the Indians of the Southeast. Most Mississippi Indians spoke Muskhogean, but the Natchez and Tunicas spoke a slightly different dialect.

It is difficult to assign a precise location for the various Indian nations which lived within the boundaries of the present state of Mississippi because they moved often and their hunting grounds extended over large areas. The Alabama Indian nation illustrates this point very clearly. According to the records kept by members of Hernando De Soto's expedition through Mississippi in 1540–1541, a battle between the Spanish and the Alabamas occurred within the modern boundaries of Mississippi. But the next time the Alabamas are mentioned by European explorers, they are found along the confluence of the Alabama and Tombigbee Rivers. The Alabamas are not unique in this regard. Several other Indian nations, especially the smaller ones, are known to have moved several times during the period of European colonization.

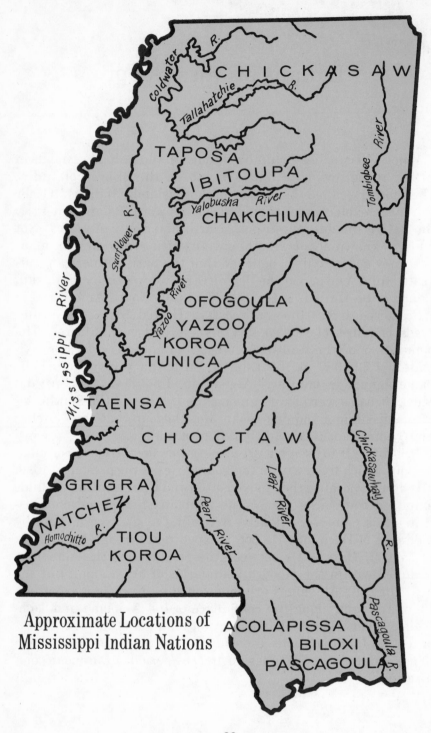

Approximate Locations of
Mississippi Indian Nations

General Characteristics of Mississippi Indian Nations

The Indians of Mississippi lived in harmony with the environment of the southern woodlands. Although their agriculture and commerce were primitive by our standards, they took great care to maintain the ecological balance they found in nature. When an Indian hunter killed a deer, he apologized to the dying animal. He spoke of the cycle of life that would be sustained by the deer's meat and the warmth its skin would provide the hunter's family during the winter days when snow covered the land. Hunters took care not to disturb the nesting places of animals, but treated them with reverence, acknowledging the animal's right to share in the bounty of the pristine wilderness.

Early European travelers often referred to the Indians' love for the land and their willingness to face any danger in defense of it. One writer compared the Mobile Indian's defense of their village to the ancient Battle of Thermopylae where the three hundred Spartans died defending their homeland. Like the Spartans many Mobilians, including their Chief Tuscaloosa, died before De Soto captured their village. Often when Choctaw warriors went into battle Choctaw women accompanied them, standing by their side holding a quiver of arrows, encouraging their men to fight bravely. Julius Caesar, during his conquest of Gaul, described a similar custom among the Gallic nations.

The vocabularies of the woodland Indians were enriched by their natural habitat. Boundaries, holy places, and children were named for things in nature. A letter was known among Indians as a "barking tree." Although none of the Mississippi Indian nations had a written language, they did develop a form of written communication called "pictography." This system used pictures and symbols, but it was a very effective method of communication.

Food Gathering

Until the appearance of large numbers of white settlers, the southern woodlands provided the Indians with a bounty of food. Practically all southeastern Indians developed a form of agriculture which was supplemented by wild game and fish. They developed ingenious trapping and fishing techniques, some of

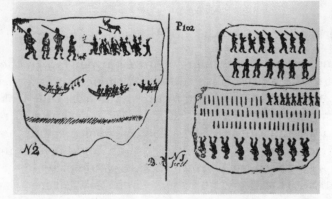

Pictography. Although Mississippi Indians did not have a written language they were skillful in communicating through pictures and signs. These two pictographs relate messages about an enemy attack.

A hunting scene as drawn by an early European explorer.

which are used even today. When hunting alone, an Indian draped a deer skin over his head and shoulders. With barely a sound and always from the down-wind side, he approached his game for a close-range shot with his bow. When hunting in groups, hunters surrounded the game and forced the animal to run in circles until it collapsed. Their fishing techniques were also ingenious. In small ponds or lakes, Indians waded into the water, kicking the bottom to stir up the mud. When the water was muddied, the fish came to the top for air and were then easily caught in nets. Grabbling was also practiced by Mississippi Indians. This is a technique of diving below the surface and reaching into sunken, hollowed-out logs to grab large fish which might be hiding in the log. Stupefying was another form of fishing. The Indians discovered that the roots of certain herbs or plants when crushed and spread over the surface of a pond or lake, would stupefy or stun the fish, making them lose control of their muscular functions and float to the surface. Indians then simply gathered the fish as they floated to the top of the water. Trotlines, sieves, nets, and other devices were also used to catch fish.

Because swine are not native to the United States, Indians had never tasted pork before De Soto's expedition in 1540. But they immediately developed a fondness for pork and were willing to trade almost anything for this delicacy. When De Soto refused to trade or if the Indians had nothing of value to exchange, they would go to any length and risk any danger to satisfy their taste for pork. Indian raids against his swine was a constant problem to De Soto. They often drove the hogs into the countryside where they would later capture them. The swine De Soto lost in the Southern woodlands may have been the origin of the wild hog population, sometimes known as "razor-backs," which are found in several Southern states.

Family Life

The social organization of Mississippi tribes was based on the clan which was made up of several families with a common ancestry. The clan farmed and hunted together and defended their territory as a unit. Within each clan, the different families lived together as a family unit which usually included aunts, uncles, nieces, nephews, and grandparents. The clans were exogamic which meant that clan members must marry outside the clan. The marriage ritual was elaborate and usually was accompanied by a celebration. Divorce or separation was easily attained by the male and only required the approval of the two families. Among Mississippi Indians, marriage was an economic and political alliance between two families rather than a union of two individuals.

Like many primitive people, Mississippi Indians destroyed children who were born with physical deformities. Although descent was usually traced through the mother, Indian families were patriarchal or male dominated. For example, women did practically all the farming and household chores. When a man killed a deer, he told his wife where it was and sent her into the forest to fetch it home, clean it, and cook it. Adultery among men was not condemned, but among women it brought shame and severe punishment. Indian women, had they known of the term and dared to use it, would perhaps have referred to their men as male chauvinists.

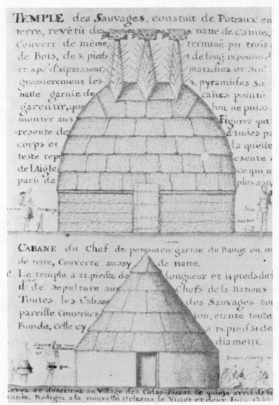

The sacred temple and cabin of the chief of the Acolapissa Nation.

Religion

All Mississippi Indians practiced some form of organized religion and all believed in some form of life after death. They worshipped many gods, some of whom they believed to be kind and friendly and others they believed to be evil, jealous, and unfriendly. Their religious beliefs were closely tied to their natural habitat and most of their ceremonies were designed to appease the unfriendly gods, whom they felt needed more attention than the friendly ones.

Probably the most important ritual among the southeastern Indians was the "Green Corn Ceremony" which took place in late August. It was held in anticipation of and in hope of a bountiful harvest. This occasion always attracted large numbers and sometimes required the use of temporary shelters to house all those attending the ceremony. One interesting feature of the Green Corn Ceremony was that it was the season for forgiving. Standing feuds and other disagreements were often settled during the ceremony, so everyone could start anew. It is believed that the Green Corn Ceremony marked the beginning of a new year among the Indians.

Tribal folklore among Mississippi Indians included a creation story, a great migration, and a flood epic which described the use of rafts on which both men and animals escaped the relentless and rising waters.

Burial traditions among the Indian nations varied widely. Among the Indians traditionally associated with Mississippi, only the Natchez practiced human sacrifice upon the death of a tribal leader. The Chickasaws usually buried their dead with their favorite possessions below the deceased's cabin floor. The Choctaws first laid their dead on a raised platform to allow the body to decompose. Then specially trained people called "bone pickers" removed the flesh from the skeleton before it was buried.

Recreation

Among Mississippi Indians organized games and other sporting events were very popular and highly developed. Singing and dancing for both religious and recreational purposes were observed by early travelers. The Choctaw language specifically lent itself to musical expression. One early traveler described it as "very agreeable to the ears . . . gentle and musical . . . the women in particular so fine and musical as to represent the singing of birds."

In a male dominated society, as might be expected, most recreational customs centered around a masculine routine. "Chunky" was a game in which a disc or a small wheel was rolled at high speed as warriors ran alongside the disc and threw spears at the moving target. Mississippi Indians also played their own version of the modern game of horseshoes.

The most popular game among Mississippi Indians was "stickball," from which the modern game of lacrosse has developed. Stickball, as played by Mississippi Indians, was much more physical and rugged than any modern American sport. The game was played on a large open field with as many as two or three hundred players on each side. Uprights, similar to football goal posts but much closer together, were built at each end of the field. The object of the game was to throw a small ball through the uprights. In each hand a player held a stick to which a small leather cup was attached. A player cradled the ball in the cup as he ran toward the opponent's goal. If he was surrounded and could not proceed toward the uprights, he passed the ball to a teammate. There were no out-of-bounds and when a player went into the crowd to retrieve the ball, he was usually hit, kicked, tripped, and beaten by the spectators. The first team to score one hundred goals was declared the winner. The games sometimes lasted for several days and drew crowds of up to 10,000. Men and women often wagered practically everything they had on the outcome. So fierce and competitive, and on some occasions so critical was the outcome of the game, that the Choctaws called stickball "the little brother of war."

These drawings of a Choctaw ball player and a stickball game were made by George Catlin in the 1830s.

Tribal Government

The Natchez nation was ruled by an autocrat, or dictator, but other Mississippi nations developed a more democratic form of government. Most nations were organized by towns or villages which exercised a certain degree of local self-government. The entire nation was a confederation of those towns or villages. Both the Choctaws and Chickasaws developed a tribal council

39

The Natchez chief, called the Great Sun, was treated like a king.

composed of men called "Mingos" or chiefs. These Mingos ruled the nation with the advice of tribal elders. The rule of law among Mississippi nations followed custom and tradition. In a case of murder, the victim's relatives had the right of vengeance. If the person judged guilty escaped, a brother or some other close relative of the guilty person was executed to avenge for the crime.

The Calumet

All important council meetings, either among various Indian nations or between nations and white men, were opened by the smoking of the *calumet*, or the peace pipe. The importance of this custom was first mentioned by a French traveler who wrote: "We stayed in their village three days—as long as their calumet lasted." So binding was the tradition of the calumet that many Indian affairs were limited to three days, the normal period of time a calumet lasted.

The smoking of the Calumet, or peace pipe, was a high ceremony among Mississippi Indians.

The Large Indian Nations

Natchez

The Natchez, who were sometimes called the "Sunset Indians," may have at one time numbered as many as 200,000 and ruled over territory extending from the Gulf of Mexico to the Ohio Valley. In 1690, they numbered approximately 4,000 and were located in several villages along St. Catherine's Creek near the present city of Natchez. Most scholars believe that the band of Indians led by Chief Ouigaltanqui, mentioned by Spanish explorers in 1541, were actually the Natchez. Natchez are first mentioned by name by René Robert Cavalier, Sieur de La Salle in 1682.

From the beginning of French explorations in the lower Mississippi valley, the Natchez and the French were hostile to each other. In 1699 a French missionary began living among the Natchez, and in 1700 Pierre le Moyne, Sieur d'Iberville visited their villages. Anxious to develop trade in the lower Mississippi valley, the French established a trading post among the Natchez and in 1716 built Fort Rosalie. French trade in this area developed rapidly, and Fort Rosalie soon became a flourishing commercial center in the Louisiana Province.

As the encroachment upon Indian land and hunting grounds increased, several tribal chiefs planned a revolt to drive the French out of the lower Mississippi Valley. The Natchez attack of Fort Rosalie on November 28, 1729, was supposed to be one phase of a larger, coordinated revolt against the French by several other nations including the Koroas, Yazoos, Tious, and the Chickasaws. For some reason, however, the Natchez attacked before the other nations were ready, and they lost the element of surprise in the combined assault. Nevertheless, Fort Rosalie was captured by the Natchez. About 200 whites were killed and many captives were taken. The next year, a combined French and Choctaw force recaptured Fort Rosalie and by 1731 the French had practically destroyed the Natchez tribe. Most of those who were not killed or sold into slavery escaped into the Chickasaw country. A few Natchez were granted refuge among the Cherokees in Georgia. After 1731, the Natchez lost their tribal identity, but a few descendants of the Natchez living among the Cherokee in the Oklahoma territory continued to speak the language as late as 1925.

The Natchez was one of the most interesting and unusual of all the American Indian nations. Four social classes existed among the Natchez. At the top of the social order was the sun class. This was the class from which the hereditary chiefs, called the Great Sun, were chosen. They were believed to be descended from the sun and ruled with absolute authority. Below the sun class were the nobles, the honored people, and the stinkards were at the bottom of the social scale. The stinkards were the workers and laborers. The sun class spoke a special "court" language which differed from the dialect used by the lower classes.

Several other unusual customs attracted the attention of the French settlers living among the Natchez. The French observed the practice of human sacrifice and eventually persuaded the Natchez to abandon that tradition. When a Great Sun died, tribesmen volunteered to be strangled in order to accompany their Chief on his journey into the spirit world. Mothers gladly volunteered their young children, for it was considered an honor to be selected for sacrifice.

Love, courtship, and marriage among the Natchez were not as formalized as in our society, and one warrior often had several wives. Chastity before marriage was not considered to be of special significance, although fidelity on the part of the woman after marriage was of utmost importance. Natchez marriage customs, according to accounts left by French explorers, required members of each class to marry down into the class below them. Since there was no class below the stinkards, they married up into the sun class. The purpose of this unusual practice was probably to maintain as nearly as possible, a numerical balance among the classes. However, a stinkard could not become a Great Sun. A Natchez chief inherited his position only through his mother who must be of the sun class.

Choctaw

A Muskhogean speaking nation numbering approximately 20,000 in 1700, the Choctaws were the second largest nation in the southeast. Choctaw villages numbering well over one hundred were scattered throughout southeastern Mississippi and adjoining areas of Louisiana and Alabama. Hernando De Soto was probably the first European to encounter the Choctaws. He called them "long hairs" because the men wore their hair long, down to their shoulders. The French often referred to them as "flat heads" because Choctaw infants, like those of many other American Indians, were kept for long periods of time in cribs or cradle boards which flattened the tops of their heads.

The Choctaws were the most agricultural of all the southeastern Indians. Although there were a few bands of Choctaws who allied with the British, especially the group led by Chief "Red Shoes", they normally allied with the French.

According to oral tradition, their ancestors were led to Mississippi from the far west where the sun disappears by two brothers named Chatah and Chickasah. The legend has it that on each night of their journey a sacred stick was placed in the ground, and on the following morning the nation migrated in the direction the stick was leaning. One morning they found the stick in an upright position or not leaning in any direction. They took this as a sign from the Great Spirit to settle at that location. However, because of some disagreement between Chatah and Chickasah, the nation divided into two groups. The groups became known as the Choctaws and the Chickasaws.

Another legend among the Choctaws explains their origin in quite a different way. This story tells of a sacred mound they called Nanih Waiya. At some point in the remote past, this mound opened up and the Muskhogean, the Cherokee, and the Chickasaw nations came forth out of Mother Earth. Sometime later, the mound opened again and the Choctaw nation came forth.

Both of these legends, which indicate some ancient relationship between the Choctaws and the Chickasaws, help explain the many similar customs, traditions, and characteristics of the Choctaws and Chickasaws. The story of the dispute between Chatah and Chickasah is especially interesting because, in contrast to the peaceful Choctaws, the Chickasaws were known as fierce warriors who were almost constantly at war either with neighboring nations or with the European invaders, especially the French.

Among the Mississippi Indians the Choctaws were perhaps the tribe that most quickly and thoroughly adopted the ways of the white man. Gradually the Choctaws sold or traded or lost their land to the white men; first the French, then the Spanish, then the English, and finally the Americans. By the 1830's this once large nation which occupied a vast area had no more land and was forcibly removed from Mississippi to the western territory which had been set aside for the Indian nations of the southeast.

Chickasaw

A Muskhogean nation of about 4,500 to 5,000, the Chickasaws were clustered in several villages called Long Town near the Pontotoc Ridge at the time of European exploration. The Chickasaws once ruled over hunting grounds that extended up into Tennessee along the Cumberland River. They were also famous for the Chickasaw horse. This tall, lean, very fast mount, which they bred and developed themselves, was used by Chickasaw war parties.

After the Natchez attacked Fort Rosalie in 1729, the Chickasaws allowed members of the Natchez nation who had escaped the French counterattack to live among them. For the next several years French officials in Natchez considered launching an attack against the Chickasaws. The French wanted to punish the Chickasaws for aiding the Natchez. They also wanted to stop the Chickasaws from interfering with French trade on the Mississippi River, especially at Chickasaw Bluffs near the present city of Memphis.

In 1736, the French mounted a major offensive against the Chickasaws. The plan was for Pierre d' Artaguette, with about one hundred-forty troops and three hundred Indian allies, to attack the Chickasaw villages from the north coming down from a French fort in Illinois. Jean Baptiste le Moyne, Sieur d' Bienville, with about five hundred troops and a large number

An early drawing of a Chickasaw Indian.

of Choctaw warriors, was to attack from the south. But the timing of these two French officers was not coordinated, and d' Artaguette who arrived before Bienville was captured and put to death. By the time Bienville arrived, the Chickasaws had fortified their villages at Long Town. British traders who were living among the Chickasaws helped them prepare for the approaching battle. On May 26, 1736, Bienville's force was defeated at Ackia, near Tupelo. Having suffered heavy losses, the French retreated southward to Mobile.

Even though the Chickasaws were allies of the British, they could not hold back the western expansion of English colonies on the Atlantic coast. Gradually they, too, were forced to sell their lands and move to Oklahoma.

Small Nations of Mississippi

Acolapissa

When Bienville came to Mississippi in 1699, the Acolapissas were living along the Gulf Coast about eleven miles above the mouth of the Pearl River. A small Muskhogean-speaking nation numbering about 1,000 in 1700, the Acolapissas were frequently raided by English and Chickasaw slave traders. When the

French offered protection from the English and the Chickasaws, the Acolapissas became French allies. After moving to several different locations in southeast Louisiana and Mississippi, the Acolapissas finally merged with the Houma Indians in 1739.

The Acolapissas, who were known in their own language as "Those who listen and see," are noted for several unusual traditions which attracted the attention of French explorers. For example, the entire Acolapissa nation gathered around their temple twice each day for morning and evening prayers. The circular temple was located in the center of the village and contained the nation's sacred relics. Members of the Acolapissa nation were thoroughly tatooed.

Biloxi

This nation who called themselves the "first people," spoke a Siouan dialect and probably migrated from the Ohio Valley to the Gulf Coast not too long before the French explorer, Pierre le Moyne, Sieur d' Iberville, landed at Ship Island in 1699. After Iberville encountered a scouting party of Biloxi Indians on the Gulf Coast, his younger brother, Jean Baptiste le Moyne, Sieur d' Bienville, visited their village which was located several miles inland on the Pascagoula River. The Biloxi nation shifted its location several times during the French period and finally moved west of the Mississippi River when the French lost this territory to England in 1763. Eventually they moved to the Indian territory in Oklahoma. When a Biloxi chief died, he was mourned by his relatives and friends who brought food to the tribal temple where the chief was buried among other former chiefs. The mourners remained in the temple for some time and spoke the praises of their departed chieftain.

Chakchiuma

The Chakchiumas, known as the "red crawfish people," were probably a part of the Choctaw-Chickasaw group before it divided into several nations. Their language was similar to the Choctaw-Chickasaw dialect, and traditions among the tribal elders tell of the great migration from the west when the Chakchiumas, Choctaws, and Chickasaws came to the Mississippi territory. It is likely that these three nations, along with several smaller ones, were one large nation before the period of European colonization. After the advent of the white man, the size of the Chakchiuma nation was greatly reduced. In a battle with De Soto's conquistadors, the Chakchiumas lost several warriors and an entire village when Niko Lusa, the "Black Chief," set fire to one of his villages in an effort to trick De Soto. After the French occupied Mississippi, the Chakchiumas suffered additional losses when the French attacked them for killing a French missionary who had settled among them. This French attack reduced the nation to about one-fifth of its former size. All of the Chakchiuma losses, however, were not at the hand of the whites. Their location between the Choctaws and Chickasaws placed them in jeopardy from both these large nations, especially when they were at war. Following a great battle in 1770 in which the Chakchiumas lost many warriors, the remaining Chakchiumas merged with the Choctaws and Chickasaws.

Grigra

The name of this nation is derived from the frequency of the two syllables "gri" and "gra" in their speech. The Grigras, who spoke a Tunican dialect, numbered about 200 and had been adopted by the Natchez prior to the European period. Before joining the Natchez, the Grigras may have lived along the Yazoo River where several other small Tunican-speaking nations were located. The French usually referred to the Grigras, not as a nation, but as a village—sometimes, the Gray Village of the Natchez. Although the Grigras were given refuge among the Natchez, they occupied the lowest status in the Natchez social structure and were not allowed to retain their tribal identity (customs and traditions) to the same extent as were the Tious, another small nation adopted by the Natchez. The Grigras' temple and village were burned by Bienville in 1723, and they are not mentioned in French sources after that time.

Ibitoupa

In the Muskhogean language, the word Ibitoupa means "people at the source of a stream," and is the name given to a small band of about 50 people who were very closely related in language and culture to the Chickasaws. In 1699, this small band was living on the lower course of the Yazoo River, but by 1722 they had moved further up the Yazoo. It is possible that the Ibitoupa united with other small nations like the Chakchiuma and Taposa before finally merging with the Chickasaw. There is no mention of the Ibitoupas after 1730.

Koroa

A Tunica-speaking nation located along the lower course of the Yazoo River, the Koroas joined the Natchez in their war against the French in 1729. Koroa warriors killed a French missionary and destroyed Fort St. Peter, a French post on the Yazoo River, but suffered heavy casualties when the French retaliated. Within a few years the Koroas were either destroyed or merged with other nations. They were probably absorbed by the Choctaws and Chickasaws soon after 1731. Years later, a famous Choctaw Chief, Allen Wright, claimed to be of Koroan descent.

Ofogoula

Known as "dog people" among their neighboring nations, the Ofogoulas were living in southwest Ohio and southeast Indiana during the early French period. They later migrated to the lower Yazoo River by way of Kentucky, Tennessee, and Arkansas. In 1729, the Ofogoulas refused to join their neighbors, the Yazoos and Koroas, in attacking the French. Instead they joined the Tunicas who were allies of the French. After the fighting had subsided, the Ofogoulas settled near Fort Rosalie where they remained until 1784 when they moved to the west bank of the Mississippi River just above Point Coupé, Louisiana. Nothing more was heard of this nation until the early 1900's when the last surviving Ofogoula Indian was found living among the Tunica nation near Marksville, Louisiana. The famous Indian scholar, John Swanton, transcribed the language spoken by this

48

Ofogoula woman and discovered that the Ofogoula language was very similar to the dialect spoken by the Biloxis.

Pascagoula

Known among the French as the "bread people" because of a special kind of bread they baked, the Pascagoulas were closely associated with their Biloxi neighbors. Located several miles inland on the Pascagoula River, this Muskhogean-speaking nation maintained very friendly ties with the French during the entire period of French occupation of the lower Mississippi valley. They moved down to the Gulf Coast after the French arrived and continued to live there until 1764, when the nation resettled near the Red River in present-day Louisiana. As late as 1829 there were over one hundred Pascagoula Indians living near the Biloxi nation on the Red River in east Texas. By 1911 the Pascagoulas, like many other nations, had lost their tribal identity.

Taensa

Although most members of this nation lived in Louisiana and are most often associated with Louisiana history, one village of Taensas was located in present-day Mississippi. The Taensas spoke a dialect very similar to the Natchez and, like the Natchez, was one of the few southeastern Indian nations that practiced human sacrifice.

Taposa

Very little is known about the Taposas except that they were located on the Tallahatchie River just above the Chakchiuma. The Taposas probably spoke a Muskhogean dialect similar to that of the Chickasaws. When the Natchez attacked the French in 1729, the Taposas aided the Natchez. But after the Natchez were defeated, the Taposas were probably absorbed, perhaps first by the Chakchiuma and later by the Chickasaws.

Tiou

When the Tiou nation was first mentioned by European explorers in the 1680's, it was located on the upper Yazoo River and was identified as a small band that spoke the Tunican dialect. By 1699, however, at least some of the Tious had settled among the Natchez who adopted them into the lower social class. The Tious may have abandoned their Yazoo villages to escape Chickasaw slave raids. Sometime later the Tious were found living among the Baygoula tribe in Louisiana, just across the Mississippi border. During the Natchez war of 1729 the Tious supported the Natchez. They were virtually destroyed by the French in 1731.

Tunica

The Tunicas, who called themselves "the people" or "those who are the people," were the largest nation that spoke the Tunican dialect. Numbering about 1,575 in 1698, the Tunicas were also the closest and most consistent French ally among the Mississippi Indians. Although the main body of the nation was located on the south bank of the lower Yazoo River, bands of Tunicas traveled widely throughout the southeast conducting an active salt trade. In approximately 1706 the Tunicas abandoned their villages on the Yazoo River and resettled among the Houmas near the mouth of the Red River. In 1730–1731 the Natchez attacked the Tunicas because they supported the French, killing the Tunica chief and many warriors. However, the Tunicas survived this attack and continued to live in southeast Louisiana. Although their tribal identity was eventually lost, several Tunicas were later found living among the Choctaws in Oklahoma.

Yazoo

The Yazoo nation, which spoke a Tunican dialect, was located on the south side of the Yazoo River several miles above its mouth. The Yazoos were closely associated with the Koroa and were anti-French. In 1727, the Yazoos killed a French missionary who was stationed among them and then attacked the Tunicas. Very little is known about the outcome of this battle, and afterwards, the Yazoos are rarely mentioned again in contemporary sources. It is likely that most of the Yazoos were absorbed by the Choctaws and the remainder by the Chickasaws. The Yazoo and Koroa tribes illustrate the drastic decline in Indian population. Their combined population was estimated at 600 in 1698; 175 in 1722; 150 in 1731. By 1740, they had lost their tribal identities.

Indian Removal

One of the unfortunate pages of American history deals with the forced removal of thousands of Indians from the southeastern United States to the Indian territory west of the Mississippi River. The long, laborious, hapless journey is described as a "Trail of Tears."

Through a series of treaties beginning in 1801 the Choctaw Indians surrendered their land to the United States. Finally, under the terms of the Treaty of Dancing Rabbit Creek of 1830, they exchanged their remaining land in Mississippi for land in the Indian territory. Heads of Choctaw families who wished to remain in Mississippi were promised 640 acres of land, plus additional acres for each child. But few Choctaws ever received any land. Most of those who had originally chosen to remain in Mississippi later migrated to Oklahoma.

The Chickasaws gave up their land in north Mississippi under the terms of the Treaty of Pontotoc in 1832. This cession conveyed 6,283,804 acres to the United States. Chickasaw families were not given an opportunity to remain in Mississippi, but they were promised all the money from the sale of their lands. Like the Choctaws who got little or none of the land promised them, the Chickasaw tribe received practically none of the money from the sale of their land. Both nations felt that the American government had either tricked them or cheated them out of their land. When the Confederate States of America was established in 1861, the Choctaws and Chickasaws sided with the South and each tribe provided soldiers to the Confederate army. Indian leaders argued that the United States had not paid them for their land as they had promised, and that they were only trying to reclaim what was rightfully theirs. After the Civil War, the United States government again refused to pay the Indians on the grounds that the nations had rebelled against the government.

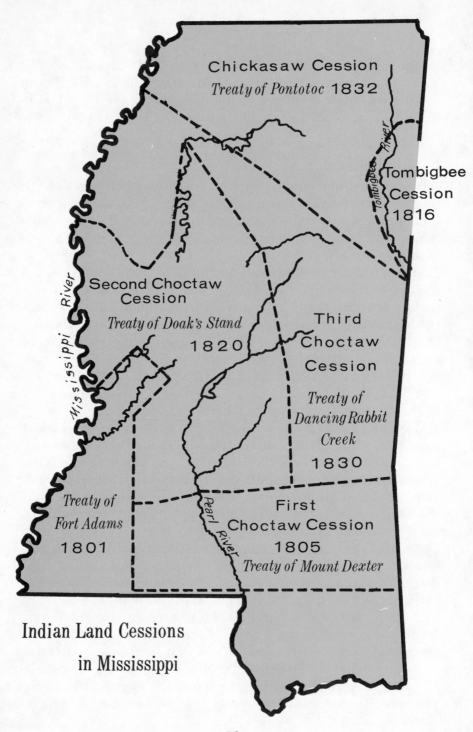

Chickasaw Cession
Treaty of Pontotoc 1832

Tombigbee Cession 1816

Mississippi River

Second Choctaw Cession

Treaty of Doak's Stand 1820

Third Choctaw Cession

Treaty of Dancing Rabbit Creek 1830

Treaty of Fort Adams 1801

Pearl River

First Choctaw Cession 1805
Treaty of Mount Dexter

Indian Land Cessions
in Mississippi

Mississippi Band of Choctaws

For many years the American government's Indian policy was conducted on a trial and error basis. Frequent changes and modifications of that policy caused great hardships for America's native inhabitants. But a proud band of Mississippi Choctaws who refused to leave Mississippi endured all those hardships and retained their tribal identity. In 1918, their plight was brought to the attention of the Bureau of Indian Affairs which soon opened a branch office in Mississippi. Over the next few years, the Bureau of Indian Affairs bought land for a reservation on which the Choctaws could live peacefully and preserve their traditions, language and cultural heritage. The reservation includes about twenty-seven square miles located in several counties in east Mississippi. Since 1918, the Mississippi band of Choctaw Indians has made significant progress in reestablishing their tribal customs and traditions. But perhaps most important of all, they are living on the land of their ancestors—near the sacred mound of Nanih Waiya.

The European Period

The circumstances which eventually displaced and all but destroyed Mississippi's native population and culture were born of the great rivalry among European nations to establish colonies in the new world. For many years, the area that later became the state of Mississippi, was a focal point of that rivalry. Each of the three strongest European nations—France, Spain, and England—ruled this land at some time during the period of colonization. And each left its legacy which all Mississippians, red, black, and white, share as our common heritage. An understanding of that great colonial struggle is necessary to an understanding of Mississippi's history.

A. KEY TERMS—Explain the following terms. If necessary, use a dictionary or encyclopedia.

1. Bering Straits
2. Muskhogean language family
3. pictography
4. "razor-backs"
5. clan
6. exogamic clans
7. patriarchal
8. Green Corn Ceremony
9. Chunky
10. autocrat
11. St. Catherine's Creek
12. stinkards
13. "long hairs"
14. Battle of Ackia
15. Long Town
16. Pierre d'Artaguette
17. Bureau of Indian Affairs
18. ecological balance
19. tribal folklore
20. "bone pickers"
21. Chickasaw horse
22. Indian land cessions
23. migrate
24. Oklahoma
25. Indian artifacts

B. MATCHING EXERCISE

1. Christopher Columbus
2. grabbling
3. "barking tree"
4. stickball
5. Mingos
6. Calumet
7. Great Sun
8. Nanih Waiya
9. Tunica nation
10. Indian removal

a. "little brother of war"
b. salt traders
c. peace pipe
d. sacred mound
e. Indian expression for letter
f. Choctaw and Chickasaw Chiefs
g. Bahama Islands
h. "Trail of Tears"
i. Natchez Chief
j. Indian form of fishing

C. MAP EXERCISE

On a map of Mississippi, identify the approximate locations of the Mississippi Indian nations. Also identify on that map the location of as many towns, cities, counties, rivers, and other Indian place names as you can. For as many of these place names as possible, explain the Indian meaning of those words.

D. COLLECTION AND DISPLAY OF INDIAN ARTIFACTS

Conduct a search for Indian artifacts in your neighborhood. If any are found, or if any collectors of artifacts will make their collections available to your class, make a display of these.

CHAPTER III

The European Period, 1540-1798

As Europe emerged from the Middle Ages a flourishing trade with China and India led European nations to seek a short-cut to the riches of the Orient. This search opened the Age of Exploration when courageous seamen ventured out into the unknown and uncharted oceans. One of their most spectacular discoveries was the western hemisphere. Can you imagine their surprise when they discovered that the ocean route from Europe to Asia was blocked by a vast land mass totally unknown to them? Soon after the discovery of the western hemisphere European nations began establishing colonies to develop the natural resources of this New World.

Colonial Rivalry in North America

During the Age of Exploration and Colonization, several European nations held claims to some portion of the territory which is now the United States. Smaller countries, such as Sweden and the Netherlands, eventually lost their American colonies to one of the three major colonial powers: Spain, France, and England.

Spanish colonial activity in North America centered primarily along the Gulf of Mexico, extending from Florida to Texas. French colonies were initially established in the region of Canada, and English settlements were located along the Atlantic seaboard between Spanish Florida and the French colonies in the north. While colonial activity was restricted to the coastal areas, conflict among these three nations was minimal. But as explorers opened the interior regions and settlers moved inland, a contest for empire developed and provoked a series of colonial wars. The struggle over territory that would later become Mississippi was one phase of this larger, three-way struggle for an American colonial empire.

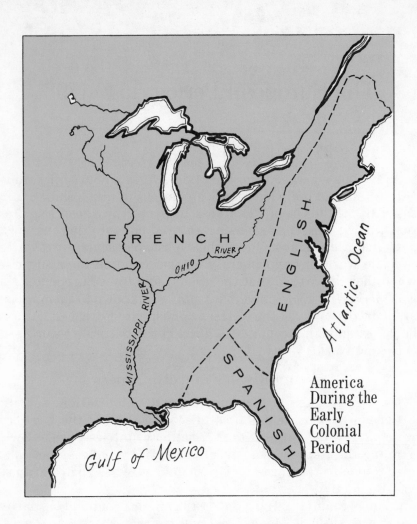

America
During the
Early
Colonial
Period

Early Spanish Activity in Mississippi

From their bases in the Caribbean, Spanish conquistadors, conquerors or soldiers, began exploring the Gulf of Mexico. In 1513 Juan Ponce De Leon discovered Florida. Soon afterward, Alonso de Pineda conducted an expedition along the Gulf Coast and sighted the mouth of either the Mobile or the Mississippi River. Pineda's voyage increased Spanish interest in the Gulf region, and in 1528 another expedition under Panfilo de Narvaez was made along the coast. Narvaez's exploration was a total failure because of internal dissension, hostile Indians, and the loss of the makeshift ships which were to be used in sailing to the Texas coast. However, an account of the Narvaez expedition by Cabeza de Vaca inspired further exploration of this region.

Hernando De Soto

Perhaps the first white man to touch Mississippi soil was Hernando De Soto. An adventurous conquistador, De Soto was only thirty-six years old when he was appointed governor of Cuba and began his exploration of the southeastern United States. He had already served under Francisco Pizarro in Peru, but he dreamed of leading his own expedition and finding even greater riches than those that had been found among the Incas and Aztecs of South America.

On May 30, 1539, De Soto landed at Tampa Bay with a large expedition that included 620 men and women, 223 horses, a drove of swine, and a pack of dogs. Among his men were priests, a physician, carpenters, and smithies who were needed to repair the metal armor worn by De Soto's soldiers. From Tampa Bay De Soto marched northward through Georgia, South Carolina, and North Carolina before turning back southwestward.

De Soto reaches the Mississippi River.

The greatest battle of De Soto's expedition occurred near the present city of Mobile just before he entered Mississippi. In this fierce battle 3,000 Indians, including Chief Tuscaloosa, were slaughtered by De Soto's army. The Spaniards also sustained heavy losses. Eighteen soldiers and twenty horses perished in the battle. De Soto also lost the pearls which were the only treasure he had found during his expedition.

After this battle De Soto refused to return to the Gulf of Mexico where ships and supplies were waiting for him. Instead, he marched northwestward and in December 1540 his expedition entered the present state of Mississippi and set up a winter camp along the Pontotoc Ridge. At first De Soto and the Chickasaw Indians lived on friendly terms. However, when the Indians stole supplies from the Spanish, especially pork for which they had developed a fondness, De Soto punished them severely. In some cases he cut off their hands, and in some extreme cases he executed them. In March 1541, as he prepared to continue his explorations, De Soto demanded that the Chickasaws provide him with enough men to carry the expedition's supplies. This demand was taken as an insult by the brave Chickasaw warriors. To avenge themselves, they attacked De Soto's camp. During a two hour battle both the Chickasaws and the Spanish suffered heavy losses. After about a month's delay during which De Soto repaired his armor, weapons, and other equipment, the expedition moved west again. Another costly battle was fought with the Alabama Indians before De Soto finally reached the Mississippi River on May 5, 1541.

De Soto spent about a month building rafts to ferry his men and supplies across the great river. Exactly where this historic crossing took place has been the subject of controversy for many years. Although some people claim to know the exact route De Soto took across our state and the precise place where he ferried the river, no one will ever know for certain. This information will forever remain a part of history's buried treasure.

After failing to find any gold in Arkansas or Texas, De Soto returned to the river near Natchez where he soon died from a long-festering wound suffered in some earlier battle. Appropriately, Hernando De Soto was buried in the turbid waters of the great river which will ever be associated with his name. After De Soto's burial the survivors of his expedition, which was by then less than half its original size, sailed down the Mississippi River to the Gulf Coast where they were rescued by Spanish ships.

The Southern Death Cult or Buzzard Cult

After De Soto's expedition left Mississippi soil, the southern woodlands were undisturbed for another one hundred and thirty years. But the peace and stillness of this pristine wilderness had been broken. Squirrels, deer, bison, bear, and Indian braves had heard the sounds of gunfire; Indians had grown ill and died of white men's diseases for which they had no natural immunity. The terror and the mystery surrounding these invaders sparked a religious revival and cultural renaissance among Indians in the Southeast called the "Death Cult" or "Buzzard Cult." Very little is known about this brief flowering of culture or about the mysterious decrease in the Indian population between De Soto's time and the arrival of the French in the 1670's. But ethnologists and anthropologists, those who study people and culture, have estimated that the Indian population in Mississippi declined by eighty percent during that one hundred and thirty year period.

Decline of Spanish Activity

Following De Soto's failure to find any treasure, Spanish interest in the area of Mississippi waned. The Spanish did, however, establish several forts and towns in Florida.

Louisiana Province

Originally, French explorers or voyagers were more interested in finding a Northwest Passage across the United States than they were in establishing colonies. Of course they had no idea how large the continent was in those early days. After hearing Indian stories about a river that "lost itself in the great sea," Count Louis de Frontenac, Governor of Canada, commissioned

Louis Joliet and Father Jacque Marquette to locate and explore this river. They found a river which the Indians called the 'Mississippi'. But it flowed South to Mexico, not West to China. After sailing down the Mississippi River to a point approximately where the town Rosedale is now located, Marquette and Joliet returned to Canada with a glowing description of both the trading potential and the strategic importance of this river. The French quickly realized that control of the Mississippi River would open up a vast area of trade and could also serve as a barrier to block the western expansion of the English colonies on the Atlantic Coast.

La Salle's Expedition

Convinced of the importance of the river, King Louis XIV of France commissioned René Robert Cavalier, Sieur de La Salle to explore and fortify the river and claim its great valley for France. La Salle, with his trusted and devoted lieutenant, Henri de Tonty, organized an expedition in Canada and started the long descent of the Mississippi River in February, 1682.

La Salle established friendly relations with Indians all along the river and at last reached the mouth of the Mississippi on April 9, 1682. To celebrate this momentous occasion, La Salle held a formal and elaborate ceremony. His men lined up with their muskets in hand. First they sang some French songs. Then they fired several volleys with their muskets while shouting, "Long live the King!" La Salle then planted the flag of France in the southern soil and proclaimed in a loud voice that all the lands and tributaries of this mighty river belonged to Louis, King of France. In honor of the King, the new province was named Louisiana.

La Salle's next major undertaking was to fortify the mouth of the river to give France effective control over the whole interior of this great continent, the vast size of which Europeans were by then learning to appreciate. After returning to France for more supplies and men, La Salle sailed back to the mouth of the river by way of the Caribbean Sea. Unfortunately he could not locate the mouth of the river and sailed too far west. He actually

Sieur de La Salle.

landed at Matagorda Bay, Texas. In the meantime, Tonty, who was waiting for La Salle at the mouth of the river, grew impatient and returned to Canada. On his way back up the river, Tonty left a letter with the Taensa tribe telling La Salle he had returned to Canada. La Salle, realizing that he had missed the river, set out on foot to find it. His rebellious crew, which had given him trouble from the very beginning of the voyage, assassinated their captain, buried him in the wilderness, and walked back to the French settlement in Canada.

Significance of the Mississippi River

It soon became apparent to the governments of Spain, France, and England that the Mississippi River would be an important factor in the success of their colonial enterprises. Consequently, all three nations became involved in an effort to occupy and control that lengthy waterway. Each nation attempted to establish a permanent settlement at the mouth of the river. Only the French were successful, although Spain did establish a settlement at Pensacola which formed the basis of her claim to Florida. English ships did not arrive at the mouth of the Mississippi River until France had already firmly established her claim to that area.

Establishment of Biloxi

A French expedition under Pierre le Moyne, Sieur d' Iberville, a Canadian-born naval officer, arrived at Ship Island on February 10, 1699. Three days later, Iberville and a small detachment went ashore. They met a band of Biloxi Indians who later took them to their village a few miles inland on the Pascagoula River.

The French expedition under Iberville lands on the Gulf Coast.

Iberville's purpose was to locate the Mississippi River and establish a French colony there. For the next several weeks, Iberville and his younger brother, Jean Baptiste le Moyne, Sieur de Bienville, explored the Gulf Coast looking for the Mississippi. Finally on March 2, 1699, they found a river they believed to be the Mississippi. After sailing up the river for several days, they arrived at an Indian village where they were greeted as if they had been expected. It was the Taensa village where

Tonty had left the letter for La Salle fourteen years earlier. Iberville was then certain that he had found the Mississippi, but he decided that the swampy river banks were not a suitable location for a colony. He went back to the Gulf Coast and built Fort Maurepas which served as the French capital of the Louisiana Province for a short time.

Capital Moved to Mobile

Fort Maurepas did not prove to be a desirable capital for the Louisiana Province. It was not located on a river and thus could not provide access to the interior regions where the French hoped to develop fur trading with the Indians. In 1701 the French settlement was moved to Fort Louis on the Mobile Bay. Until then the colony had been under the control of French authorities in Canada. With the establishment of the new capital, Louisiana was divided from Canada and existed as a separate French province.

Bienville Becomes Governor

When the capital was moved from Fort Maurepas to Mobile Bay, Bienville was also appointed governor of the Louisiana Province. Bienville spent almost fifty years in French Louisiana and served as governor on several occasions. During his first term as

Jean Baptiste Le Moyne, Sieur d'Bienville.

governor, he urged the French government to send both men and women to the province because he considered a large population essential for a prosperous colony. Bienville also made special efforts to maintain harmony with the Indians. In 1706 accusations of corruption, stemming from famine conditions in the province, were brought against Bienville and he was temporarily suspended. He was reinstated the next year, however, when the charges were investigated and found to be without basis. But economic failure continued to plague the Louisiana Province. In 1714 the King of France granted a fifteen-year franchise to Antoine Crozat, who was allowed to operate the province as a business venture. Crozat removed Bienville and installed Antoine de la Mothe, Sieur de Cadillac as governor.

Fort Rosalie

Perhaps the most significant accomplishment during the Crozat period was the building of a fort on the Mississippi River near the present site of Natchez. In order to make trade along the Mississippi River safer, Cadillac ordered Bienville to take a detachment of soldiers to punish the Natchez Indians for murdering four Canadian traders. Bienville negotiated a settlement with the Natchez chiefs who agreed not only to surrender the guilty warriors, but also to provide the material with which to construct a fort. In 1716 Fort Rosalie was completed and became one of the major centers of French activity in the territory which later became Mississippi.

The Mississippi Bubble, 1717–1731

When he failed to acquire the wealth he had expected, Crozat returned the Louisiana Province to the King. Louisiana was then leased to John Law, a Scottish gambler who had recently been appointed French Minister of Finance. John Law combined several small French trading companies into one large corporation called the Mississippi Company. He published pamphlets about the Louisiana colony telling of its fertile soil, balmy climate, and exotic plants. But he greatly exaggerated the colony's wealth. Because of these glowing accounts, thousands of Frenchmen bought stock in the Mississippi Company, and the price of the company's stock became greatly inflated. Stock prices, like a balloon or a bubble, rose higher and higher. When the colony failed to show any real profit, the company went broke in 1731. The stock was then worthless; the "Mississippi Bubble" burst and French investors lost millions of dollars. After the failure of the John Law scheme, the control of the colony was placed under various French governmental agencies.

Transfer of Capital to New Orleans

When John Law took over the Louisiana Province, Bienville was again appointed governor. One of the first things he did was to move the capital from Mobile back to Biloxi where he built a fort on the mainland called New Biloxi. Bienville later moved the capital to New Orleans in 1722.

The Black Code

When French landowners moved to Louisiana from the Caribbean Islands, they brought their slaves with them. The slave population increased so rapidly after 1719 that Bienville found it necessary to issue special laws regulating the institution of slavery. These laws, known as the Black Code, were issued in 1724. They were not as strict as the slave codes passed by Mississippi and other southern states in later years. Bienville's code prohibited the separation of husbands and wives. Children under fourteen years old could not be separated from their mothers. Slaves who were freed by their owners became naturalized French citizens with all the rights and privileges of Frenchmen.

Population Growth

During his long service to the colony, Bienville consistently encouraged French settlers, especially women, to come to the lower Mississippi valley. Since the female population of the colony was very small, many Frenchmen had married Indian women. Bienville disapproved of these marriages because he considered a large mixed population a threat to the peace and progress of the colony. Some Indian chiefs also opposed this practice. Bienville developed an interesting scheme to get more French women to come to the colony.

The Casquette Girls

As early as 1704, twenty young French girls were brought to Biloxi to be married to the soldiers and settlers. Within a short time all but one had married. But the girls did not adjust very well to the frontier conditions, and in 1706 they vowed to leave their husbands and return to France. This "petticoat insurrection," as it was called, did not succeed because the French captains would not give the girls passage back to France. Over the next several years, perhaps as many as 500 young women known as "fillies á la casquette," or casquette girls, were brought to the colonies. Each of the girls was given a casquette, or small suitcase, containing a wedding dress and other personal articles. The girls came from orphanages, brothels, and prisons. Some of them were even sold by their parents. The casquette girls were usually under the care of the Ursuline nuns until a suitable marriage arrangement was made.

The Attack of Fort Rosalie

Following the building of Fort Rosalie in 1716, the French population in and around the fort steadily grew. By 1729 the population had reached about 550. These French settlers claimed large tracts of land and began farming operations. As long as the Frenchmen remained traders and trappers, they were welcomed among the Indians. But when they claimed the right of private ownership of land, a practice unknown among the Mississippi tribes, the Natchez Indians resorted to violence in an effort to drive the French from their hunting grounds. As we learned in Chapter II, this resistance climaxed with the attack of Fort Rosalie on November 28, 1729. Warriors from the Natchez tribe slipped into Fort Rosalie in small groups with concealed weapons and took up strategic positions inside the fort. At a given signal they attacked the garrison. They killed approximately 236 men, set the slaves free and took the women and children captive. This attack was supposed to be coordinated with simultaneous attacks of other French forts by other Indian nations along the Yazoo River. However, some of the tribes did not carry out the planned attacks, and the Natchez had to do most of the fighting. In March 1730 the French recaptured Fort Rosalie and easily defeated the Natchez, most of whom were killed in the counterattack. About four hundred Natchez Indians were captured and sold into slavery. Most of those who escaped fled north into Chickasaw country, but a few Natchez fled into Georgia where the Cherokees accepted them into their tribe.

The Battle of Ackia

For the next several years, Bienville planned to attack the Chickasaws for aiding the Natchez. And as you remember from Chapter II, he was also determined to punish the Chickasaws for attacking French traders sailing down the Mississippi River from Canada. But the attack failed and Bienville was defeated by the Chickasaws at Ackia in 1736.

The Removal of the French from the Mississippi Valley

The struggle for a colonial empire climaxed in the French and Indian War, 1754–1763. France and Spain, with their Indian allies, declared war against England, which also had some allies among the Indians. The war was settled by the Treaty of Paris in 1763. Under the terms of this treaty, France ceded all of its land in North America east of the Mississippi River to England. To Spain, an ally during the war, France gave all of its land west of the Mississippi. The only French territory east of the Mississippi River that was not ceded to England was the city of New Orleans which France gave to Spain. Because Spain lost the war, Spanish Florida was transferred to England. Therefore, Mississippi passed from French to English control.

Mississippi Under British Rule, 1763–1783

English Claims to Mississippi

As early as 1733 England had some claim to the northern part of Mississippi. Under its original English charter, the colony of

Georgia included all the area between South Carolina and Florida extending from "sea to sea." Although France had never recognized England's claim to this land, English possession was clearly and legally established by the Treaty of 1763. But English officials soon realized that there would be many problems in trying to govern the vast territory which they had recently acquired. As land-hungry Englishmen pushed into the interior after the French and Indian War, they encountered strong Indian resistance. In order to have more time to work out an agreement with the major Indian nations, the English government issued the Proclamation of 1763 which temporarily prohibited immigration into the new territory. The area affected by the Proclamation was the land west of the Appalachian Mountains to the Mississippi River and between the Great Lakes on the north and the 31° parallel on the south. This policy was not intended to permanently prohibit expansion into that area. The restriction was a temporary measure designed to keep the Indians and the white settlers from fighting over the land.

British West Florida

In 1763 the English government also established two colonies from the Florida territory which had been ceded to them by Spain. These two colonies were British West Florida and British East Florida. The boundaries of British West Florida were the Mississippi River on the west, the Chattahoochee River on the east, the 31° parallel on the north, and the Gulf Coast on the south. When these boundaries were first established, British authorities were not aware that Fort Rosalie was north of the 31° parallel. When they realized this, the British moved the northern boundary of West Florida from the 31° parallel up to the 32°28" parallel which is approximately where Vicksburg is located. Revising this boundary placed Fort Rosalie within British West Florida, but it would later cause a dispute between Spain and America.

British Indian Policy

In 1765 the British government held an Indian Congress at Mobile which was attended by Indian leaders from throughout the Southeast. The purpose of this conference was to reach an agreement by which the white settlers and the Indians might live in peace. Out of this conference came pledges of friendship and trade agreements. British officials also promised Indian leaders not to sell whiskey, or "fire water," to their braves. The most important result of this meeting was that several Indian nations ceded large areas of their land to the British. The Choctaws surrendered some of their land around Natchez and Mobile. Both of these settlements began to grow rapidly under British control.

Development of the Natchez District

As British West Florida grew, the colony was divided into four districts. One of those was the Natchez District which included the area from the confluence of the Yazoo and Mississippi Rivers extending southward in a triangular shape to the Gulf Coast. British soldiers and officers were given land grants of 200 to 5,000 acres in the Natchez District in payment for their services during the French and Indian War. The British changed the name of Fort Rosalie to Fort Panmure which continued to be the center of activity in the district. A flourishing river trade and profitable agriculture continued to attract many settlers into the Natchez District. The town of Natchez was founded and soon became an important center of Britain's southern colonial enterprise. Although tobacco was the principal crop in the Natchez District, some settlers also grew cotton, corn, and indigo.

Natchez During the American Revolution

Because a large number of Natchez residents were former British military officials, the Natchez District remained loyal to the British government when the thirteen American colonies rebelled in 1774. Some colonists who opposed the revolution moved to Natchez from the Atlantic colonies. William Dunbar, one of Mississippi's most distinguished early citizens, came to Natchez from Pennsylvania under these circumstances.

Because of its strategic location on the Mississippi River, Natchez was very important to the American colonies which were receiving supplies and aid from the Spanish in New Orleans.

The Willing Expedition

The Continental Congress sent a former Natchez resident, James Willing, on an expedition down the Mississippi River to Natchez and New Orleans. The purpose of his mission was, first of all, to encourage the Natchez citizens to join the American cause. If they would not join the rebellion, Willing was to persuade them to remain neutral and not interfere with the supplies being shipped up the Mississippi to the American colonies. Secondly, he was to go to New Orleans to purchase additional supplies from Spain and arrange for their shipment to the Atlantic colonies. When Willing arrived at Natchez on February 21, 1778, he was greeted cordially but found many Natchez residents who were loyal to the British. Probably exceeding his authority, Willing arrested several loyalists, confiscated their property, and took them as prisoners to New Orleans. After selling some of their property, Willing became something of a problem to the Spanish authorities in New Orleans who ordered him to leave the city and take his English captives with him. Spain was not yet at war with England, and they could not risk provoking an English attack on New Orleans to rescue the English prisoners. When Willing finally left the area, he was captured by an English warship.

Spain Declares War on England

The American Revolution which kept England busy on the Atlantic coast made her vulnerable to a Spanish attack along the Gulf Coast and in Florida. Seeing this situation as an opportunity to recapture Florida, Spain declared war on Great Britain in 1779. Bernando de Galvez, Spanish governor of Louisiana, immediately attacked Fort Panmure (Fort Rosalie) which the Spanish captured without much difficulty. Within two years Spain had reoccupied most of Florida.

Natchez Revolt

The British citizens at Natchez refused to acknowledge the Spanish conquest of Florida. On April 22, 1781, Captain John Blommart, a Natchez mill owner, led an uprising and recaptured Fort Panmure. But the Natchez revolt was only temporarily successful. Spanish forces regained the fort on July 23, 1781. During this turbulent period of transition from English to Spanish control, the Natchez population declined slightly.

Treaty of Paris, 1783

Under the provisions of the Treaty of Paris of 1783, which ended the American Revolution, England recognized the independence of the thirteen colonies and ceded to the United States of America the territory south of Canada and east of the Mississippi River down to Spanish Florida. The boundary between America and Spanish Florida was not clearly settled by the treaty. America claimed that the boundary should be the 31° parallel which was established as the original northern boundary of British West Florida in 1763. Spain, however, claimed that the boundary should be the 32°28″ parallel as amended by the British in 1764. What was at stake in this dispute was Natchez, and Spain was not going to give up this territory unless they were forced to do so. Since the young American republic was in no condition to take on Spain so soon after her revolution against Great Britain, the area between the 31° and the 32°28″ remained in Spanish possession for the next twelve years.

Mississippi as a Spanish Province

Under Spanish control the Natchez District experienced continued growth and prosperity. Spain's liberal land grants and low taxes attracted many settlers to the Natchez area. Both Jews and Protestants were guaranteed religious freedom by the Spanish government. The migration of English and Americans into the Natchez District was so rapid that by 1787 a majority of the District's population spoke English rather than Spanish.

Mississippi Gulf Coast After the Treaty of Paris, 1763

Mississippi Gulf Coast After the Treaty of Paris, 1783

Governor Gayoso

In 1789, Manuel Gayoso, de Lemos was appointed governor of the Natchez District. A popular and intelligent governor, Gayoso ruled the District wisely and had the respect and cooperation of most of its citizens. *Concord*, Governor Gayoso's mansion at Natchez, was frequently the scene of the kind of parties, balls, and other festivities for which Natchez would later become famous.

Spanish Forts

Fort Rosalie, originally built in 1716, was run-down and in need of repair when Gayoso came to Natchez. But Gayoso decided to build several new forts rather than repair Fort Rosalie. In 1791 the Spaniards built Fort Nogales at the point where the Yazoo River flows into the Mississippi, and in 1795 they constructed a fort on Chickasaw Bluffs (Memphis). These two forts gave Spain effective control over the lower Mississippi and its tributaries.

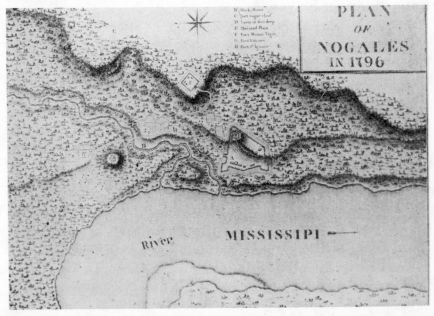

Realizing the strategic importance of the high bluffs overlooking the great bend in the Mississippi River at Walnut Hills Spanish authorities built Fort Nogales at that location in 1791. The settlement of Walnut Hills, later became the city of Vicksburg. During the Civil War, Vicksburg provided the Confederacy with almost total control over the Mississippi River traffic.

Pollution in the Natchez District

The Spanish settlers in the Natchez District developed a diversified economy which included manufacturing, agriculture, logging, and cattle raising. There were, however, certain side effects of manufacturing that were not looked upon favorably by cattlemen. Livestock was an important part of the District's economy. There were over 14,500 head of cattle, 5,500 sheep, and 20,000 hogs in the Natchez District. In 1793 a group of cattlemen complained to Governor Gayoso that the chemical waste from the indigo factories was polluting the creeks and streams and was harmful to their livestock. In response to their complaints, Governor Gayoso fined the factory owners and ordered them to discontinue dumping their wastes into the streams.

Importation of Slaves

Slavery existed in the lower Mississippi Valley long before the white man came. Most Indian tribes practiced slavery in one form or another. But Europeans brought to America a form of slavery that was somewhat different from the kind found among the Indians. The form of slavery practiced by Europeans and Americans is known as chattel slavery. This means that slaves were considered the personal property of their owners in the same way that household goods, furniture, a wagon, or livestock are considered private property. Slaves, like other personal property could be bought, sold, traded, or inherited and moved about whenever the owner moved from one location to another.

As the cotton culture began to show signs of increasing importance in the Natchez economy, Spanish authorities encouraged settlers to bring their slaves into the Natchez District by offering additional land grants to settlers who did so. In the 1790's, black males were valued at about $400 and females at about $300.

Slave Revolt in 1795

In 1795 rumors about a possible slave revolt circulated throughout the Natchez District and Louisiana. The militia was mobilized and Spanish authorities arrested a group of slaves at Pointe Coupé, Louisiana, who were believed to be the leaders of the revolt. After several of these slaves were executed, the rumors of revolt and the fear bred by those rumors were quieted. But rumors of revolt would continue throughout the period of slavery. Southern whites lived in an almost constant state of fear of a massive slave uprising until the system of slavery was finally abolished.

Population Increase

Population growth in the Natchez District kept pace with economic development. By the end of the Spanish period the white population numbered approximately 4,500 and slaves numbered about 2,400.

Georgia Claims to Mississippi

On two occasions within a ten-year period the state of Georgia claimed the land between Tennessee and the 31° parallel. Georgia made its first claim in 1785 and established Bourbon County. Large tracts of land in Bourbon County were sold to several Yazoo land companies which were authorized by Georgia to settle the area. However, Spanish officials disregarded those sales and because Spain was in actual possession of the territory Georgia did not press its claims. In 1795 the Georgia legislature again authorized the sale of land by the Yazoo companies. These sales were invalidated, however, when it was learned that many Georgia legislators had been bribed to vote for the bill allowing the sales. At the next election every member of the state legislature who ran for re-election was defeated and the new legislature revoked the sales.

America Acquires Mississippi

Treaty of San Lorenzo

In 1795, while Spain was engaged in a war in Europe, America pressed its claim to the land north of the 31° parallel. Spanish officials were reluctant to give up this land, but because they were already pre-occupied with the European war, they did

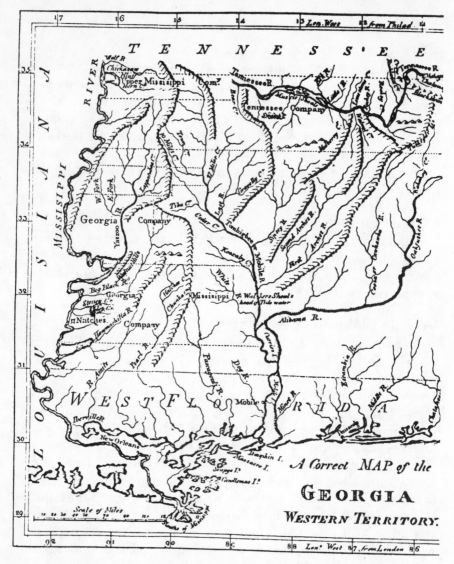

An early map showing the western lands claimed by the state of Georgia.

not want to risk another war with America. In a war with America, Spain was sure to lose New Orleans and perhaps more. To save as much of their American colonial empire as possible, the Spanish gave up their claim to the land north of the 31° parallel. Under the terms of the Treaty of San Lorenzo, Spain further agreed to allow Americans free navigation of the Mississippi River and the privilege of depositing goods in New Orleans without having to pay duties or taxes on those goods. Spain also promised to do what it could to restrain the Indians living in Spanish Florida from attacking American settlements along the border.

The Spanish authorities, especially Governor Gayoso, did not want to leave Natchez. They had homes and friends there and delayed their departure as long as possible. But after the 31° parallel was surveyed and marked in 1798, the Spanish had no more excuses to remain in Natchez. On the morning of March 30, 1798, Spanish authorities officially transferred the territory to the United States of America and left Natchez by river for New Orleans. As the American flag was raised over Fort Rosalie, accompanied by a fifteen gun salute, Mississippi became an American possession. A few days later, Fort Nogales was transferred to American control, and a bill was introduced in Congress to establish the Mississippi Territory. Mississippi would remain a territory for eighteen years before gaining admission to statehood in 1817. Those eighteen years were very important and interesting years and will be the subject of the next chapter.

A. KEY TERMS—Explain the following terms. If necessary, use a dictionary or encyclopedia.

1. Age of Exploration
2. colony
3. conquistador
4. De Soto's Expedition
5. Renaissance
6. ethnologist
7. anthropologist
8. Count Louis de Frontenac
9. Rene' Robert Cavalier, Sieur de La Salle
10. Henri Tonty
11. Fort Maurepas
12. Antoine Crozat
13. Fort Rosalie
14. The Black Code
15. Casquette Girls
16. Battle of Ackia
17. French and Indian War, 1754–1763
18. Proclamation of 1763
19. The Willing Expedition
20. Treaty of Paris, 1783
21. Fort Nogales

B. MATCHING EXERCISE

1. Juan Ponce De Leon
2. Hernando De Soto
3. Marquette and Joliet
4. Iberville
5. Bienville
6. John Law
7. Manuel Gayoso, de Lemos
8. Bourbon County
9. 31° parallel
10. Treaty of San Lorenzo, 1795

a. governor of Louisiana Province
b. explorers of the Mississippi River
c. Spanish Governor of Natchez District
d. Yazoo Land Companies
e. discovered Florida
f. settled dispute between Spain and America
g. established French settlement at Biloxi
h. border dispute between Spain and America
i. discovered the Mississippi River
j. The Mississippi Bubble

C. MAP EXERCISE

On a map of Mississippi, draw a dotted line tracing the approximate route of Hernando De Soto across the state. On that map also locate the following places:

Fort Maurepas
The 31° parallel
The 32°28″ parallel

The Battle of Ackia
Fort Nogales

D. MAKING A TIME LINE—Arrange the following events in the correct order in which they took place:

American Revolution
Battle of Ackia
De Soto Expedition
Establishment of Biloxi
Establishment of Fort Rosalie
French and Indian War
La Salle Expedition
Marquette and Joliet Expedition
Mississippi becomes American Territory
Ponce De Leon's discovery of Florida
Treaty of San Lorenzo

CHAPTER IV

The Mississippi Territory, 1798–1817

On April 7, 1798, just one week after the Spanish evacuated Natchez, the United States Congress established the Mississippi Territory. Americans living on the Atlantic Coast did not know very much about their country's most recently acquired possession. Mississippi was an untamed frontier out on the rim of the young American republic. In 1798 it took as long for a letter to get from Mississippi to Philadelphia as it did for a letter to get from Philadelphia to Europe. The Mississippi Territory was inhabited for the most part by Indians and quarrelsome whites who reacted to the transfer from Spain to America with mixed feelings. Although most territorial inhabitants were happy about becoming Americans, many of them were disturbed by the legal tangles they were certain to encounter in trying to establish title to their landholdings. Mississippians held land grants from either France, Spain, or England. Complicating land titles even more were the Georgia claims dating back to 1785. Conflicting land claims engendered strife, political factions and dissension in the territory for several years following its creation.

Territorial Boundaries

The new territory included the area bounded by the 32°28″ parallel on the north, the Mississippi River on the west, the 31° parallel on the south and the Chattahoochee River on the east. Of the nearly five thousand residents in the territory about four thousand lived in the Old Natchez District and the remainder lived in scattered settlements between the Pearl and Tombigbee Rivers.

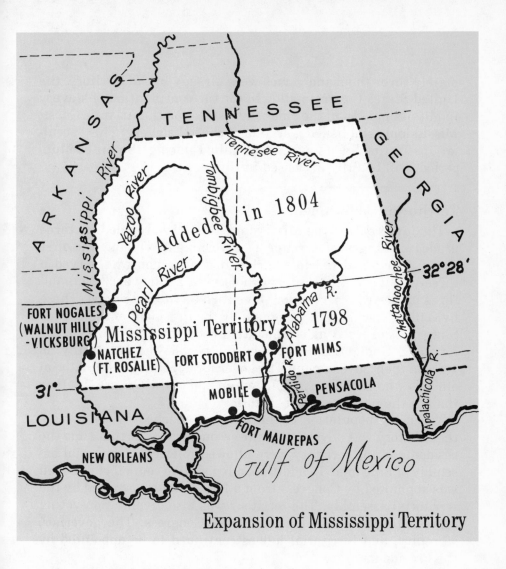

Expansion of Mississippi Territory

Map labels: ARKANSAS, TENNESSEE, GEORGIA, Mississippi River, Yazoo River, Tennessee River, Tombigbee River, Pearl River, Alabama R., Chattahoochee River, Perdido R., Apalachicola R., Added in 1804, Mississippi Territory 1798, 32°28', FORT NOGALES (WALNUT HILLS -VICKSBURG), NATCHEZ (FT. ROSALIE), FORT STODDERT, FORT MIMS, 31°, MOBILE, PENSACOLA, LOUISIANA, FORT MAUREPAS, NEW ORLEANS, Gulf of Mexico

Slavery in the Mississippi Territory

The law which established the Mississippi Territory was patterned after the Land Ordinance of 1785 and the Northwest Ordinance of 1787 which established the Northwest Territory and provided for its government. There was, however, one very important difference in those laws and the act which created the Mississippi Territory. Recognizing that slavery had existed in this area from the early French times and aware that approximately three thousand slaves were already in the territory, the United States Congress allowed for the continuation of slavery in Mississippi. As in the older slave states on the Atlantic Coast, Mississippi established a system of chattel slavery. This "peculiar institution," as slavery was called during the antebellum period, will be fully discussed in Chapter Six.

Territorial Government

The law creating the Mississippi Territory provided for three grades or stages of territorial government. During the first grade, territorial officials included a governor who served a three-year term, a Secretary who served a four-year term, and three judges who served for the entire territorial period. These five officials, who were appointed by the President of the United States, also served as a legislative body to enact laws for the territory. Under the first grade, the people had practically no voice in their government. The governor appointed all territorial officials who were responsible to him and to the Congress rather than to the people of the territory.

When the population of the territory reached five thousand, the territory was advanced to the second grade. At that time the residents of the territory were allowed to elect a territorial assembly of nine men. In addition, a legislative council of five men was appointed by Congress from a list of names provided by the territorial assembly. The territory was also given a non-voting representative in the United States Congress. The governor, secretary, and territorial judges continued to be appointed by the President.

The territory advanced to the third and final stage of territorial status when its population reached sixty thousand. At that time, the residents elected delegates to a constitutional convention to draft a state constitution. After this constitution was approved by Congress, the territory was admitted as a co-equal member into the union of states.

Governor Winthrop Sargent, 1798-1801.

Governing the Territory
Administration of Governor Winthrop Sargent, 1798–1801

The first governor to serve the Mississippi territory was Winthrop Sargent of Massachusetts. A graduate of Harvard University and a major in the American Revolutionary Army, Sargent was serving as secretary of the Northwest Territory when President John Adams appointed him governor of Mississippi. John Steele served as secretary of the territory under Governor Sargent and Peter Bryan Bruin, Daniel Tilton and William McGuire were territorial judges. From the very beginning of his three year term Governor Sargent faced one problem after another. Both he and Secretary Steele were so ill at times that they could hardly fulfill their duties. None of the three judges were of much help to Governor Sargent as all three were very rarely in the territory at the same time.

One of the most pressing problems facing Governor Sargent was the high crime rate among the rowdy and unruly frontiersmen who inhabited the territory. Conflicting land claims was another problem. Sargent's biggest problem, however, was his politics. He was a member of Alexander Hamilton's Federalist Party which favored the development of commerce and industry in preference to agriculture. The majority of the people in the territory, especially those in the backwoods settlements along the Tombigbee River, belonged to the Democratic-Republican Party. This party, under the leadership of Thomas

Jefferson, favored the development of agriculture. Throughout Sargent's short rule there was constant dissension between the Natchez businessmen and the backwoods farmers. Sargent almost always sided with the Natchez aristocrats.

In an effort to improve conditions in the territory, a small group of Democratic-Republicans led by Cato West and Narsworthy Hunter, brought charges of misrule against Governor Sargent. They petitioned the United States Congress to advance Mississippi to the second grade of territorial government, even though the population had not quite reached five thousand. Upon the recommendations of the congressional committee which investigated the charges against Sargent, Mississippi was advanced to the second grade of territorial government on May 10, 1801.

Administration of Governor William Charles Cole Claiborne, 1801–1805

When Governor Sargent's three year term expired in 1801, President Thomas Jefferson did not reappoint him. Following his retirement from public office, Sargent remained in Mississippi and settled on his estate at *Gloucester*. He later served as President of the Bank of Mississippi. In his place, President Jefferson appointed W. C. C. Claiborne. This twenty-six year old Tennessean had served as chairman of the congressional committee which recommended that Mississippi be advanced to the second stage of territorial government. Claiborne was extremely popular in Mississippi. When he arrived in the territory on November 23, 1801, he found that the Democratic-Republican Party had already begun to make changes in the territory. The capital had been moved to the small town of Washington, six miles east of Natchez, the original capital. In addition to the three existing counties of Washington, Adams, and Pickering (which was later renamed for President Jefferson), two new counties, Wilkinson and Claiborne, were soon established. Claiborne was an efficient and capable governor, but like Sargent before him, he also faced several difficult problems.

Kentucky Triangle

The problem requiring the most immediate attention was lawlessness in the territory. An indication of the seriousness of crime in the territory is the fact that a jail was the first public building erected in Mississippi. The Natchez Trace and the Mississippi River, the two main transportation routes into Mississippi, were plagued by lawless gangs of robbers who made both life and property unsafe in what may be called the "Kentucky Triangle."

Flatboats, known as "Kentucky Arks," carried a variety of commodities from Kentucky and Tennessee down the Mississippi past Natchez on the way to New Orleans. After selling their goods in New Orleans the boatmen dismantled their boats and sold the lumber. They then embarked upon the long and dangerous return to Kentucky and Tennessee by way of the Natchez Trace, which was then known as the "Devil's Backbone." Year after year these hardy flatboatmen braved this treacherous triangle. The slow moving and clumsy flatboats were easy prey to the cut throats and robbers who clustered in bands along the great river.

One of the favorite hideouts of the river pirates was the canebrakes near Walnut Hills (Vicksburg). These pirates were such a menace in the territory that Governor Claiborne offered a $2,000 reward for the head of Sam Mason—the most notorious bandit of them all. The reward specified dead or alive, but if Mason were killed, the reward would not be paid unless his head were presented as positive proof. According to legend, a member of Mason's gang, Wiley "Little" Harpe, killed the famous bandit one night as he slept. Harpe decapitated Mason, covered the head with clay, wrapped it, placed it in a box, and brought it into town to claim his reward. However, just before receiving the money, Harpe was recognized by a man whom he had recently robbed. Although he strongly denied that he was the infamous "Little Harpe," the bandit was asked to remove his shirt. On the left side of his chest, his accuser said, would be found a two-inch scar that had been inflicted upon the robber in their recent encounter. The exact size and location of the scar, as predicted, was

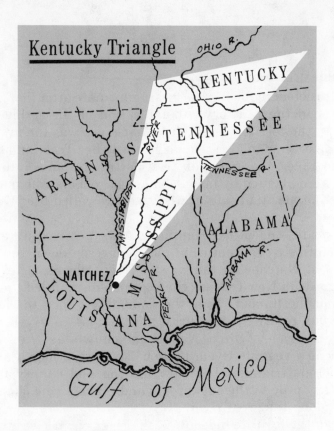

Kentucky Triangle

sufficient identification for the territorial officials. "Little Harpe" and a fellow member of the gang who accompanied him to town were both tried and convicted. After their execution they were decapitated and their heads were impaled upon stakes at the north and south entrances to town. This gory sight was to be a warning to other robbers of the fate awaiting them if they were captured and convicted.

This brand of justice plus a steady growth in the territory's population gradually reduced the dangers of frontier travel. After the Natchez Trace was made an official United States mail route in 1801, travel along the "Devil's Backbone" became much safer. The introduction of steam powered vessels on the Mississippi River in 1811, which made flatboats obsolete, also made river transportation much less dangerous. The river pirates were gone, but another equally interesting group of rascals, the riverboat gamblers, followed their footsteps.

Indian Cessions

One of the most striking features of territorial demography, which is the study of population, was the growth rate of Mississippi during its first decade. Territorial population increased from 7,598 in 1800 to 42,353 in 1810. Such a dramatic increase would create problems under any circumstances, but in a frontier environment where Indians claimed vast areas of land the problems were enormous and often led to violent conflict. As white settlers steadily encroached upon Indian lands, territorial officials resorted to the practice of buying land from the two large nations still located within Mississippi. During the territorial period there were three major land purchases, or Indian cessions as those purchases were called. In the first cession, executed by the Treaty of Fort Adams in 1801, the Choctaws gave up their claims to the land in the Old Natchez District. In 1805, by the terms of the Treaty of Mount Dexter (near Macon), the Choctaws sold approximately four and one half million acres to the United States government. Most of this land, known as the First Choctaw Cession, was located in the Piney Woods.

In 1816, the Choctaws, by the Treaty of Choctaw Trading House, and the Chickasaws, by the Treaty of Chickasaw Council House, sold several hundred thousand acres in the upper Tombigbee River valley to the federal government. These two purchases, known as the Tombigbee Cession, opened up some of North Mississippi's most fertile soil to white settlers. But even after these cessions, several million acres of land within the boundaries of Mississippi were still claimed by the Choctaws and Chickasaws. By 1832, however, practically all of this land had been purchased by the government.

Conflicting Land Claims

Still another problem facing Governor Claiborne and other territorial officials, was the confusion over land titles among Mississippi's white inhabitants. Citizens holding Spanish and English land grants or titles issued later by Georgia, claimed that those deeds were valid and should be honored under American law. Many of these people had already spent years clearing and improving their land. Like the Indians, they were willing to fight if necessary to hold onto their land.

Although the confusion caused by the various land claims was not solved immediately, the situation was greatly relieved on April 24, 1802 when the state of Georgia relinquished its claim to any land in Mississippi. In the following year, a federal land law established the validity of land grants made by England and Spain and also honored the titles held under Georgia law. Two federal land offices were established in 1803 at Washington, the territorial capital, and at Fort Stoddert on the Mobile River. Territorial residents could go to the land offices closest to them to have their titles validated.

Incorporation of Natchez, 1803

Although it was no longer the territorial capital, Natchez was the largest and fastest growing settlement in the Mississippi Territory. This growth made it necessary for Natchez to have a city government to regulate and supervise its development and maintain law and order among its citizens. On March 12, 1803, the territorial legislature incorporated the city of Natchez. This law established city limits and provided for elected officials who were authorized to collect taxes, to maintain order, and to perform other duties normally associated with governmental authority.

Louisiana Purchase, 1803

While land titles were being settled in the Mississippi wilderness, one of the most spectacular land deals in the history of man was being negotiated by American agents in Paris, France. It all started in October 1802, when American merchants were told that they could no longer deposit their goods in New Orleans without paying a fee. A month later Governor Claiborne wrote Secretary of War Henry Dearborn that there were rumors that Spain would soon sell Louisiana back to France. The Spanish Governor of Louisiana, Claiborne wrote, had told some ladies who had in turn told a "few others." After learning that Spain did intend to return Louisiana to France, President Jefferson opened negotiations for its purchase. He did not want to buy all of Louisiana, just New Orleans. However, when Napoleon Bonaparte, Emperor of France, offered to sell all 828,000 square miles of the Louisiana Territory for just $15,000,000—about 3¢ an acre—Jefferson accepted the deal. America bought an empire, just to get a city.

On December 20, 1803, Louisiana was transferred to the United States in official ceremonies in New Orleans. W. C. C. Claiborne accepted Louisiana on behalf of the United States. Claiborne remained in New Orleans and was later appointed governor of the Louisiana Territory when it was established in 1804.

Expansion of the Mississippi Territory

Following the Louisiana Purchase America entered an era of western expansion that not only shaped America's national character but also stimulated the development of sectional differences. To facilitate this expansion west, the United States government added the land between Tennessee and the 32°28″ parallel to the Mississippi Territory in 1804. At that time, most of this land was occupied by Choctaws and Chickasaws. In that same year, 1804, another federal judge was assigned to the eastern section of the Mississippi Territory. This additional judge was needed because of the increase in the number of cases in the Tombigbee settlements. The backwoodsmen argued that they needed a full-time rather than a part-time judge.

Administration of Robert Williams, 1805–1809

During the year and a half between Claiborne's assignment in Louisiana and Robert Williams' appointment as governor of Mississippi on March 1, 1805, Cato West served as acting governor of Mississippi. Although West was a capable and competent official, he was unable to control the intense political and sectional rivalry within the territory.

Governor Williams, who came to Mississippi from North Carolina, was not very successful either. The aristocratic merchants in Natchez and the backwoods farmers east of the Pearl

River were in constant disagreement over economic issues. The eastern half of the territory even tried to separate from the western half. The Tombigbee settlers were far away from the territorial capital, and it was very difficult to get to the capital during the rainy months when many of the small rivers and creeks were flooded.

There was also trouble along the Spanish border. The area south of the 31° parallel down to the Gulf Coast was Spanish territory, but many Americans were also living there. Among the Americans south of the 31° line were the notorious Kemper brothers, Nathan and Samuel. In 1804, they led an unsuccessful revolt against the Spanish and were captured. They were later rescued by American troops. For the next several years American citizens below the 31° parallel hatched several plots to free that area from Spanish control.

The Burr Conspiracy

In 1806 while Governor Williams was in North Carolina making plans to move his family to Mississippi, rumors began to spread throughout the territory that an invasion force led by Aaron Burr was headed down the Mississippi River. No one knew exactly what Burr intended to do. Some rumors had it that Burr was going to lead a secession movement in the Louisiana Purchase Territory. Other rumors suggested that he was going to invade Mexico. Still another rumor had Burr attacking the Spanish south of the 31° parallel. Not knowing what to expect, Acting-Governor Cowles Mead called out the militia and ordered the arrest of Burr. When Burr landed at Bruinsburg at the mouth of Bayou Pierre, he had only nine ships with less than seventy-five men and only a few arms—hardly the makings of an invasion force. Burr surrendered himself voluntarily to the militia on January 17, 1807, and allowed his ships to be searched. Judge Thomas Rodney set a special hearing for February 2, 1807, and then released Burr on $10,000 bond.

At the hearing there was practically no evidence to indicate that Burr had committed any crime. Even the Attorney General, George Poindexter, admitted that Burr was not guilty of violating any territorial law and he recommended that the jury be dismissed and that Burr be released. Judge Rodney did dismiss the jury on February 4 but ordered that Burr be held in custody until further notice. Within a few days, however, Burr disappeared. The whereabouts of Burr remained a mystery until late in February, when he was arrested near Fort Stoddert, north of Mobile on the Mobile River. At the time of his arrest, Burr was wearing old, shabby clothes, but his gentlemanly manner had aroused suspicion. He was taken to Washington, D.C., where charges of treason were brought against him. But once again very little evidence could be produced showing his guilt. Finally all charges against him were dropped, and he was released.

Administration of David Holmes, 1809–1817

On March 4, 1809, in one of his last official acts, President Jefferson appointed a native Virginian, David Holmes, governor of the Mississippi Territory. Holmes was a very popular and efficient territorial official. He was elected the first governor of the state in 1817.

Annexation of the Gulf Coast

As you have already learned, Mississippians living along the 31° parallel had been involved in border incidents with Spanish troops for several years. As the American population along the border increased, so did the desire to annex the Gulf Coast to the Mississippi Territory. In September 1810 a group of Americans captured the Spanish fort at Baton Rouge and established the Republic of West Florida. They immediately asked for annexation to the United States. On October 27, 1810, President James Madison issued a proclamation stating that the area south of the 31° parallel was already an American territory. He based that claim on the Louisiana Purchase of 1803. Madison said that the eastern boundary of the old Province of Louisiana had been the Perdido River and that all the area along the Gulf Coast had been included in the Purchase of 1803. Because Spain was involved in the Napoleonic Wars in Europe, Spanish authorities were unable to resist this American claim and allowed the Gulf Coast region to be annexed by the United States. There was some question among American officials as to which territory, Louisiana or Mississippi, the newly acquired possession should be attached. It was finally decided that the area south of the 31° parallel between the Mississippi River and the Pearl would go to Louisiana and the area between the Pearl and the Perdido Rivers would go to Mississippi.

The War of 1812

The basic cause of the War of 1812, between England and America, was the freedom of the seas. As far as the Mississippi Territory is concerned it was primarily an Indian War. For about a year before the war, which began on June 18, 1812, British agents in the United States had been forming alliances with various Indian nations. The British promised to return their land to the Indians if they helped defeat the United States. Tecumseh, the famous Shawnee warrior, was very helpful to the British in organizing the Indian tribes. In 1811, Tecumseh came to Mississippi to enlist the Choctaws and Chickasaws in his great confederation of Indian nations.

Tecumseh's Speech

To a large assembly of Choctaws, Chickasaws, and a few representatives from the Creek nation Tecumseh delivered a terrific and terrifying speech. Although there was no copy made of the original address, some years later several different versions of the speech appeared. The following is one of the best versions of Tecumseh's speech. Undoubtedly embellished by the historian, it appears in J. F. H. Claiborne's, *Mississippi As A Province Territory and State:*

> In defiance of the warriors of the dark and bloody ground, once our favorite hunting range, I have come from the great lakes of the North, and passed through their settlements like the wind at night. No war-whoop was sounded, no track was made, no fire was kindled, but see! there is blood on our war clubs!

The pale faces felt the blow, but knew not whence it came.

Accursed be the race that has made women of our warriors, and harlots of our women. They have seized our country, and our fathers in their graves reproach us as slaves and cowards. Listen! Do you not hear their voices in the wailing winds?

The Muscogees were once a mighty people. The pale faces trembled at your war-whoop, and the maidens of my tribe, on the distant lakes, sung the prowess of your warriors, and sighed for their embraces. And when our young men set out on the war-path the Shawnee sachems bade them, "Be brave like the Muscogee"!

But now your blood has become white; your tomahawks have no edge; your bows and arrows were buried with your fathers. You sleep while the pale face ploughs over their tombs, and fertilizes his fields with their sacred ashes.

Oh, Muscogees! Brethern of my mother! Brush from your eyelids the sleep of slavery, and strike for vengeance and your country!

The red men have fallen as the leaves now fall. I hear their voices in those aged pines. Their tears drop from the weeping skies. Their bones bleach on the hills of Georgia. Will no son of those brave men strike the pale face and quiet these complaining ghosts? Let the white race perish!

They seize your land; they corrupt your women; they trample on the bones of your dead!

Back whence they came, upon a trail of blood, they must be driven!

Back—aye, back into the great water whose accursed waves brought them to our shores!

Burn their dwellings—destroy their stock—slay their wives and children, that the very breed may perish.

War now! War always! War on the living! War on the dead! Dig their very corpses from their graves. The redman's land must give no shelter to a white man's bones!

This is the will of the Great Spirit, spoken in the ear of my brother, the mighty Prophet of the Lakes. He sends me to you.

All the tribes of the North are dancing the war dance. Two mighty warriors across the seas will send us arms—at Detroit for us, at Pensacola for you.

I will soon return to my country, to wash my hands in the blood of the pale face. My prophets shall tarry with you. They will stand by your side and catch the bullets of your enemies. When the white men approach your towns the earth shall open and swallow them up.

Soon shall you see my arm of fire stretched athwart the sky. You will know that I am on the war-path. I will stamp my foot and the very earth shall shake.

Shortly before this speech, British authorities had told Tecumseh about a comet that would soon appear. Also while he was on his way south from the Great Lakes region a great earthquake had occurred. Tecumseh mentioned both of those natural phenomena in his speech. The southern tribes had heard of these great events and were impressed with the supernatural powers claimed by Tecumseh and his brother, the "Prophet." However, the Choctaws and Chickasaws did not join Tecumseh in his war against the Americans. But the Creek nation did and soon after his speech Creek war parties attacked white settlements along the southern frontier.

Andrew Jackson and the Southwest Campaign

General Andrew Jackson of Tennessee was placed in command of the American troops in the southwest and was ordered to march against the Creeks. The Indian attacks had spread fear and panic among the settlers in communities near Creek villages.

Panic of 1813

Whites in the scattered settlements along the Tombigbee River hastily abandoned their homesteads and gathered at the residence of Samuel Mims, which later became known as Fort Mims because it was protected by a stockade. Soon over 500 men, women, and children had taken refuge inside the fort. Included in that number was a small detachment of troops under the command of Major Daniel Beasley. Although warned that the Creeks planned to attack the fort, Major Beasley failed to take the precaution of closing the front gate to the fort. At noon on August 30, 1813, a group of Creek warriors attacked Fort Mims and killed all but about thirty-six of the settlers within its walls. The fear that swept across the southern countryside, along with the news of the attack, was described as the Panic of 1813.

Heroic Hester

The loss of life among white settlers would undoubtedly have been even greater if it had not been for a slave woman known only as Hester. Although wounded in the attack, Hester made her way to the Mobile River, found a canoe, and rowed several miles downstream to Fort Stoddert where she warned General Ferdinand L. Claiborne of the Creek attack.

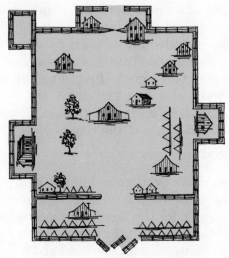

PLAN OF FORT MIMS

The End of the Creek War

Within a year after the attack of Fort Mims General Jackson had achieved several significant victories against the Creeks, including the Battle of the Holy Ground, December 23, 1813, and the Battle of Horseshoe Bend, March 27, 1814. Accompanying General Jackson in his campaign against the Creeks were the Mississippi Dragoons under the command of Colonel Thomas Hinds. Following their defeat the Creeks were forced to sign the

95

Treaty of Fort Jackson on August 9, 1814. Under the terms of this treaty the Creek nation agreed to lay down their arms. They also ceded millions of acres of land to the United States.

Battle of New Orleans

After the defeat of the Creeks, General Jackson was ordered to New Orleans to defend that city against a British invasion. When the Battle of New Orleans took place on January 8, 1815, the War of 1812 was already over but neither the British naval commanders nor General Jackson had received the official news. This famous battle, which was a great victory for America, made General Jackson a national hero and helped him win the presidential election several years later. General Jackson's command at New Orleans included an unusual combination of troops. In addition to his own troops (the Tennessee Volunteers) Jackson again had the aid of Colonel Hinds and his Mississippi Dragoons. There were also two battalions of free blacks fighting with General Jackson. Even the famous pirate, Jean Lafitte, contributed to the defense of the city of New Orleans.

Pushmataha

Another hero made even more famous by his exploits during the Creek War was Pushmataha, the Choctaw chief. When Tecumseh had called for the Southern nations to join him in war against the whites, Pushmataha had counseled against such action. And when General Jackson marched against the Creeks, Pushmataha led a force of Choctaw and Chickasaw warriors into battle under the American flag.

This Choctaw chief's ancestry was not known exactly, but he often claimed: "I had no father, no mother, no brother, no sister. The winds howled, the rain fell, the thunder roared and the lightning flashed; a pine tree was slivered, and from its splinters stepped forth Pushmataha with his rifle on his shoulder."

In 1824, Pushmataha visited Washington, D.C., where he met President James Monroe, Secretary of War John C. Calhoun, and Marquis de Lafayette, the French hero of the Revolution. He was especially pleased to meet Lafayette. Remembering the

Pushmataha, Choctaw chief.

friendship between the French and Choctaws many years earlier, Pushmataha said to Lafayette:

> We heard of you in our distant villages. We longed to see you. We have taken your hand. For the last time we look on the face of the great warrior whose fathers were the friends of our fathers. We go. Tis the last time we shall meet. We shall soon be in the land of shadows.

His words were prophetic. Soon after his meeting with Lafayette the aging chieftain became gravely ill with pneumonia. General Jackson visited Pushmataha several times just before his death. On one of those visits, Jackson asked the old warrior if he had any last wishes. Pushmataha answered, "When I am dead, fire the big guns over me." A short time later he died and was buried with full military honors. The big guns sounded his death.

Mississippi Becomes a State

After the War of 1812 Mississippi's population grew rapidly and soon reached the level necessary for advancement to the third grade of territorial status. During this final stage a constitutional convention was assembled at the territorial capital. After the constitution was completed and state officials were elected, the United States Congress officially admitted Mississippi to statehood. This process, which will be more fully discussed in the next chapter, was completed on December 10, 1817.

Life in the Territory

Mississippians who had been living in the territory since its establishment in 1798 must have remarked on the eve of statehood, "My, how things have changed!" Those hardy pioneers who fought their way through Indian territory and cut their way through the wilderness to get to Mississippi could hardly have imagined that in less than twenty years there would be over 75,000 people living in the territory. They would not have believed that they would soon be hearing steamboat whistles announcing the arrival of mail, goods, and passengers from the East.

Transportation

In the early days of the territory, flatboats were the most important means of transportation. These "Kentucky Arks," which were used exclusively for downstream traffic on the Mississippi River, were about 40 feet long, 12 feet wide, and 8 feet deep. The trip from Kentucky to New Orleans usually took about six months. At the end of the long journey the boats were dismantled and the lumber was sold along with the cargo of horses, cattle, hogs, chickens, pelts, iron, apples, whiskey, hemp, corn, tobacco, etc. On some occasions these flatboats also carried settlers down river to Natchez.

Similar in some respects to the "Kentucky Arks," were the keelboats which were used not only for downstream traffic but upstream as well. These shallow draft boats were pointed at both ends and had running boards on each side for the crew to stand on as they poled the boat or pulled it upstream by grabbing overhanging tree limbs and bushes. This latter method was called "bushwhacking." When boats were being pulled along in this manner, they were easy prey for the river pirates who hid in the bushes along the banks waiting for an opportunity to attack.

Keelboats were also pulled against the river's current by tying a long rope to a tree upstream and then pulling the craft to the point where the rope was tied. By repeating this over and over, the crew gradually moved the boat upstream. Some boats were

Flatboats were primary form of transportation during the early territorial period.

equipped with a winch or crank to wind in the rope which made upstream travel less difficult than pulling the rope by hand. Ocean-going vessels were sometimes brought from New Orleans up to Natchez by using this method, but not too often because it usually took eighty days to travel the 300 miles between the two cities.

Poling a Keelboat upstream.

The Steamboat

In 1811 river transportation was revolutionized by the advent of steam powered vessels. Nicholas Roosevelt of New York built the first steamboat to travel the Mississippi River. His boat, the **New Orleans**, stopped at Natchez in December 1811 on its maiden voyage from Pittsburgh to New Orleans. For several years afterwards the ship made regular runs between New Orleans and Natchez. Roosevelt's original design was later modified by Henry Shreve, and a new era of river travel dawned. By 1860 steamboats plied most of the river systems throughout the state and connected the interior sections of the state with the commercial centers along the Mississippi River and the Gulf Coast.

The Natchez Trace

The earliest and most important overland route into the Mississippi Territory was the Natchez Trace. Originally a Chickasaw Indian trail through central Mississippi, the Trace was extended to Natchez after the territory was established. In 1801, the trail was surveyed and designated as an official United

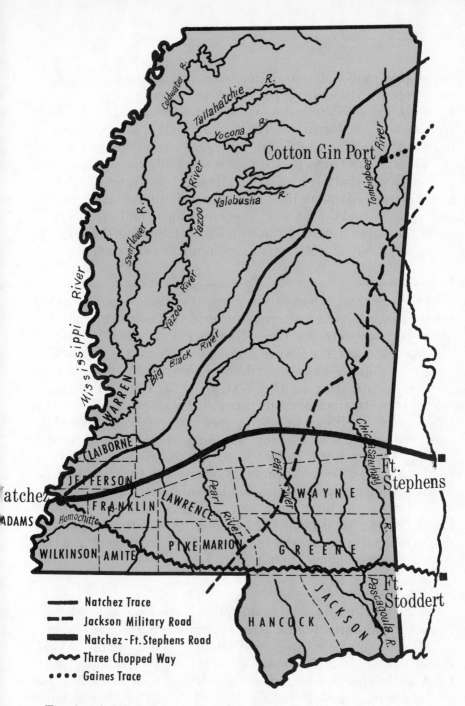

Territorial Transportation Routes and
Original Fourteen Counties of Mississippi, 1798-1817

States post road and mail route. After negotiating land cessions with Indian nations along the Trace, the territorial government was authorized to widen the roadbed to sixteen feet and extend it from Natchez to Nashville, Tennessee. Neither land pirates nor unfriendly Indians could deter the ever increasing number of travelers on the Trace. By 1818 there were fifty inns, lodges, and trading posts scattered along the Trace from Natchez to Bear Creek on the Alabama line. In 1934 the United States government established the Natchez Trace as a National Parkway, and since that time a hard surface highway, following the original Trace as closely as possible, has been under construction.

Other Roads

As the territorial population grew, it was necessary to build roads connecting the scattered settlements. The most important of these roads were the Three Chopped Way between Natchez and Fort Stoddert, the Gaines Trace which connected Cotton Gin Port with Muscle Shoals, Alabama, and the Natchez to Fort Stephens road. During the War of 1812, General Jackson learned that the lack of roads through the Mississippi Territory was a great hindrance in getting men and supplies to New Orleans. After the war Jackson was authorized to build a road through the territory. Known as Jackson's Military Road, this route extended from Columbia, Tennessee, through Muscle Shoals, Alabama, crossed the Tombigbee River where the town of Columbus was later built, and then proceeded through east Mississippi to Madisonville, Louisiana. Since all the overland routes crossed many creeks and rivers, ferry boats were in widespread use throughout the territory.

Cotton Culture

Cotton was introduced into the lower Mississippi valley by the French in the early 1720's. They probably brought a few plants into Mississippi from the French colonies in the Caribbean Sea. During these early years many different varieties of cotton were tried in the humid Mississippi climate but none of them grew well enough to make cotton a profitable crop. The time and cost involved in separating the lint from the seed, which was done by hand, also discouraged the growth of the cotton culture. However, the invention of the cotton gin and the development of the Petit Gulf seed had an enormous impact on cotton production in Mississippi. These developments increased the cash value of cotton and it soon became Mississippi's major export.

A Slave Mechanic

In 1795 a slave mechanic, whose name is unknown, was given a verbal description and a drawing of Eli Whitney's cotton gin. From this information, this slave craftsman built a workable model of the most important machine in Southern history. The Whitney gin was inexpensive to produce and very soon several of the machines were in use in south Mississippi. The major value of the mechanical method of separating the lint from the seed was the fact that one machine could do the work of many hands and the slaves who had been performing that slow and tedious job were free to work in the fields growing more cotton.

An early Whitney gin.

Mexican-Petit Gulf Variety

With an inexpensive method of ginning available, the only other thing necessary to make cotton the state's major cash crop was the development of a variety that would grow well in Mississippi. It had been known for some time that Mexican cotton would grow in a damp climate, but Spanish officials in Mexico had forbidden its exportation. According to tradition, Walter Burling of Natchez visited Mexico in 1806. While having dinner with a Spanish official who was a friend of his, Burling asked for permission to take some Mexican seeds back to Natchez. This official explained his government's policy prohibiting the exportation of cotton seeds. But with a grin, he told Burling that there was no policy that would prohibit him from taking Mexican dolls home with him. Acting upon this suggestion, Burling bought several dolls which he stuffed with cotton seed and brought them back to Natchez. A few years later, Dr. Rush Nutt, a planter and scientist, developed the Petit Gulf variety of cotton from the Mexican seeds brought to Mississippi by Burling. The Petit Gulf variety was ideally suited for Mississippi's growing conditions. Within a few years cotton became the crown prince of Mississippi's economy by replacing tobacco, indigo, and hemp as the state's chief crop. By the end of the 1830's cotton became King.

Cattle Herding

In the eastern section of the Mississippi Territory large herds of cattle and swine roamed the Piney Woods and canebrakes between the Pearl and Tombigbee Rivers. They grazed on the grass and reeds along the small creeks and rivers and foraged in the woods for acorns and nuts. Once a year the Piney Woods herdsmen drove their livestock to market in Mobile and other nearby towns. Cattle raising on the open range provided a living income for thousands of east Mississippians until the Civil War.

Industry and Commerce

By no means was everyone in the Mississippi Territory engaged in agriculture or cattle raising. In Natchez, Port Gibson, Vicksburg, and other settlements mercantile establishments conducted a thriving business. There was a textile plant, six distilleries, two newspapers, and a bank in Natchez. There were also several tanneries, tinsmiths, saw mills, barbershops, blacksmith shops, stables, and taverns located in the Mississippi Territory.

Education in the Territory

Public education as we know it today did not exist in the territory. Most children were taught by private tutors or were sent to private academies. Jefferson College was established at Washington in 1802, but did not open because of financial problems until 1811. Jefferson College's most famous professor was John James Audubon, the naturalist whose bird paintings are still very popular. The college closed in 1826 and later became a military school.

Many territorial residents were interested in the accumulation of any useful or scientific information that could improve agriculture production. Several prominent men in the territory established the Society for the Acquirement and Dissemination of Useful Knowledge. The society's most prestigious member was William Dunbar who often corresponded with Thomas Jefferson and other well-known scientists and educators of his day. One member of the society was reprimanded by his church for using his telescope. The church criticized him for invading the privacy of God.

Early Newspapers

Throughout most of the antebellum period Mississippi's newspapers were not published merely as news journals. They were usually established to promote the cause of a particular political party, a faction within a party, or even an individual candidate seeking public office. This fact explains the existence of so many newspapers that were published for just a few years or in some cases only a few months. Editors were strongly committed to what they believed to be a righteous cause. They considered themselves defenders of the truth. The names of their papers bear this out. Two of the first papers published in the territory were the **Herald** and the **Messenger**. Later journals were styled the **Guardian**, the **Sentinel**, the **Clarion**, and the **Pilot**. More often than not, editors viewed their rival editors as false prophets who would lead the people to doom and destruction or worse. Many editors, who usually wrote their fiery editorials with cocked revolvers close by, were almost constantly involved in controversies which often led to duels.

Marschalk—Poindexter Feud

One of these controversies which fortunately did not lead to a duel, was between Andrew Marschalk and George Poindexter. Marschalk brought the first printing press into Mississippi in 1798 and soon afterwards began publishing a newspaper. George Poindexter was one of the territory's most prominent political figures. These two strong-willed men belonged to opposing political parties. After a series of editorials criticizing Judge Poindexter appeared in Marschalk's paper, the editor was called before the judge and fined twenty dollars for contempt of court. Marschalk said that he would gladly pay the fine because that was just what he intended—contempt for Judge Poindexter. When the editorials continued, Judge Poindexter saw Marschalk on the street one day and started chasing him with a brickbat, threatening to hit the editor if he could catch him. Marschalk then had Poindexter put in jail. But the judge let himself out of jail by signing the papers ordering his own release. Their running battle continued until Marschalk's death in 1837.

Religion in the Territory

Life was hard during the frontier days in the Mississippi Territory. The rugged settlers took everything seriously—their work, their play, their whiskey-drinking, and especially their religion. Both the Spanish and French established missions in the Mississippi Territory, and Roman Catholicism was the dominant religion until 1763. British settlers naturally brought the Anglican faith with them into the frontier wilderness. Very soon, however, as migration from the Atlantic Coast increased, other denominations including Baptists, Methodists, and Presbyterians appeared in the territory. These religious groups, which were especially opposed to drunkenness and gambling, played an important role in taming the Mississippi frontier.

Territorial Architecture

The earliest white settlers in Mississippi lived in log cabins because timber was the only building material available to them. Starting out with a one room cabin, settlers would add rooms as they prospered or as the size of their families increased. Eventually an architectural style, known as a "dogtrot house," developed in the Southern frontier. A dogtrot house consisted of two or three rooms on one side of an open hallway with a similar number of rooms on the other side. A single roof covered the rooms on both sides of the hall. If a farmer became wealthy, he might close in the hallway, add a second floor and tall white columns to give his home a more stately appearance.

A dogtrot house.

This log cabin served as the Pike County sheriff's office in 1815.

Concord, the home of Spanish governors, was built at Natchez.

There were very few large mansions in Mississippi during the territorial period. The few which did exist were built by the wealthy planters living along the Mississippi River near Natchez. The best examples of these are **Concord**, built by Governor Gayoso, **Gloucester**, built by Winthrop Sargent, and **Forest**, built by William Dunbar. Most of the large mansions for which the South has become famous were built during the early years of statehood. Those formative years will be the subject of the next chapter.

A. KEY TERMS—Explain the following terms. If necessary, use a dictionary or encyclopedia.

1. land grants
2. political factions
3. chattel slavery
4. territorial assembly
5. administration
6. governor
7. judge
8. commerce
9. industry
10. aristocrats
11. "Kentucky Triangle"
12. Sam Mason
13. Wiley "Little" Harpe
14. demography
15. Natchez
16. Washington
17. Fort Stoddert
18. Louisiana Purchase
19. Cato West
20. George Poindexter
21. David Holmes
22. Republic of West Florida
23. confederation
24. Andrew Jackson
25. Hester
26. Treaty of Fort Jackson
27. keelboats
28. Nicholas Roosevelt
29. Three Chopped Way
30. Petit Gulf Cotton
31. Walter Burling
32. cattle herding
33. William Dunbar
34. Andrew Marschalk
35. dogtrot

B. MATCHING EXERCISE

1. slavery
2. Winthrop Sargent
3. W. C. C. Claiborne
4. "Kentucky Arks"
5. Natchez Trace
6. Tecumseh
7. Panic of 1813
8. Colonel Thomas Hinds
9. Pushmataha
10. Eli Whitney

a. second territorial governor
b. organized Indian confederation
c. followed attack of Fort Mims
d. famous Choctaw Chief
e. "peculiar institution"
f. commander of Mississippi Dragoons
g. first territorial governor
h. "Devil's Backbone"
i. cotton gin
j. flatboats

C. MAKING A TIME LINE—Arrange the following events in the correct order in which they took place:

Addition of territory north of 32°28"
Burr Conspiracy
Winthrop Sargent appointed governor
W. C. C. Claiborne appointed governor
Establishment of Mississippi Territory
Louisiana Purchase
War of 1812

D. MAP EXERCISE

On a map, sketch the early roads in the Mississippi Territory and the original fourteen counties. Also include the boundaries of Indian land cessions.

CHAPTER V

Early Statehood, 1817–1851

One of the challenges facing the young American republic in its early years was sectionalism. This problem was caused by the differences in geography and climate which existed in various parts of the country. People in each of these regions, or sections, developed local customs and traditions and different economic interests. Representatives and senators in the United States Congress almost always supported laws and policies that were good for their section. But, unfortunately, what was good for one section was not always good for another. One of the causes of sectionalism can be seen in the controversy over the protective tariff. A protective tariff is a tax placed on manufactured goods that are brought into America from foreign countries. This tax is added to the cost of the products when they are sold to the American people. The purpose of this tax is to protect American manufacturers from the competition of manufacturers in other countries. Tariff laws were understandably supported by congressmen from those states in the Northeast where most of the nation's factories were located. But, it is also understandable that congressmen from agricultural states would oppose such laws because they made the prices of manufactured products higher than they would be without tariffs.

Another issue that caused serious sectional differences was slavery. In the southern agricultural states slavery was the primary system of labor. But in the Northeast white wage earners did most of the work. Over the years a sectional controversy developed over whether or not America should continue to allow slavery. Eventually, this issue became the single most important sectional controversy in American politics. Almost all other sectional differences or controversies were related in one way or another to this question. Perhaps it will be easier to understand sectionalism on the national level by observing a similar development within Mississippi during its early years.

Sectionalism in Mississippi

Settlement patterns during the territorial period were almost certain to produce sectionalism within Mississippi. The first immigrants into the territory settled in the Old Natchez District or in the backwoods areas between the Pearl and Tombigbee Rivers. The Natchez District, which was much more heavily populated than the backwoods, dominated the territorial assembly and the Tombigbee settlers felt they were being neglected. They complained that the capital was too far away from their settlements and that most of the laws seemed to favor the commercial interests along the Mississippi River instead of the rural farm settlements. On several occasions, the backwoods farmers proposed that the territory be divided so they could have their own capital and territorial assembly in the eastern part of the territory. But by 1817, when Mississippi was ready to become a state, the population in the eastern section of the state had outgrown the Old Natchez District, and the situation was reversed. The western half of the territory was then in favor of separating the territory into east/west divisions.

The problem of how to divide the territory was also complicated by the fact that there was another settlement in the northern part of the territory on the upper Tombigbee River. There seemed to be only one thing that everybody agreed upon: that the Mississippi Territory should be divided in some way. And everyone's idea of how it should be divided was determined by the interests of the different sections in which they lived. Finally, it was decided that the territory should be divided by a line running south from the Tennessee border down through the middle of the territory to the Gulf Coast. The western half of the territory became the state of Mississippi in 1817. The eastern half became the state of Alabama in 1819. This solution certainly did not satisfy everyone, and sectionalism continued to be a major factor in Mississippi politics for years to come.

Sense of Place

Another very important factor in the development of sectionalism in America and within the different states, is the fondness that people develop for the locality where they are born and grow up. This feeling is sometime called a sense of place. This awareness of and fondness for one's place of birth seems to be much stronger in Southerners than in most other Americans. During our nation's first two hundred years Southerners developed an attachment for and a loyalty to their section that has been the subject of study by sociologists, historians, writers, and even movie-makers and television producers. No one has been able to fully explain it, but hardly anyone denies that this very strong sense of place exists among Southerners. It was certainly noticeable in Mississippi at the time of its admission to statehood.

The Constitution of 1817

On March 1, 1817, President James Madison signed the Enabling Act, a law which provided for Mississippi's admission as the twentieth state in the federal union. In preparation for this major step a constitutional convention was held from July 7 to August 15, 1817, at the Methodist church in Washington, the territorial capital. This convention was composed of forty-eight delegates who were elected from the fourteen counties located in the area that had been divided from Alabama.

A special Committee of Twenty-One was appointed to draft a constitution. George Poindexter was the chairman of this committee and actually wrote most of the state's first constitution. Since Poindexter was from Natchez and was associated with the economic interests of that section, the constitution reflected the influence of the Natchez aristocracy. Only white, male citizens who either owned some kind of property or were in the state militia were eligible to vote. John Burton, a delegate from Amite County, proposed that the voting age be set at eighteen, but his proposal was defeated. The constitution established a bicameral state legislature, that is, two houses consisting of a senate and a house of representatives. Members of the senate were required to own three hundred acres of land or other property valued at $1,000 and members of the house of representatives were required to own one hundred fifty acres or property valued at $500.

112

The Governor was required to own six hundred acres or $2,000 worth of personal property.

Because of these property requirements, it is obvious that only the wealthy exercised any real power in running the state government. But it should be pointed out that practically all the states in the Union at that time had some property requirement both for office holding and for voting. In the 1830's Mississippi and most states dropped those requirements.

Admission to Statehood

After the adoption of the constitution the voters of Mississippi elected the officials created by that constitution. David Holmes, who was then serving as governor of the territory, was elected Mississippi's first governor. George Poindexter was elected as the state's representative to the United States Congress, and Walter Leake and Thomas H. Williams were appointed by the state legislature as Mississippi's first United States Senators. (Senators were not elected by the people of their states until after the passage of the Seventeenth Amendment to the United States Constitution in 1913). After these steps had been taken, the United States Congress passed a law formally admitting Mississippi as a co-equal member of the union of states on December 10, 1817.

Economic Development

The future of Mississippi was bright in 1817, and its citizens set themselves to the task of developing its natural resources. The state's most abundant natural resource was land. It was available to almost anyone "for the taking." There were, however, several obstacles that had to be overcome before the state could realize the maximum benefit from this resource.

Internal Improvements

In 1817 there were very few roads or bridges in Mississippi, especially in the remote sections that were sparsely settled. Also, many of the state's rivers, another valuable natural resource, were not navigable for any great distances because of sunken logs, trees that had washed out along the banks, and other obstructions. In order for settlers to occupy and develop the land which was then available, they had to be able to get to it. Consequently, internal improvements was one of the most important issues to come before the state legislature in the early days of statehood. Internal improvements are such things as roads and bridges which are financed by public funds. The re-

Snagboats like this one were used to keep the rivers clear of fallen trees and sunken logs.

moval of snags from the state's river system, at public expense, was another example of internal improvements. Later, and in other parts of the nation, internal improvements included the construction of canals and railroads.

Mississippians living near the Pearl River were especially anxious for the state to improve the navigation of the Pearl River which would enable them to transport their goods down river to the Gulf Coast. This would save them the extra time and cost of taking their products overland to Natchez and then shipping them down the Mississippi River. However, if traffic on the

Pearl River increased, commerce along the Mississippi River would decrease and this would be bad for business in Natchez. Natchez residents also realized that roads and bridges into the back-country would cause a rapid population growth of that region and would result not only in business losses but in political losses as well. Therefore, legislators from the counties along the Mississippi River usually voted against internal improvements. But they could not prevent the inevitable growth of the interior section of the state which began developing much more rapidly after the Indian Cessions of 1830 and 1832.

The Movement of the State Capital

The Constitution of 1817 provided that the location of the state capital would be determined by the legislature. The site of the new capital soon became a sectional issue as Piney Woods residents began to demand that the capital be moved from Natthez to a more central location. The worst fears of Natchez businessmen seemed to be coming true. They were not only losing trade along the Mississippi River, but would soon lose even the state capital.

In 1821 the legislature appointed a special committee to recommend a site as near the center of the state as possible for the location of a new state capital. The committee recommended Le Fleur's Bluff on the Pearl River. This bluff was named for Louis Le Fleur, a French trader who first came to Mobile in 1792 and later established a trading post on the bluff that now bears his name. Le Fleur married a Choctaw Indian girl named Rebecca, who bore him a famous son, Greenwood Leflore.

The first
State Capitol
in Jackson.

115

While a town site was being laid out at Le Fleur's Bluff, the state capital was moved temporarily to Columbia in Marion County. The legislature met for the first time at the new capital city, named for General Andrew Jackson, in December 1822. For several years after the establishment of Jackson the location of the state capital continued to be a topic of controversy. Immediately after the Civil War, serious consideration was given to the matter of moving the capital to north Mississippi, but no action was taken. As late as the 1880's, a bill was introduced in the state legislature to transfer the capital to Meridian. To put an end to any further wrangling over its location, the Constitution of 1890 established Jackson as Mississippi's permanent seat of government.

Flush Times

As we have already seen, most of the small Indian nations left Mississippi when the French ceded the territory to the British in 1763. Only the Choctaws and Chickasaws remained within Mississippi at the time the Territory was established. In 1830 and 1832 these two large nations finally gave up their remaining tribal lands and agreed to move out west where they were given land in Oklahoma. These cessions, which more than doubled the area open for white settlement, caused a land rush and population explosion that transformed Mississippi's economic and social system.

At a banquet celebrating the acquisition of this land, Robert J. Walker of Natchez declared:

> Already the feet of thousands press upon the borders of this new purchase—to pitch their tents in the wilderness—Kentucky's coming, Tennessee's coming, Alabama's coming, and they're coming to join the joyous crowds of Mississippians.

These settlers were attracted to this newly acquired area because the land was very cheap. Under a federal law passed in 1832 an individual could buy land from the government for $1.25 an acre with a minimum purchase of fifty acres. Within a few years over seven and one half million acres of good cotton land in north Mississippi were sold by the United States government. Mississippi's population soared from 136,621 in 1830 to 375,651 in 1840. The economic expansion of the early 1830's was known as the "Flush Times" when "a golden canopy covered the land."

Towns sprang up over night. Slaves were imported into the state in ever increasing numbers. The state's economy was booming. Several new banks were chartered to supply the money and credit necessary for the purchase of land and farm supplies and slaves. Prices for everything were rising in this period of inflation. For example, land prices had risen from $1.25 an acre in 1832 to $40.00 an acre in 1836. Young black men and women were being sold for $1,600 each.

The Second Mississippi Bubble

The state's rapid economic growth in the 1830's created a period of inflation similar to the "boom" period under John Law in the 1730's. Settlers moving into Mississippi in the 1830's did not have much gold or silver so they had to borrow the money to buy land, slaves, farm animals, and equipment. To meet the ever increasing demand for credit, the legislature authorized railroad companies to lend money just like banks. This law made things worse, however, because "fly-by-night" railroad companies were organized solely for the purpose of lending money at high interest rates. These companies were not interested in building railroads. During the 1830's twenty-two railroad corporations were chartered, but all of them combined laid only 83 miles of track. The lenient credit policies, or easy terms, offered by the railroad companies and state banks put millions of dollars of paper money (promissory notes and certificates of credit, etc.) into circulation. Real money or specie, (which is gold or silver), was scarce but everybody and anybody could get credit. It was an insult to deny a man credit. The only thing a man had to do to get a loan was to sign a piece of paper promising to repay the loan at a later date. This was called a promissory note. Upon receiving a loan the borrower put up his land as security or collateral for the loan. If the borrower failed to pay back the loan, the bank could confiscate or take his land. It should be remembered that the value of land was very high during the first few years of the Flush Times and men could borrow large sums of money on their land. With such easy credit available, many Mississippians over extended themselves. They bought too much land and too many slaves. They were deeply in debt, and prices were rising.

By 1836 many people realized that the boom period had reached such a point that an economic collapse was inevitable. President Andrew Jackson was so concerned about the rate of inflation that he ordered the federal land offices to accept only specie in payment for land purchases. He hoped that this policy would discourage the continued use of paper money which he believed to be the major cause of rising prices. This order, known as the Specie Circular, caused an immediate slowdown in the state's economic growth. Individual land owners quickly followed the government's example and they too refused to accept paper money as payment for land. Since most people did not have any gold or silver, the price of land began to drop because no one could buy land. People who had borrowed money using their land for security were now in real trouble. The value of land had decreased so much, so quickly, that most of these borrowers owed the banks more money than they could get for their land if they sold it. To make matters even worse, the Bank of the United States, the major financial institution in America, tightened its credit policy which made bank loans much harder to obtain.

Mississippi banks and the people who had borrowed from them faced still another serious and unexpected problem. In 1833 about one million dollars of federal surplus funds had been deposited in two Mississippi banks. This money had been immediately loaned to Mississippi farmers. But in 1836 the Congress passed a law which provided that those funds be distributed among all the states. Mississippi's share of the funds was about $500,000. Therefore, the two banks had to collect the federal funds which they had already loaned to Mississippi farmers.

When the banks started calling in the loans, people were not able to repay them. The banks had no alternative but to confiscate their property. Thousands of Mississippians lost everything—their land, homes, tools, and slaves. Some others, however, gathered up all their personal property, including slaves, and migrated to Texas. They often left secretly at night, to keep from having to surrender their property. When the sheriff came to their farms to confiscate their goods and noticed that they had already left, he scribbled "G.T.T." on the court order authorizing foreclosure. They had "Gone to Texas." The boom was over and the state's economy collapsed.

The Panic of 1837

This collapse was called the Panic of 1837. The word panic describes the emotional crisis that people experience when they realize that they are about to lose everything they had worked so hard to get and to build. The optimism and enthusiasm that was wide-spread during the boom period had turned into pessimism and bitterness at the time of the collapse. In an effort to soften the blow and to make additional money available for loans, the legislature chartered the Union Bank and bought $5,000,000 worth of the bank's stock. This purchase of stock by the state of Mississippi was necessary to help get the bank started because few citizens were able to buy stock—they were broke and were just trying to hold on to their land and slaves. To get this $5,000,000 the legislature issued state bonds. The state in essence borrowed the money. But disaster struck within a year, and the Union Bank went bankrupt. The state was left with the worthless bank stock, but still owed the five million dollars it had borrowed to buy the stock. The legislature faced an impossible situation. It had no money; its tax revenues were barely enough to meet its operating costs; and it also owed, in addition to the Union Bank bonds, for other bank stock it had bought a few years earlier. A public controversy developed over the course of action the state should take. The state legislature finally decided to repudiate, or not repay, the bonds. This decision caused a bitter political debate which continued until 1890 when the

119

new state constitution declared that the bonds had been issued illegally by the legislature and were not a valid debt against the state.

By the mid-1840's Mississippi's economy had recovered, and the people once again enjoyed prosperity.

King Cotton

One of the most important developments during the Flush Times was Mississippi's growing dependence upon a one-crop cotton economy. Just as Mississippi was entering the Flush Times an industrial revolution in the English textile industry increased the demand for southern cotton. This demand, coupled with the availability of cheap land and a ready supply of slaves, caused many Mississippi farmers to abandon other crops in favor of cotton. The production of cotton could make a man rich within a few years. And those cotton-rich aristocrats, living in big white mansions, quickly became the economic and social models for other white Mississippians. Although only about eight percent of the population was able to achieve that lifestyle of leisure, it remained the "Great Mississippi Dream" until the Civil War.

Parties, Politics, and Expansion

One of the things that made Mississippi attractive in the 1830's, in addition to its cheap land and economic opportunity, was its democratic politics. The Constitution of 1817 had already become very unpopular by 1832. The establishment of many new counties within the Indian Cessions in north Mississippi and a need for several additional court districts made many changes in the constitution necessary. The shift in political power from the Old Natchez District to the rapidly growing northern part of the state also brought about a shift in political philosophy. For one thing, the people wanted the right to elect judges. Under the 1817 constitution, all judges were appointed. The people also wanted to abolish the property requirements for office holding and voting. The dissatisfaction with the old constitution was shown in 1831 when the people voted four to one in favor of a state convention to draft a new constitution.

Constitution of 1832

On September 10, 1832, forty-eight delegates met at Jackson to draft a new state constitution. Only about half of them had any political experience outside their local communities. One of the wealthy delegates from Adams County remarked, "the many young and inexperienced men we have in this body give rise to wild and extravagant schemes . . . [They are] in favor of what they call **Reform**." The changes in the 1832 constitution, which may have seemed "wild and extravagant" to the wealthy, conservative delegates, reflected the spirit of reform which was so popular in the 1820's and 1830's. This period is known as the "Rise of the Common Man." Although it may seem strange to modern day Americans, the leaders of reform in that period gave hardly any serious thought at all to extending the right to vote to either women or free blacks. It was difficult enough to win that right to vote for all white males.

One of the most important changes in the 1832 constitution was the removal of all property qualification for holding public office and voting. These provisions brought even the highest offices of state government within the reach of all white male citizens. In addition, all judicial officials and many other officers who had been appointed under the 1817 constitution were to be elected by the people.

Another very important provision of the new constitution was the abolition of imprisonment for debt. Even as late as the 1830's people could still be put in jail if they did not pay their debts. Although it was not actually enforced very often, imprisonment for debt was still legal throughout America. But Mississippi's 1832 constitution authorized the legislature to devise some means for the collection of debts other than imprisonment. Mississippi was one of the first states in the nation to abolish this system.

By today's standards of democracy the Constitution of 1832 may not appear very progressive. But for the period during which it was adopted, it was considered a major victory by the reform leaders of that day. Many people were attracted to Mississippi because of its democratic spirit.

Public Building Program

The new constitution expanded the services of state government and created several new agencies to administer those services. The creation of new state agencies caused something of a problem. At that time the only building the state owned was a two-story building located in Jackson. That small capitol could not house all the new agencies. The new constitution also required the governor to live in Jackson during his term of office. But there was no suitable residence in the capital for the governor and his family. Therefore, the first legislature to meet following the adoption of the constitution appropriated $105,000 for the construction of a state capitol building and a mansion for the governor.

The State Capitol

The law authorizing the construction of the capitol also provided for the appointment of a state architect. William Nichols was appointed in 1835. Things did not go smoothly for Nichols, however, and a long series of problems ranging from a shortage of labor and supplies to the Panic of 1837 delayed the completion of the capitol until 1839.

The Old Capitol, built in 1839, is now a state historical museum.

By 1903, state government had again outgrown the capitol building. Moreover, its condition was so dilapidated that costly repairs would have been necessary for the old building to continue as the state capitol. Rather than spend the money to repair the old capitol, the legislature voted to build a new capitol to be located on the site of the state penitentiary which was no longer in use.

When the legislature decided to build a new capitol, Jackson businessmen urged the legislature to tear down the old capitol and sell the lot for commercial development. But because the old capitol was a direct link to Mississippi's past and had been the scene of so much of the state's history, that suggestion was rejected. Instead, the building was preserved and later renovated. The old Capitol now serves as a state historical museum. Governor William Winter took the oath of office in this historic building on January 22, 1980.

The Governor's Mansion

Mississippi's antebellum Governor's Mansion also has an interesting history. Serving as the official residence of every governor since 1842, the Mansion is known throughout the country for its architectural beauty and its tradition of hospitality. During the Civil War it was used as a Confederate hospital and as a headquarters for General William T. Sherman. The Mansion has sometimes been the focus of controversy because of the expensive repairs needed to maintain the building. But even when its physical condition and appearance were not a source of pride to the people, its tradition of hospitality was.

In 1972, the Mansion was in such poor condition that it was not safe for the First Family to live in it. Many people favored tearing it down and building a new Governor's Mansion in a Jackson suburb. But Mississippi's First Lady, Carroll Waller, led an effort to preserve the Governor's Mansion which she called the "home of our heritage." Through the cooperative efforts of the Department of Archives and History, the state legislature, the Building Commission, and especially Governor William L. Waller, the Mansion was not only saved but was restored to its original splendor.

One of the earliest pictures of the Governor's Mansion.

The money to beautify the Mansion's gardens was contributed by private individuals and businesses. Several hundred dollars was raised by the school children of Mississippi through a "Dimes for the Mansion" fund raising project. The dimes which the school children contributed were used to construct the gazebo on the Mansion's west lawn. On June 8, 1975, at the formal reopening following its restoration, the Governor's Mansion was designated a national historic landmark.

Political Parties

Mississippi has always been famous for its fiery brand of politics. Its citizens have traditionally taken politics seriously and have been very active in the support of the party of their choice. In antebellum Mississippi there were two major parties, the Whigs and the Democrats. These two parties nominated candidates for local and state-wide offices and party members usually turned out in large numbers to support their candidates. In those early days political debates were held several times during a campaign. Those debates were not like political rallies of today, where candidates appear to make a short speech and then hurry on to their next engagement or to a television appearance. In those days the rallies often lasted for several hours, maybe even all day. Sometimes, if a platform was not available, candidates stood on tree stumps to make their speeches. When one candidate was finished, his opponent took the stump to criticize or correct the previous speaker who was usually standing by to listen. If a candidate heard something he felt was untrue, or unfair, or insulting to him, he might interrupt the speaker and demand that he retract or clarify his statement. Often the audience demonstrated their agreement or disagreement by cheering, applauding, or booing the candidates. Under such circumstances, and especially since Mississippians of those days had a very strong sense of personal honor, it was not unusual for fights to break out among the huge crowds. Quite frequently even the candidates themselves engaged in fist fights. On some occasions these fights might lead to someone drawing a pistol, which most Mississippians carried with them at all times. When this occurred someone was usually wounded, at times even killed.

The Whig party was the smaller of the two major parties in antebellum Mississippi. Its members were usually large planters and merchants. Most of the state's leading lawyers also belonged to the Whig party. Whig strength in Mississippi was concentrated in the river counties and in the Delta, but Whigs were also strong in the larger towns throughout the state. After the plantation system spread into the Brown Loam region and the prairie counties in east Mississippi, Whigs also became strong in those sections. Because they usually supported Henry Clay and were strongly allied with the merchants and businessmen in the Northeast, Whigs tended to be more national than sectional in their attitudes. During the secession crisis of 1861 most of the state's Whig newspapers and party leaders opposed secession. Some of the leading Whig statesmen included George Poindexter, Charles Lynch, Seargent S. Prentiss, William L. Sharkey, Luke Lea, and James L. Alcorn.

The Democratic Party was widely scattered throughout the state and was made up of farmers, small merchants, mechanics, craftsmen, and other working people living in Mississippi's small towns. They were less aristocratic, more democratic and progressive, more sectional in their attitudes and were devoted to their hero, Andrew Jackson. The movement for secession found its grestest support among the Democrats. Jefferson Davis, L. Q. C. Lamar, Albert Gallatin Brown, John J. McRae, Samuel Gholson, Tilghman M. Tucker, and Ethelbert Barksdale were among the state's leading Democrats. During the 1850's when the question of slavery became the major issue in Mississippi politics, many Whigs drifted into the Democratic Party which was in favor not only of maintaining but expanding slavery into the western territories.

Western Expansion

In the decades following the American Revolution, organizations or societies devoted to the abolition of slavery were established in the United States. Initially these societies did not have widespread appeal among politicians or the general public in northern states. In fact, until the 1830's there were more abolition societies in the South than there were in the North. But as the rate of western expansion greatly increased during the 1840's, national attention was focused on the question of whether slavery should be allowed in the new western states. Since 1820 slave expansion had not been a major issue. Under the Missouri Compromise of 1820 it was agreed that new states were to be admitted to the Union in pairs—one being a free state and the other being a slave state. The Missouri Compromise also provided that slavery would be allowed below the 36°30″ parallel but not above that line.

When Texas petitioned for statehood in 1845, there was an equal number of free and slave states in the Union. If Texas, where slavery was legal, were admitted to the Union that balance would be upset in favor of slave states because there was no free state ready for admission. The controversy surrounding the admission of Texas intensified sectional feelings and stimulated the growth of abolition societies in the free states.

The Texas Question

Since the early 1800's Mexico had owned what is now the American Southwest which included the present states of Texas and California. In an effort to develop Texas and to attract immigrants into that area, Mexico offered large tracts of land at very cheap prices. During the 1820's many Americans took advantage of this offer. Within a decade Texas was largely populated by Americans from Tennessee, Alabama, and Mississippi. Those people carried Southern customs and traditions with them. One of those customs was slavery. By 1836, Americans in Texas were no longer content to live under Mexican rule, so they rebelled against the Mexican ruler, Santa Anna. The revolution was successful, and soon afterwards Texas asked the United States to annex the area they had freed from Mexico. Texas was so large that some consideration was given to dividing it into five states. Since slavery was legal in Texas, this division would mean that five new slave states would be added to the Union. Northern and Midwestern free states were bitterly opposed to the admission of five slave states because there was no immediate prospect for a similar number of free states being added to the Union. The Texas question placed a severe strain on the uneasy truce that had existed between the free and slave states since the Missouri Compromise of 1820.

For almost ten years the Texas question remained a national controversy. The control of the national government was at stake. The admission of Texas, especially if it were divided into several states, would give the slave states control over the national government. Mississippi politicians and newspapers were naturally in favor of admitting Texas to the Union, and the state's congressmen supported such action in the United States Congress.

One aspect of the Texas question, however, troubled some Mississippians and made them reluctant to annex Texas. Mexico, which had not recognized the independence of Texas, vowed to go to war with the United States if Texas were annexed. Politicians and abolitionists in free states used this threat of war as an argument against annexing Texas. Missis-

Greenwood Leflore, a Choctaw chief, who remained in Mississippi after the Choctaw Nation moved to Oklahoma, became a wealthy planter-slave owner, and built this mansion, "Malmaison", near Greenwood, the city named in his honor. Leflore served in the State Legislature for several years.

sippi Whigs believed that an unpopular war with Mexico would further agitate the issue of abolition. Additional controversy over slavery, the Whig leaders feared, would do more in the long run to endanger the institution of slavery than to preserve it. Later events would prove them right.

Mexican War, 1846–1848

Historians call the decade of the 1840's the period of America's "Manifest Destiny." During those ten years many Americans believed that it was the destiny of this country to occupy all the land between the Atlantic and the Pacific Oceans. Most Mississippians felt that way and were enthusiastic in their support of the war against Mexico. Such a war, they believed, would not only settle the Texas question, but would also lead to the acquisition of the Southwest, including California.

Within about a year after the admission of Texas in 1845 the United States was at war with Mexico. Mississippians raised two regiments of volunteers and served with distinction in that short but important war. Jefferson Davis resigned his seat in Congress to lead one of Mississippi's regiments. A Mississippian, John Anthony Quitman, was appointed military governor of Mexico City during American occupation of the Mexican capital. Many other prominent Mississippians, including Earl Van Dorn, Alexander K. McClung, Reuben Davis, and Charles Clark, also served in the Mexican War.

Wilmot Proviso

The Mexican War had broad popular support in Mississippi and it provided several men an opportunity to "make a name for themselves." But the war was very unpopular in the North. Abolitionists claimed that the war was designed to increase the political power of the South. They pointed out that most of the land that would be acquired as a result of the war was below the 36°30″ parallel and would eventually become slave states. To prevent this from happening, David Wilmot, a congressman from Pennsylvania, introduced a bill to exclude slavery from any of the territory that America might acquire from Mexico. This bill, called the "Wilmot Proviso," ignited a bitter sectional debate in Congress. The law was not passed, but Mississippians and other Southerners were angry that northern states would try to prevent them from taking their slaves into the western territory. By the time the war was over in 1848, some Mississippians were talking about secession and the formation of a Southern nation. One of these men, General John Anthony Quitman, was elected governor of Mississippi in 1849.

The United States
in 1848

The First Secession Crisis

In May 1849 a group of Mississippi's leading politicians, planters, and businessmen held an informal meeting in Jackson to discuss the "threatening relationships" between the North and South. The major topic of discussion at this meeting was the Southern slave owners' right to expand the institution of slavery into the territory recently acquired from Mexico. Everyone at the meeting agreed that the area below the 36°30″ parallel should be open to slave expansion. A few months later a state convention was held in Jackson to discuss the issue of slave expansion. William L. Sharkey, a member of the state supreme court, presided at this meeting. It was decided that a convention representing all the slave states should be called to design a plan of action to protect the rights of southern states in the western territories.

The Nashville Convention

On June 3, 1850, representatives of nine southern states, including Mississippi, assembled at Nashville, Tennessee. The purpose of the Nashville Convention was to formulate a southern strategy to guarantee that slavery would be allowed in the Utah and New Mexico Territories which Congress had recently established. But there were several other matters before the Congress that were also important to Mississippi and the South. For one thing, the population of California had grown so rapidly during the "Gold Rush" of 1849, that it was eligible for statehood. By 1849 the numerical balance between free and slave states had been restored. California's admission would again disrupt that balance. The California question was naturally an issue of sectional concern.

Two other matters that increased sectional antagonism was the Southern demand for a stronger fugitive slave law and the growing support for the abolition of slavery in Washington, D.C. For several years slave owners had been complaining that northern sheriffs and police officials had not tried to capture fugitive slaves. They charged that some sheriffs had hidden

A street scene in a Mississippi town during the mid-1800s.   131

runaways and helped them escape. Therefore, Southerners demanded that Congress pass a new statute to require northern law enforcement authorities to arrest fugitive slaves and return them to their owners. On the other hand northern abolitionists were determined to abolish the slave market in Washington, D.C. They called the public sale of slaves on the streets of Washington a disgrace to the world's largest democratic country.

While the Nashville Convention was considering what course of action the South should take in regard to these and other issues, a compromise designed to ease sectional tension was introduced in the United States Congress. The need for such a compromise was obvious because the American people, both in the North and in the South, were becoming very emotional over the issue of slavery. Politicians and newspapers in both sections were becoming more abusive in their criticism of each other. The bad feelings in both sections were dividing the country.

The Compromise of 1850

Henry Clay of Kentucky had already become known as the "Great Pacificator" for his ability to work out compromises between the North and the South. He had been instrumental in designing the Missouri Compromise in 1820 and a tariff compromise in 1833. Once again this great statesman was able to work out a compromise which reduced the sectional animosity that threatened the Union. Clay introduced a series of bills which became known as the Compromise of 1850. This compromise established the right of the citizens in Utah and New Mexico to decide by a popular vote if slavery would be allowed in their territories. The public sale of slaves was prohibited in Washington, D.C., but slavery would still be allowed. Also, a strong fugitive slave law was passed. The Compromise provided that California would be admitted as a free state.

The reaction to the Compromise in Mississippi was sharply divided. The two senators from Mississippi in 1850 were Jefferson Davis and Henry Stuart Foote. Senator Davis opposed and voted against the Compromise. Senator Foote, however, not only

John Anthony Quitman,
Governor-General of Mississippi.

favored it but cooperated closely with Henry Clay to help pass the Compromise.

Governor John Anthony Quitman was violently opposed to the Compromise. In fact, he was convinced that the Compromise was so detrimental to Southern interests that the South's only recourse was secession from the Union. He therefore called upon the state legislature to assemble a special secession convention with the authority to sever Mississippi's connection with the United States. In response to Governor Quitman's request, the legislature authorized a special election to be held in September 1851 for the purpose of electing delegates to a secession convention.

The Election of 1851

The legislature's call for a special election sparked a great public debate and caused a major reorganization of political parties in Mississippi. Senator Foote resigned his seat in the Senate, returned home, and organized the Union Party. This party was composed of both Whigs and Democrats who had one thing in common. They were opposed to secession. They wanted Mississippi to stay in the Union. The Union Party nominated Foote for governor along with a slate of delegates to the convention who were pledged to vote against secession. Governor Quitman organized a States Rights Party and was renominated for governor. The States Rights Party nominated delegates pledged to secession.

The election of 1851 was hotly contested, and both Quitman and Foote campaigned vigorously. On one occasion Quitman became so angry at some remarks Foote made that he physically attacked Foote. After that fight, Foote and Quitman did not make any more joint appearances during the remainder of the campaign. By September the Union Party had built up a substantial lead. The election results showed an overwhelming support for Foote and his stand against secession. The Union delegates were elected by a majority of more than seven thousand votes. This defeat so disappointed Quitman that he withdrew as a candidate for governor. His withdrawal left the States Rights Party in a position of having to find someone else to run for governor in an almost hopeless situation. The party leaders were fortunate enough to secure Jefferson Davis as their candidate. Senator Davis was extremely popular in Mississippi, but he could not overcome the tremendous lead the Union Party had built up. Foote was elected governor in November, 1851.

The Convention of 1851

After this vigorous campaign the convention delegates assembled in Jackson on November 10, 1851. What was supposed to be a secession convention turned out to be something quite different. Instead of passing an ordinance severing the ties between Mississippi and the Union, the convention passed a resolution reprimanding the legislature for calling the convention. The delegates also declared that, even though they did not agree with all its provisions, the state of Mississippi would accept and abide by the Compromise of 1850. However, the delegates asserted that a state did have the constitutional and legal right to withdraw from the Union. They also declared that if the relations between Mississippi and the Union did not improve over the next few years, Mississippi might be forced to take that step.

Events over the next decade produced the very conditions that some of the convention delegates had anticipated. The decade between 1851 and 1861, which began in an atmosphere of compromise and cooperation, climaxed in sectional bitterness, controversy, secession, and finally in war. We will study that important decade in a later chapter.

Many of the customs and traditions that distinguish Mississippians from other Americans had their origins in the social and economic conditions of the antebellum period. In order to provide a better understanding of the forces and circumstances that continue to influence our society, the following chapter will deal exclusively with life in antebellum Mississippi.

A. **KEY TERMS**—Explain the following terms. If necessary, use a dictionary or encyclopedia.

1. sectionalism	14. Whigs
2. protective tariff	15. Democrats
3. sense of place	16. Western expansion
4. John Burton	17. abolition societies
5. bicameral legislature	18. Missouri Compromise of 1820
6. Walter Leake	19. annexation
7. Thomas H. Williams	20. Manifest Destiny
8. internal improvements	21. Jefferson Davis
9. Louis Le Fleur	22. Compromise of 1850
10. promissory note	23. Secession Convention of 1851
11. specie circular	24. Constitution of 1817
12. Panic of 1837	25. Constitution of 1832
13. King Cotton	26. depression

B. **MATCHING EXERCISE**

1. George Poindexter	a. caused Mexican War
2. Flush Times	b. David Wilmot
3. Constitution of 1832	c. supported Compromise of 1850
4. Annexation of Texas	d. removal of property requirements
5. John Anthony Quitman	
6. Wilmot Proviso	e. called to plan a Southern strategy
7. Nashville Convention	
8. Henry Stuart Foote	f. Chairman of Committee of Twenty-one
9. Convention of 1851	
10. William Sharkey	g. accepted Compromise of 1850
	h. second Mississippi Bubble
	i. Chairman of Nashville Convention
	j. opposed Compromise of 1850

C. **WRITING EXERCISE:**
1. Write an essay explaining the causes of the Flush Times and also the reasons why that period of economic growth ended in a depression.
2. Write an essay entitled, "The First Secession Crisis of 1851."
3. Write an essay explaining the need for internal improvements in Mississippi during the period of early statehood.
4. Suppose you were a delegate to the Secession Convention of 1851. Write a speech you would like to have delivered at that convention.
5. Suppose you were a registered voter in Mississippi in 1851. Would you have voted for Henry Stuart Foote or Jefferson Davis in the governor's race? Explain your answer.

CHAPTER VI

Antebellum Society

Throughout the antebellum period Mississippi remained basically agrarian or rural. Its white population was primarily of Anglo-Saxon (English) and Scottish descent because most of the people who migrated to Mississippi came from the south Atlantic states which had been populated by settlers from England and Scotland. Although many different African tribes were represented among Mississippi blacks, very few of them had been born in Africa. Since the importation of slaves was illegal after 1808, most Mississippi slaves, especially those brought into the state during the 1830's and 1840's were native born Americans.

Mississippi slaves actually lived in two different worlds. Their primary environment was the slave quarters where they lived according to standards and priorities they developed themselves. Slaves also lived in the white man's world, which was their secondary environment. In the white man's world they lived by standards of conduct over which they had no control. Throughout the antebellum period, Mississippi was actually two different societies—one black and one white. The customs and traditions of those two communities were a world apart from each other. After 1840, the slave community was the larger of those two societies. And in an indirect way, the slave community had an enormous influence on the white man's world. We will study the slave community in greater detail later in this chapter.

White Mississippians lived their lives for the most part in rural isolation. Facing the hazards of a frontier environment, they developed a rugged individualism and a strict code of honor. They learned to be self-reliant and independent. Although very suspicious of strangers, antebellum Mississippians were famous for their generous hospitality to neighbors and friends. According to Reuben Davis, they lived by a simple but stern creed:

> A man ought to fear God, and mind his business. He should be
> respectful and courteous to all women; he should love his friends

and hate his enemies. He should eat when he was hungry, drink when he was thirsty, dance when he was merry, vote for the candidate he liked best, and knock down any man who questioned his right to these privileges.

There were many forces that influenced the customs, traditions, and attitudes of antebellum white Mississippians. An examination of some of those influences should be helpful in our understanding of Mississippi history.

Religion

The southern part of America was greatly affected by a religious revival which swept the Southland during the 1730's. Called the Great Awakening, this religious movement spawned the development of a large number of small denominations, and its influence lasted much longer in the South than in any other part of the country. Even today, the South is known as the "Bible Belt" because religious activity seems to play a greater role in the daily lives of its people than in other parts of the country.

One of Mississippi's most famous churches, the Antebellum Presbyterian Church in Port Gibson.

Southern churches were noted for their evangelistic fervor, their emotionalism, and their acceptance of a literal translation of the Scriptures. Southerners perceived the eternal conflict between God and Satan as a larger dimension of their own personal, human struggle. The conflict between good and evil in their own personal experience was a manifestation of that cosmic conflict which the Scriptures so vividly described. To most Mississippians, there were no shades of good or evil— something was either good and right or evil and wrong. Sunday after Sunday, year after year, Mississippians were warned that God would reward the good and punish the wicked. Heaven or hell were the only alternatives, and mankind would be held directly and personally accountable for its actions. Over the years they developed a habit of thinking. Compromise and moderation were not considered virtues to them. A man must stand up and be counted. To straddle the fence on any issue, whether it was religious or political, was a sign of weakness. A man was either for you or against you.

Newspapers

Mississippi newspapers in the antebellum period also had a strong influence on how Mississippians looked at their world. They read their newspapers closely and were again confronted with a manner of thinking that placed great emphasis on one choice over another. Few Mississippi editors ever recommended a policy of compromise. Instead, most of them took definite sides on the issues of their day. Not only did they take sides, but they could almost never see anything good in the positions held by their opponents. They spoke with an air of authority and certainty which reinforced the prevailing attitude of good versus evil, or right against wrong. This thought pattern was clearly evident in Mississippi's official position on sectional issues and especially at the time of the second secession crisis in 1861. Mississippians were advised that they faced only one of two choices—submission to the dictates of Northern abolitionists or secession from the Union. Over many years they had formed the habit of thinking in those terms, and, unfortunately, they could see no other option. To submit would have been unmanly, so they seceded.

Politics

Still another strong influence on antebellum Mississippians was politics. To the drudgery of their rural isolation politics brought a measure of excitement. But politics and the strife of rival factions also kept the people stirred-up almost constantly. Many politicians in the pursuit of public office tended to exaggerate the problems facing the people and often oversimplified the solutions to those problems. Mississippi politicians provided one more influence on the people's behaviour patterns in which they were given a choice of either/or.

Education in the Antebellum Society

Most school age children in antebellum Mississippi lived on farms widely scattered throughout the state. Since farming required very little formal educational training, there was practically no demand for a state-wide system of public education. In 1844 Governor Albert Gallatin Brown recommended to the legislature the establishment of such a public school system but no action was taken. The children in families who could afford to do so were taught by private tutors and were later sent to colleges in Europe or northern states. However, there were public schools in a few counties and in practically all the towns of any size such as Jackson, Natchez, Woodville, Vicksburg, and Columbus.

Sixteenth Section Lands

It was not the cost that discouraged the development of public education because school funds were available from the sixteenth section lands. When the Mississippi Territory was established, all the land lying within its borders was surveyed and divided into townships, which were then further divided into sections. There were thirty-six sections in each township. A section is 640 acres. The sections were numbered from 1 to 36.

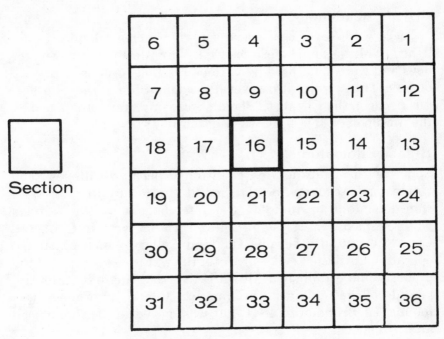

Section

Township

Every sixteenth section in the township was set aside for school purposes. These sixteenth sections could not be sold, but instead were to be leased or rented. The rent money was to be used for the support of public schools in the counties where the sixteenth section was located. Franklin Academy, established at Columbus in 1821, was the first public school in the state to be supported by the revenue from sixteenth section lands. The Academy had an enrollment of 400 in 1840.

Chickasaw School Funds

The Chickasaw Cession of 1832 was not divided into townships and sections, so the federal government set aside 174,500 acres in that area which were to be used in the same manner as were the sixteenth sections. Only the counties established within the Chickasaw Cession receive the revenue from the lease or rental of this land.

Private Academies

There were several preparatory schools or academies established in Mississippi before the Civil War. Most of them were for boys and were sponsored by various religious groups or private donors. There were also several academies for girls. The first girls' school, the Elizabeth Female Academy, was established by the Methodist Church at Washington in 1818.

Higher Education

Some of these academies eventually became colleges. The Hampstead Academy, established at Clinton by the Presbyterian denomination in 1826, was later bought by the Baptists who renamed it Mississippi College. An academy in Claiborne County eventually became Oakland College which continued operation until the Civil War. After the war the state bought the property and established Alcorn University, the first state supported college for blacks in America. Centenary College was founded at Brandon in 1841, but was moved to Louisiana soon after it opened.

University of Mississippi

When Mississippi became a state, the United States Congress granted one township of land to the state for the purpose of supporting a university. However, the revenue from the sale of that land was lost during the depression of 1837. After Mississippi recovered from those hard times, the matter of establishing a state supported university was again considered. Governor Albert Gallatin Brown enthusiastically endorsed the proposal, and the legislature authorized the establishment of a state university in 1844. There was a long and heated debate over where the university should be located. Finally, by a margin of *one vote*, Oxford was selected over Mississippi City on the Gulf Coast. William Nichols, the architect who had designed the capitol and the Governor's Mansion, was employed by the Board of Trustees to construct the university's first buildings. One of those original structures, the Lyceum, now serves as the university's administration building. The University began classes in

1848. After the Civil War Mississippi established several other state supported colleges and universities.

Law and Justice

The Bloody Code

Just as life on the frontier was hard and sometimes cruel, so was frontier justice also harsh and stern. Until 1832 persons who were convicted of robbery, forgery, burglary, or murder were executed. Many other crimes carried such severe penalties that Mississippi's system of criminal law was called the "Bloody Code." Juries sometimes refused to convict people of minor crimes because the penalties were so severe. Branding of criminals, the public pillory, and the use of the lash or whip were all part of the criminal justice system in Mississippi. But the new constitution of 1832 abolished the "Bloody Code" and provided for a new legal system which reduced the number of capital crimes and the penalties for many other crimes.

Duelling

It has been said that one of the reasons the South developed such a polite society was the **Code Duello**, or the duelling code. Long after duelling had disappeared in other parts of the country, it continued to be a feature of the Southern code of honor, especially in the deep South states of Louisiana, Texas, Alabama, and Mississippi. Even though duelling was illegal in Mississippi after 1837, it was often resorted to as a means of settling disputes between men whose honor or dignity had been offended. In an effort to discourage the practice, the state legislature passed a law which required the survivor of a duel to pay all the debts of the man who was killed.

The Prentiss-Foote Duel

One of the most famous duels in Mississippi involved Seargent S. Prentiss and Henry Stuart Foote. Both of these men were outstanding lawyers in Vicksburg and were often on opposite sides in some of the state's most celebrated legal cases. On one occasion when the trial arguments became unusually heated, Prentiss struck Foote in the face in the courtroom. Since this, of course, was a breach of Foote's honor, he challenged Prentiss to a duel. Early one misty morning the two men, their seconds, and a small crowd of on-lookers crossed the Mississippi River at Vicksburg and met at a famous duelling spot just inside Louisiana. At the appropriate time the two men faced each other. Foote fired first, but missed. Prentiss then fired and wounded Foote in the shoulder. The two men were apparently satisfied and the matter seemed to be settled.

But for some time afterwards there was talk that Prentiss, who was crippled and walked with the aid of a cane, had taken unfair advantage of Foote by using his cane to steady himself and thus had gotten off a better shot. This insinuation so angered Prentiss that he boastfully offered Foote another opportunity, declaring that he would not use his cane. So once again, early one morning about dawn, the retinue crossed the river. Again the two distinguished men faced each other. As before, Foote fired, and as before, he missed. As Prentiss leveled his pistol, this time without the aid of his cane, his gun misfired; it did not discharge. This meant that the whole affair would have to be repeated at a later date.

Once more, for the third time, Foote and Prentiss, with their seconds, crossed over into Louisiana. But by then the unusual circumstances of this duel involving such well known personalities had attracted widespread attention. On the morning of the third duel a large crowd, including several young boys, accompanied the duellers across the river. To get a better view, some of the boys climbed a large oak tree near the field where the two men faced each other. Just before the announcement was made allowing the men to fire, Prentiss observed the boys in the trees. In that great vocal style that had won him fame as an orator, Prentiss called out to them: "Boys, you should come down here and stand by my side, it will be much safer." After the laughter subsided the duel was resumed.

The firing commenced. Foote fired first and missed for the third time. Prentiss then fired and, for the second time, wounded Foote in the shoulder. The matter was at last settled to the satisfaction of both men and to the great amusement of those who had observed the duel. Many years later Henry Stuart Foote wrote an autobiography. He recalled his famous duel with Prentiss. Foote admitted that he had heard the story many times about Prentiss calling out to the boys in the tree. It was not true, Foote claimed, but because it was such a good story, he had not bothered to correct the error.

How Antebellum Mississippians Lived

Although most antebellum Mississippians lived on plantations and farms, there were several towns and cities in the state. Columbus, Port Gibson, Rodney, Woodville, Pontotoc, Coffeeville, Natchez, Water Valley, Grenada, Canton, Vicksburg, Jackson, and Corinth were among the leading towns before the Civil War. Each of the counties in Mississippi had a county seat, but most of those consisted of nothing but a courthouse, a jail, and one or two stores. Population statistics show how slowly towns grew in antebellum Mississippi. In 1830, 98% of the people lived in rural areas of the state and in 1860, 97.4%.

Natchez

The largest town in Mississippi was Natchez, which actually was more like two different towns than one single town. After a visit in 1820, John James Audubon described the two sections of Natchez as an "upper town" and a "lower town." The upper town, which was the part of the city that was built up on the high bluffs overlooking the river, was described as a model of luxury and comfort. But the lower town, commonly known as "Natchez-under-the-hill" because it was built on the landing below the bluffs, was described as "the abode of a rascally population living in crude houses made chiefly from the ruins of flatboats."

Social Customs

A combination of several circumstances such as frontier conditions, an agricultural economy, the institution of slavery, religious fundamentalism, and the love of politics shaped Mississippi's social customs. Recreation was essentially a private or family affair. Both balls and brawls were usually kept within a tightly knit circle of friends and acquaintances. The larger towns had theaters or opera houses where touring groups put on Shakespearean plays. Horse racing was especially popular in and around Natchez. Tournaments in which young men displayed their horsemanship and marksmanship were also popular. Political rallies and barbecues not only brought candidates and voters together but also provided another form of recreation.

Revival meetings, or protracted meetings as they were called back then, were not only of importance to the religious development of the people, but they also provided an opportunity for friends and relatives to spend a week or two together. Sometimes these revival meetings attracted several hundred people. When the people were all assembled, the men built a brush arbor or pavilion where the religious services took place. The women and children usually slept in wagons, while the men slept in the open air. Some of the people might stay as long as two weeks to enjoy the singing, preaching, and renewing of old acquaintances.

Social Issues

Changing social conditions during the antebellum period reflected the gradual emergence of Mississippi from frontier conditions. As we have already noted, public reaction to the cruel and inhumane punishment brought about reforms in Mississippi's penal code. The restriction of the use and sale of alcoholic beverages was another important social issue in Mississippi. In 1837 a newspaper advocating the prohibition of all alcoholic drinks was established at Natchez. The paper was named the **Cold Water Man**. Another newspaper predicted in 1849 that "the time is coming when the act of public drunkenness will place a blot on the character of its victim." During the 1850's several temperance societies were organized to promote prohibition.

Gambling was another prominent social issue. In July 1835, an anti-gambling society was organized in Natchez with John Anthony Quitman as its president. Quitman described gambling as the "greatest of all curses to civil society." His organization was only temporarily successful in driving the gamblers out of Natchez, because most of them gradually drifted back to the famous gambling houses at Natchez-under-the-hill. An anti-gambling society was formed in Vicksburg after a prominent citizen was killed while trying to arrest several notorious gamblers in that city. Most other towns were also troubled by the gambling habits of antebellum Mississippians.

Architecture

The stately two-storied mansions that symbolize the Old South are perhaps Mississippi's most famous landmarks. However, only a small minority of white Mississippians lived in those kinds of houses. The great majority of white Mississippians lived in much smaller houses with simple furnishings.

The home of Albert Gallatin Brown, one of antebellum Mississippi's most popular governors:

Built in about 1828, the B.L.C. Wailes home illustrates the architectural diversity of antebellum Mississippi.

This house, known as the Elijah Ray home near Sturgis, was built in 1850 and is somewhat typical of the period.

Isom Place, in Oxford, is a fine example of Mississippi frontier architecture. This beautiful mansion developed over many years from a single cabin built by its original owner, Thomas D. Isom, in 1835 or 1836.

Transportation

One of the greatest hindrances to the economic development of antebellum Mississippi was the lack of an adequate transportation system. Although the state legislature authorized the construction of a road system in the 1820's, the expense of such construction was almost too great for the young state.

There was, however, some progress. The best example is the Robinson Road which was built from Columbus to Jackson. To help pay for this road, the legislature provided that anyone traveling or hauling cargo on it was required to pay a toll which was determined by how far they traveled and the weight of the goods they were hauling. Some federal aid was also made available for the construction of Robinson Road.

Until 1831, when the first railroad line was built in the state, the stagecoach was the primary means of overland travel. But this form of transportation was limited to the available roads, some of which were not passable during the rainy winter months. These coaches, which were usually drawn by oxen rather than horses, were a very slow and tiresome means of travel.

The railroad was an ideal alternative to river transportation or other forms of overland travel. The first line built in Mississippi was the twenty-seven mile stretch between Woodville, Mississippi, and St. Francisville, Louisiana. Within a few years additional lines were built. By 1860, 872 miles of railroads were in service throughout Mississippi.

An Agricultural Economy

Most antebellum Mississippians made their living in one way or another from the land. Even those people living in towns depended upon the rural population for most of the trade at their stores, shops, and manufacturing establishments.

Although the production of cotton was the primary feature of antebellum agriculture, Mississippi farmers also raised a variety of other crops. After the depression of 1837, when cotton growers experienced a ten year period of declining prices, Mississippi farmers were forced to grow their own corn, wheat, cattle, pork, and other commodities which they were unable to buy. During the 1850's Mississippi farmers actually had more acres planted in corn then they had in cotton. And in the Piney Woods region livestock was the major source of income for farmers until the Civil War. Nevertheless, the real basis of Mississippi's prosperity was the production of cotton. Cotton producers can be divided into three major categories.

Planters

The wealthy planters are the best known of these three categories. But those landed aristocrats were only a small minority of Mississippians who lived off the magical white fiber. Cotton producers were classified as planters if they owned fifty or more slaves and farmed at least five hundred acres of improved land. Planters constituted only eight percent of Mississippi's white population, yet they dominated the state economically, socially, and until the 1850's, politically. It was these planters who built the great mansions and who have become symbols of the Old South popularized in movies and novels like **Gone With The Wind.** They lived in luxury, educated their children in eastern or European colleges and traveled extensively. These men were very conservative and were for the most part members of the Whig Party which was in a constant political struggle with the Democrats. Because of their great wealth they had more in common with the rich merchants and manufacturers in the northeastern states than they did with the small farmers in the hill sections and the herdsmen in the Piney Woods. The large planters, who owned most of the slaves in Mississippi, tried to keep the controversy over slavery at a minimum. They feared that sectional agitation which focused on slavery might eventually lead to secession and even war. Since they had the most to lose, they opposed any talk of secession and war. They realized that a war between the North and the South would probably result in the defeat of the South and the abolition of slavery.

Small Planters

The second category of cotton producers, the small planters, comprised about twelve percent of Mississippi farmers. These men owned between twenty and fifty slaves and farmed between two hundred and five hundred acres. These planters were ambitious and were very anxious to increase their land holdings and slaves. They hoped to eventually achieve the wealth and prestige of the great planters. Most of these small planters were Democrats who saw the abolition movement as a threat to their hopes and dreams of becoming great landowners. They favored the expansion of slavery into the western territory and endorsed the war with Mexico. The acquisition of additional slave territory would make it possible for these planters to sell their surplus slaves and would enable them to acquire more land if they ran out of land in Mississippi.

Farmers

The largest group of cotton producers in Mississippi were the small, independent farmers who comprised between sixty and seventy percent of Mississippi's white population. These farmers owned fewer than twenty slaves, or none at all, and farmed fewer than two hundred acres. Like the small planters, they also had aspirations of becoming landed aristocrats and they too favored the expansion of slavery into the western territory. Because of their numbers they were a powerful political force in the state during the 1850's. They supplied the momentum for the secession movement because they believed that slavery would be abolished in the Union as soon as the free states gained control of the federal government. The abolition of slavery would dash their dreams and hopes of wealth and would free a large number of people with whom they would be in direct economic competition.

The Southern Way of Life

In the 1850's Southerners described their cultural and social traditions somewhat vaguely as "the Southern Way of life." To most white Mississippians, even to those who had never experienced it, the Southern way of life meant life on a plantation with its wealth, luxury, and social prestige. They considered that way of life the highest form of civilization ever developed by mankind.

151

The hope that they would someday achieve that ideal was the motivation which caused many Mississippians to support secession. An editorial in the **Vicksburg Sun**, dated April 9, 1860, indicates how pervasive this hope was:

> A large plantation and negroes [sic] are the goals of every Southern gentleman's ambition. For this the lawyer pores over his dusty tomes, the merchant measures his tape, the doctor rolls his pills, the editor drives his quill, and the mechanic his plane—all, all who dare aspire at all, look to this as the goal of their ambition. The mind is used, from childhood, to contemplate it, and the first efforts are all lost if the objects in life should be changed. The mind is thus trained from infancy to think of and prepare for the attainment of this end.

Since the cornerstone of the plantation system was slavery, even non-slave owners defended the "peculiar institution" because in their minds slavery was the basis on which their Southern way of life was built.

Slavery In Mississippi

The Civil Rights Movement renewed America's interest in slavery and scholars began to re-examine that institution. Hundreds of books have been written about slavery in the last twenty years. Americans in the 1950's and 1960's, like their ancestors in the 1850's, responded to racial changes with emotional intensity. Across that century slavery cast its long shadow and Americans repeated, with slight modifications, the old arguments.

It is very difficult for Americans, especially Southerners, both blacks and whites, to study slavery without experiencing the emotion which this part of our past provokes. But the institution of human bondage was a part of our history, and we must study that institution which had such a tremendous influence on the course of American history and even now affects all of us.

Origin of Slavery

Since the dawn of civilization some men have enslaved others. In the ancient civilizations of Europe the tradition of human bondage was well-established. When Europeans came to the New

World, they found a system of slavery already in existence among the American Indians. As amazing as it may seem to us now, the moral objections to slavery did not appear until about two hundred years ago. It was not until the theory of the natural rights of man became widely accepted in the eighteenth and nineteenth centuries that objections arose to slavery on moral grounds. Therefore, when twenty Africans were brought to Jamestown and sold as servants for life in 1619, there was very little objection. A scarcity of labor in the American colonies stimulated the African slave trade, and an ever increasing number of Africans were swept into a labor system that would leave a legacy of bitterness and controversy.

The Growth of the Slave Population

When the French settlers first began tilling the Southern soil in the lower Mississippi valley, they used Indian slaves as well as African slaves. Gradually black slaves became the primary labor force, and by 1724, Bienville issued the Black Codes to regulate the slave system. Both the Spanish and the English perpetuated black slavery, and when America gained possession of the Mississippi Territory the system was continued.

Until the 1830's slaves comprised a minority of Mississippi's population. But during the great boom period of the 1830's when millions of acres of forests were converted to cotton fields, the black population soared. By 1840 slaves out-numbered whites 195,211 to 179,074. Over the next twenty years the slave population continued to grow at a faster rate than the white. In 1860, there were 436,631 slaves in Mississippi and 353,901 whites.

Slave Owners

A total of 30,943 individual Mississippians were listed in the 1860 census as slave owners. Since 5.7 persons was the average size family in antebellum Mississippi, this means that approximately 176,375 whites belonged to the slave owning class. Of the total white population in 1860 less than half of them owned any slaves or belonged to the slave holding class. You will notice from

NOTICE.

IN pursuance of a Deed of Trust execu
ted by *William Yerby*, on the 19th day
of April, 1824, for the use of *John F. Car*
michael, the undersigned Trustee, therein
named will proceed to sell to the highes
bidder, for ready money, on the 5th day o
December next, at the Court House of the
County of Wilkinson, the following

NEGRO SLAVES, to wit.

Anthony, Jack, Jim, Dennis, Ellison, Loui
sa, Martha, Rose, Jane, Lewis, Criss,
Sally, Charlotte and Chelson.

or so many thereof as may be necessary to
satisfy the several sums of money mentioned in said Deed, with the costs attendant
thereon.

Notices of slave sales appeared frequently in
Mississippi newspapers.

the following chart that almost three-fourths of the slave owners
owned less than fifteen slaves.

NUMBER OF SLAVES	NUMBER OF OWNERS	% OF OWNERS
1–5	14,498	46.9
6–14	8,493	27.4
15–49	6,257	20.3
50–199	1,638	5.3
200–500	36	.1
over–500	1	
		100.0%

154

Types of Slaves

Although the vast majority of Mississippi slaves were employed in the cotton culture, they performed a great variety of tasks. Basically, there were three types of slaves in antebellum Mississippi. The largest group were those slaves classed as field hands. This group included both men and women, and children who were brought into the labor force by the time they were five or six years old. Slave children sowed the seeds, carried water, chopped cotton and performed other tasks that did not require strength and endurance.

Field hands usually worked ten to twelve hours a day, five and a half days a week. Normally, field hands were expected to produce five to seven bales of cotton a year. Each adult field hand worked eight and one-half acres of cotton, four and one-half acres of corn, and on the larger plantations, about an acre and a half in the vegetable garden. Slaves usually produced more than they could harvest each fall. At harvest time all the slaves were put to work picking cotton and corn. When the corn had been pulled, the slaves, both young and old, spent several days doing nothing but shucking corn. Sometimes slaves from two or three neighboring plantations were assembled for this purpose. These occasions often took on a festive atmosphere, and plantation security was somewhat relaxed during the harvest season. In the off season, between harvesting and planting, field hands were assigned various tasks such as repairing fences, barns, harnesses, etc.

The second type of slave was the domestic servant. Domestic servants included cooks, maids, butlers, carriage-drivers, traveling companions, and gardeners. These slaves were given special treatment and privileges not available to the field hands. They ate better, wore better clothing, and did not work as hard as field hands. Domestic slaves were sometimes resented by field slaves because of the favored treatment they received from the whites.

The smallest of the three groups of slaves in Mississippi were those who lived in the cities and towns. Town slaves performed a wide variety of jobs for their owners. Most of them were craftsmen, brick layers, carpenters, blacksmiths, or draymen. Some worked in stables. Others were maids, cooks, butlers, and day laborers. Most of these slaves lived in a segregated, enclosed section of the town called the slave quarters rather than in the houses of their owners. Every evening at the sound of some signal, usually a bell or a horn, the slaves were required to go to their quarters within the enclosed areas. At dark the gates were locked for the night. Town slaves were usually hired-out or rented by their owners. A portion of the wages received for their services was kept by the slaves to pay for their food, clothing, and shelter. The remainder of their wages was kept by the owners. On rare occasions industrious town slaves saved enough money to purchase their own freedom and the freedom of their families.

Plantation Management and Police Control

Although Mississippi devised a set of laws called the Slave Codes to regulate almost every aspect of the slave's life, the enforcement of these codes was left primarily to the plantation owners. Planters who owned between thirty and fifty slaves usually employed an overseer to manage their farming operation. Smaller planters took charge of their farms themselves. The overseer, who was allowed wide latitude in enforcing the Slave Codes, exercised almost complete control over the plantation and the lives of the slaves on his plantation.

Slaves who left their plantations for an extended period of time were required by law to carry a written pass stating the purpose of their trip, where they were going, and how long they were to stay. In order to sell or buy any item slaves were also required to have written permission specifying the item they were buying or selling. For obvious reasons, the Slave Codes prohibited owners from teaching their slaves to read and write. Most of the Mississippi countryside was patrolled at night to guard against runaways or fugitive slaves. All able-bodied white men were required to serve a certain number of nights each year on these patrols.

Slaves who were charged with felonies or serious crimes were given a trial by jury, but they could not testify against whites in court. When convicted of a crime or charged with breaking the rules of their plantation, slaves were usually punished by a certain number of lashes from the "cat-o-nine-tails," a leather whip used for such purposes. If a slave was convicted of a capital offense and was executed, the state paid the slave owner the market value of his slave. Slaves were rarely executed, however. They were usually sold to some distant place, often in South America. The state law made slave owners accountable for cruel treatment of slaves. Criminal charges, however, were rarely brought against whites for ill-treatment of their slaves.

There was a clearly defined rewards and punishment system on most Mississippi plantations. Whipping, withholding of rations and the withholding of visiting privileges to towns or other plantations were the most common forms of punishment. Extra rations, special visiting privileges, new clothing, repairs on their quarters, hunting and fishing rights were among the rewards given to slaves. These privileges were awarded to slaves for exceeding their work quotas, for good behavior, or for performing some unusual service that came to the attention of the overseer or owner.

Runaways and Slave Resistance

Mississippi slaves were subjected to an almost total regulation of their daily lives. To many, this was unbearable, and they demonstrated their resistance in many different ways. The most direct means of expressing their resistance was to run away, but it is impossible to estimate the number of slaves who ran away for this reason. Their chances of escaping were not very good, and punishment was swift and severe. Slaves found other means of displaying their hatred for the system. The burning of barns, fences, and houses was a constant problem to slave owners and a means of slave resistance that was difficult to trace. Neglect and abuse of farm animals and equipment were other tactics resorted to by slaves who were frustrated and angered by their bondage. In some extreme cases slaves even murdered their owners. Domestic servants were sometimes accused of and punished for poisoning their owner and his family. The certainty of severe punishment of slaves who were guilty or even suspected of violence may have discouraged slaves from striking out against their white owners.

Perhaps, it is also a measure of their deep religious belief that a divine Providence would someday free them from their bondage as He had the children of Israel, that slaves did not resort to violence more often than they did.

Slave Revolt of 1835

One illustration of the severity of punishment against slaves who were suspected of conspiring to revolt can be seen in connection with the "Slave Revolt" during the summer of 1835. In Madison County rumors of a slave revolt swept through the isolated plantations of that county and spread into nearby counties of Hinds and Warren. Any slave or white itinerant, especially gamblers, who acted suspiciously were rounded-up for questioning. Before the summer was over about twelve whites and probably twice as many slaves had been hanged by white mobs caught up in the hysteria produced by rumors of a slave insurrection. The Nat Turner Revolt, which had occurred in Virginia only four years earlier, was still a vivid memory to white Mississippians.

The Slave Family

One of the most remarkable aspects of slavery in the American South was the fact that the great majority of slaves lived in monogamous family units. Recent scholarship has shown that the family unit not only existed in the slave community but was the primary group relationship. When slave families were broken-up by the sale of one of the parents, the slave parent who remained with the children continued, whenever possible, to maintain the family structure. Family ties and blood kinship were very important to slaves, and they were devoted to the effort of keeping the family intact. The one reason which slaves most frequently gave for running away was their desire to rejoin members of their family who had been sold away.

The major factor contributing to the monogamous marriage relationship among Southern slaves was the numerical balance between men and women in the total slave population. For example, in 1830 there were 98 women for every 100 men; in 1840 there were 99 women for every 100 men; and in 1850 there were 99.9

women for every 100 men. Although slave marriages and parentage were not legally valid, most slave owners not only permitted but encouraged the development of the family. On almost all Mississippi plantations, food, clothing, and other provisions were distributed to families, and the slave quarters on most plantations were designed for family-size occupancy.

The slave family and the larger black community in the quarters was the primary environment for the majority of Mississippi slaves. Their values, ideals, morals, and self-image were shaped and molded there. Within the framework of the family, slave parents were able to cushion the shock of bondage for their children and provide a frame of reference that enabled them to develop self-esteem and a positive self-concept. The white world, dominated by values and customs very different from their own, was their secondary environment. Although every facet of their lives was regulated while in that world, slaves actually spent more time in the protected circumstances of the quarters. Mississippi slaves did not give up their humanity and dignity simply because they were slaves. They endured their bondage by developing a status system according to their own values. Slaves judged each other, not by how they lived in the white world where they had no freedom of choice, but by how they lived and behaved within the slave community and in accordance with their own system of values.

Religion among the Slaves

Next to the family, religion was the most important feature of slave life in the quarters. A deep faith and hope of deliverance sustained the slaves during their long years of bondage. On most plantations slaves went to church with the white people, but after formal services in the white church, slaves usually conducted their own religious ceremonies called "praise meetings." These activities took place in the quarters and were attended only by the slaves. In these meetings slaves were much freer to express their innermost feelings through their songs, chants, spirituals, and dances, many of which were African in origin. Slaves were unrestrained at these times and often acted out their deepest anxieties, frustrations and anger in tribal dances accompanied by the rhythmic chanting and clapping of other slaves. These praise meetings were an escape for slaves and enabled them to "let off steam" which might otherwise have been expressed in some form of violence. These religious activities also enabled slaves to preserve some of the cultural features of their African heritage.

The Mississippi Colonization Society

In 1831, a branch of the American Colonization Society was established in Mississippi. The purpose of this Society was to assist free blacks who desired to return to Africa. The Mississippi Society provided funds for 571 free blacks to emigrate from Mississippi to Liberia, a country founded by the American Colonization Society on the west coast of Africa.

Free Men of Color

In 1860 there were 773 black men, women, and children in Mississippi who were not slaves. They were called free men of color. But their rights and privileges were severely limited. After the Nat Turner slave revolt in 1831, a state law was passed requiring all free blacks to leave the state. However, this law allowed free blacks who could secure good character references to remain in the state. But they were required to carry with them at all times a certificate identifying them as free men. Most of these black people had been slaves at one time or were descendants of former slaves. Some of them had been freed by their owners and others had saved enough money to purchase their freedom and the freedom of their families. The United States census of 1840 listed 1,366 free men of color in Mississippi. This was the highest number of free blacks living in the state at any time before emancipation. Some white Mississippians were concerned that the presence of so many free blacks would create a desire for freedom among the slaves. Consequently, in 1842 the legislature passed a law prohibiting the immigration of additional free blacks into Mississippi. The legislation also made it illegal for a slave owner to free any of his slaves.

William Johnson, a free man.

The Barber of Natchez

The most prominent and the wealthiest free black in Mississippi was William Johnson who owned several barbershops in Natchez and Vicksburg. Johnson also owned one thousand acres of land, five houses, a delivery service, and at least fifteen slaves. Johnson was one of the most successful businessmen in Natchez and he sometimes even loaned money to his white friends. Throughout most of his life, Johnson kept a diary of his personal and business affairs. He had been a slave who was manumitted, or set free, along with his mother. He taught himself to read and write and as a young man learned the barber's trade. Johnson was a remarkable man who overcame hardships to achieve not only substantial wealth but also the respect and admiration of many whites and blacks in Natchez.

Shifting Attitudes Toward Slavery

In Mississippi there were three major shifts in the white people's attitude toward slavery. Up until about 1820 most Mississippi whites considered slavery as an evil system of labor which should be abolished. But between 1820 and about 1836 the growth of the cotton culture greatly increased the state's prosperity and caused a slight change of attitude. During this period, when the number of slaves grew at a very rapid rate, whites began to think of slavery as an unfortunate but necessary evil which should be maintained. The state's economy depended

161

upon the continuation of slavery as a labor supply, and many people had invested a great deal of money in the purchase of slaves. In 1836, for example, a young black man and a woman of childbearing age were valued at approximately $3,200 a pair.

By 1836 the attitudes toward slavery of most Mississippians had shifted to the third and final phase. They believed that slavery was not an evil, not even a necessary evil, but a positive good. Whites justified slavery not only in economic terms, but in religious, philosophical, and racial terms. Ministers and politicians pointed out that slavery had existed in previous civilizations and that the Apostle Paul seemed to condone slavery when he instructed Philemon to return to his master and obey him. Teachers, editors, and other white leaders also justified slavery on the grounds that black Africans were not as advanced in civilization and culture as white Americans were. Although these views were accepted to a greater or lesser degree throughout the western world in the nineteenth century, the American Revolution had popularized the belief in natural rights. This means that all men, everywhere, are endowed by God and nature with the rights of life, liberty, and property. After the American Revolution, and later the French Revolution in 1789, this belief in natural rights gradually led to a world-wide movement for the abolition of slavery.

During and just after the American Revolution Northern states abolished slavery, but in the agricultural South the system survived. And as we have already seen, the institution of slavery eventually became the symbol or focus of the many differences between the Northern and Southern states. But the real issue of the controversy over slavery was not so much the abolition of slavery in the South. The fundamental issue in the dispute was the restriction of the system in southern states and the prevention of its expansion into the western territories. That was the real source of antagonism between the two sections.

Southerners argued that the restriction of slavery to the South would result in a greater majority of slaves in proportion to whites. In the event of a race war, which many white Southerners believed would some day occur, the white minority would

162

be at a great disadvantage. Southern whites also feared that a large slave surplus would drive down the price of slaves and that they would lose their investment in slaves. In 1860, the total value of the state's 436,631 slaves was $349,344,800—more than all the land, farm equipment and livestock combined.

This photograph of former slaves of Jefferson Davis was probably taken in 1863.

Most white Mississippians were therefore convinced that only by guaranteeing the right of slave owners to expand into the new western territory could they protect their economic investment, provide for the safety and security of their families, and maintain their way of life. When they finally realized in the late 1850's that the west would not be open to them and that slavery itself might soon be abolished, they were convinced that their only alternative was to secede from the Union and establish a separate country where slavery would be permitted.

During the 1850's, sometimes called the "violent decade," a series of events widened the gap between the North and the South, intensified sectional bitterness, and focused the nation's attention on the growing alienation between the free and slave states. The decade of the 1850's began in a spirit of compromise, but climaxed in secession and war. We will study that decade and the events that disrupted the Union in the following chapter.

A. KEY TERMS—Explain the following terms. If necessary, use a dictionary or encyclopedia.

1. Anglo-Saxon
2. Scots
3. primary environment
4. secondary environment
5. standards
6. priorities
7. rugged individualism
8. code of honor
9. hospitality
10. "Bible Belt"
11. tutors
12. Sixteenth Section funds
13. Chickasaw School fund
14. private academies
15. *Code Duello*

16. "Natchez-under-the-hill"
17. brush arbor
18. prohibition
19. Robinson Road
20. stage coach
21. The Southern Way of Life
22. natural rights
23. slave trade
24. census
25. overseer
26. runaways
27. Nat Turner Revolt
28. monogamous family unit
29. "praise meetings"
30. Mississippi Colonization Society

B. MATCHING EXERCISE

1. Great Awakening
2. Albert Gallatin Brown
3. Hampstead Academy
4. Oakland College
5. Bloody Code
6. field slaves
7. town slaves
8. free men of color
9. William Johnson
10. Black Codes

a. Alcorn University
b. largest group of slaves in Mississippi
c. The Barber of Natchez
d. recommended a public school system
e. blacks who were not slaves
f. religious revival in the 1730's
g. abolished by Constitution of 1832
h. laws regulating slavery
i. smallest group of slaves in Mississippi
j. Mississippi College

C. WRITING EXERCISE

1. Imagine that you are living in Mississippi in 1835. Write a two or three page letter to a friend of yours in a distant part of the country. In your letter describe the kind of house you live in, your school, your neighborhood, what you do for fun, etc.
2. Suppose you are the editor of your county newspaper in 1850. Write an editorial in defense of the Southern attitude toward slavery.
3. Suppose you are a member of an abolition society. Write an article in which you condemn slavery and recommend its abolition.

D. ARCHITECTURAL SURVEY

Make a study of your community or county to find out how many different styles of architecture are represented. Are there any historic buildings in your community? If so, write a report describing the architectural style and the history of one of those buildings.

164

CHAPTER VII

Secession and Civil War

After the Mexican War and California's admission to statehood in 1850 a group of Southern leaders called "fire-eaters," began making speeches throughout the South. These men tried to persuade the Southern people that secession from the Union was the only choice Southerners had if they wanted to maintain their traditional way of life. The most important Mississippi "fire-eaters" were John A. Quitman, Albert Gallatin Brown, John J. McRae, William Barksdale, and John J. Pettus.

Growth of Southern Nationalism

During the decade after the Compromise of 1850 an increasing number of people accepted the advice of the "fire-eaters" and Southerners began to think in terms of establishing an independent Southern nation. The feeling of sectional pride gradually gave way to a desire for a national identity, a new and independent country to be established by the slave states. The Southern agricultural states where slavery was legal had much more in common with each other than they did with the industrial states of the North or the agricultural states of the Midwest where slavery was forbidden by law and custom. Although many Southern leaders spoke out against secession, events during the violent decade seemed to play into the hands of the "fire-eaters" who became stronger and more convincing as the decade wore on.

Decline of the Whig Party

During the 1850's many Southern Whigs drifted slowly into the Democratic Party. After losing the presidential election in 1852, the National Whig Party began to fall apart. Southern slave owners were becoming more suspicious of the Northern businessmen who were gradually taking over the Whig Party. The Mississippi Whig Party suffered a series of defeats in 1853, 1855, 1857, and 1859. The Democratic candidates easily defeated their Whig opponents at the state and local levels in those four elections. In each of those years a "fire-eater" was elected governor of the state, and "fire-eaters" were sent to the United States Congress from Mississippi.

Kansas-Nebraska Bill

In 1854 Congress passed the Kansas-Nebraska Bill which was probably the most controversial federal law since 1820. This bill made slavery legal in a large part of the western territory. Southerners reacted to the Kansas-Nebraska Bill with excitement and enthusiasm, but in the North and especially in the Midwest most people were strongly opposed to the bill. This opposition was most clearly expressed in the formation of a new political party.

The Republican Party

This new organization, called the Republican Party, held its first convention in July 1854 at Jackson, Michigan. The main objective of the Republican Party was to prevent the western expansion of slavery. Most of its original members were small independent farmers who had been members of the Free Soil Party and abolitionists who had been affiliated with the Liberty Party. Within a few years, however, large numbers of Northern Whigs joined the Republican Party. By 1858 the Whig Party no longer existed as a national political organization. Southern Whigs who had no national party affiliation were forced into the Democratic Party if they wanted to have any influence at all in political affairs.

Bleeding Kansas

When the Kansas Territory was established in 1855, both pro-slavery and anti-slavery immigrants flocked into the territory. For the next two years Kansas was the scene of a violent struggle. Each group tried to gain control of the territorial legislature which would decide if slavery were to be legal or not. There was so much violence that the territory was referred to as "Bleeding Kansas." The debate over slavery had moved from the halls of Congress to the great plains of Kansas where the speeches and arguments were drowned in the sound of gunfire.

Presidential Election of 1856

In the midst of the Kansas struggle a presidential election was held. When the Republican Party nominated John C. Fremont, Mississippi "fire-eaters" called for immediate secession if he were elected. However, Fremont was defeated by the Democratic candidate James Buchanan and the secession movement was forestalled for another four years. But sectional bitterness was intensifying.

Dred Scott Decision

One of the most important Supreme Court decisions in the nation's history was made on March 6, 1857. Dred Scott was a slave who had been taken by his owner, an army surgeon, from Missouri where slavery was legal into Illinois and Minnesota where slavery was illegal. Scott filed suit in federal court seeking his freedom on the grounds that his having been taken into free territory made him a free man. In a very complicated decision the Supreme Court ruled that Dred Scott was not freed. The court further ruled that because slaves were recognized as property under the Constitution, slave owners could not be restricted from taking their slaves into any state or territory in the United States.

The Dred Scott decision meant that the only way slavery could be limited to the territory where it existed at that time, or abolished entirely, was to amend the Constitution. An amendment was not possible because it takes a three-fourths majority of all the states to ratify an amendment. In 1857 there were 18 free states and 15 slave states, more than enough to block an amendment abolishing slavery. The only other alternative was a violent sectional struggle, a war between the states, a Civil War.

John Brown's Raid

On October 16, 1859, John Brown led a raid on the federal arsenal at Harper's Ferry, Virginia. Brown's purpose was to capture a supply of arms and ammunition to be distributed among the slaves. He intended to lead the slaves in an armed revolt. However, Brown's mission was not successful. He was captured by a military force, led by Robert E. Lee. Brown was hanged in December 1859.

John Brown's raid created a crisis of fear throughout the South. For generations Southerners had lived in dread of a massive slave revolt. But they never really worried about white men leading an uprising. The Brown Raid, which was financed by Boston abolitionists, convinced many Southerners that not only was their social and economic system in danger but their own personal safety was also in jeopardy.

Governor John J. Pettus

When Governor Pettus was inaugurated in January, 1860, among the first things he did was to ask the legislature for a special appropriation of $150,000 to enlarge the state militia in the event of a slave uprising in Mississippi. The legislature allocated the funds, but there was no revolt among Mississippi slaves. Yet the fear of it continued to trouble and disturb the white people.

Election of 1860

In the midst of uncertain times the presidential election of 1860 was held. The National Democratic Convention was held at Charleston, South Carolina, in April 1860. Mississippi's representatives to that convention supported a party platform that strongly endorsed the Dred Scott decision and Mississippi's right to expand slavery into the great American West. However, when the Democratic Convention refused to adopt such a platform, Mississippi and several other Southern states walked out of the convention. Later the slave states established a Southern Democratic Party and nominated John C. Breckinridge of Kentucky for president. Northern Democrats then nominated Stephen A. Douglas of Illinois. Meanwhile, the Republican Party selected Abraham Lincoln for its presidential candidate. A fourth presidential candidate, John Bell of Tennessee, was nominated by the Union Party.

Lincoln's Election

For several years, especially since 1848, a few Southern leaders had advocated secession of the South. Their numbers grew through the decade of the 1850's, but the "fire-eaters" were not in a majority. Most Southerners did not want to secede and had indicated this in 1832 and 1851. They loved the Union and did not want to see it dissolved. It would take some dramatic event to produce the "psychic crisis" necessary for Southerners to take the step of secession. A combination of two events, first the Brown raid, and secondly, the election of Lincoln in 1860 produced that psychic crisis in the minds of Southerners.

The Secession Convention

Within a week after Lincoln's election Governor Pettus called the Mississippi legislature into session and urged the lawmakers to call a special election for delegates to a secession convention. The legislature did authorize the election and in December 1860, the voters went to the polls in one of the most significant elections ever held in Mississippi. In the election of delegates to the convention, only 41,656 voters cast their ballots. In the presidential election held a month earlier over 69,000 Mississippians had voted. This large drop in voters in only a month is probably due to the fact that people were confused and uncertain about the purpose of the convention.

The one hundred delegates elected to the convention included a broad cross section of Mississippi's white population. There were large slave holders and non-slave holders. There were businessmen and planters, teachers, editors, and lawyers. By the time the Mississippi convention met in Jackson on January 7, 1861, South Carolina had already seceded. And it was apparent that other Southern states would soon do so. Nevertheless, there was strong opposition to secession in the Mississippi convention. Among the opposition leaders were James L. Alcorn, Robert W. Flournoy, Walker Brooke, J. Shall Yerger, Miles H. McGehee, Edward F. McGehee, and A. K. Farrar. Most of these men were large slave holders who considered secession and war a greater risk to their interests than remaining in the Union.

169

Most of the support for secession came from small slave holders or non-slave holding lawyers such as Wiley P. Harris, David C. Glenn, W. S. Barry, Jehu A. Orr, James Z. George, and L. Q. C. Lamar. There was little doubt about the final outcome of the convention when W. S. Barry of Lowndes County was elected president and L. Q. C. Lamar was appointed chairman of a committee to draft an Ordinance of Secession.

Next to the final vote on the Ordinance itself, the most important vote in the convention came on a motion by Walker Brooke of Vicksburg to submit the Ordinance of Secession to a popular vote. Brooke's motion to have the act of secession ratified by the people failed by a vote of 70 to 29. This vote was probably the best indication of the number of delegates who favored secession and the number who favored remaining in the Union. Following Brooke's motion and several other less important ones, the final vote was taken. The Ordinance of Secession was passed on January 9, 1861, by a vote of 84 to 15. Some delegates who had opposed secession voted in favor of the Ordinance when they realized that any further opposition was useless.

The Bonnie Blue Flag

While the convention delegates were debating the future of Mississippi, some ladies of Jackson made a flag which they brought into the convention hall. When the final vote was announced, this flag—a field of blue with one white star—was brought into the convention hall amidst cheers, shouts, and applause. Harry McCarty, an entertainer who was performing in Jackson on the day the secession vote was taken, wrote a song entitled "The Bonnie Blue Flag" which became the most popular song of the war. Later that night, a torchlight parade was held as bands, marchers, and singers followed this flag winding through the streets of Jackson.

War Comes to Mississippi

Within a few weeks after South Carolina and Mississippi had seceded, five other Southern states, Georgia, Alabama, Florida, Louisiana, and Texas also seceded. On February 4, 1861, these seven states met in Montgomery, Alabama, to establish the Confederate States of America. They invited other slave states to join them. On February 18, Jefferson Davis of Mississippi was elected President of the Confederate States of America and Alexander H. Stephens of Georgia was elected Vice-President. During the next few weeks four other slave states—Virginia, Arkansas, North Carolina, and Tennessee—seceded and joined the Confederacy. When Virginia joined the Confederacy, the capital was moved from Montgomery to Richmond, Virginia. The other four slave states—Missouri, Kentucky, Maryland, and Delaware—did not secede.

Following the formation of the Confederacy, Southern authorities took control of the federal postal service, federal buildings, and military installations in Southern states. The first Mississippi troops used in the war, numbering about 1,500, were sent to Fort Pickens, Florida, to capture that important coastal base near Pensacola.

Until the Confederate shore batteries at Charleston fired on Fort Sumter on April 12, 1861, many Mississippi leaders including Governor John J. Pettus did not believe that a war would take place. When the governor was advised to begin training and arming the thousands of young volunteers, he rejected the idea as unnecessary. He even turned down an opportunity to purchase rifles and ammunition from a Belgian arms manufacturer because he did not think Mississippi would ever have to use them.

Union Military Strategy

Union military officials realized that immediate action must be taken to keep the South from getting military supplies from Europe. Union war ships were soon stationed all along the Southern coastlines. This blockade prevented foreign ships from bringing supplies into Southern ports. The blockade was the first phase of a four point Union strategy designed to defeat the Confederacy. The second point in the Union strategy was to gain control of the Mississippi River and thus divide the South in half. If Union forces controlled the river, Texas, Arkansas, and

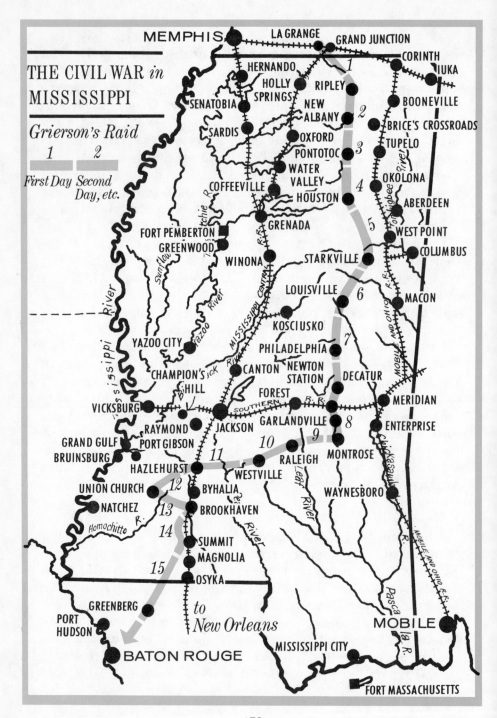

THE CIVIL WAR *in*
MISSISSIPPI

Grierson's Raid

1   2

First Day Second Day, etc.

MEMPHIS   LA GRANGE   GRAND JUNCTION
CORINTH   IUKA
HERNANDO
HOLLY SPRINGS   RIPLEY
SENATOBIA   NEW ALBANY   BOONEVILLE
SARDIS   BRICE'S CROSSROADS
OXFORD   TUPELO
PONTOTOC
WATER VALLEY   OKOLONA
COFFEEVILLE   HOUSTON   ABERDEEN
WEST POINT
FORT PEMBERTON   GRENADA
GREENWOOD   COLUMBUS
WINONA   STARKVILLE
YAZOO CITY   LOUISVILLE   MACON
KOSCIUSKO
PHILADELPHIA
CHAMPION'S HILL   CANTON   NEWTON STATION   DECATUR
FOREST   MERIDIAN
VICKSBURG   JACKSON   GARLANDVILLE
RAYMOND   ENTERPRISE
GRAND GULF   PORT GIBSON   MONTROSE
BRUINSBURG   HAZLEHURST   RALEIGH
WESTVILLE   WAYNESBORO
UNION CHURCH   BYHALIA
NATCHEZ   BROOKHAVEN
SUMMIT
MAGNOLIA
OSYKA   *to New Orleans*
GREENBERG   MOBILE
PORT HUDSON
BATON ROUGE   MISSISSIPPI CITY
FORT MASSACHUSETTS

Mississippi River — *Yazoo River* — *Tallahatchie River* — *Big Black River* — *Mississippi Central R.R.* — *Southern R.R.* — *Leaf River* — *Homochitto R.* — *Mobile and Ohio R.R.* — *Tombigbee River* — *Chickasawhay R.* — *Pascagoula R.* — *Mobile R.*

1   2   3   4   5   6   7   8   9   10   11   12   13   14   15

Louisiana would be separated from Mississippi, Alabama, Tennessee, and the other Confederate states on the Atlantic Coast. Thirdly, the Union army, especially those troops under General William Tecumseh Sherman, was ordered to divide and isolate large areas of the South. These troops were also ordered to destroy the Southern railway network, cotton supplies, livestock, and other Southern crops. The fourth phase of the Union strategy was directed toward the capture of Richmond, the Confederate capital. Mississippi was primarily involved in the second phase of the Union strategy which culminated in the capture of Vicksburg, the "Gibraltar of the Confederacy."

Ship Island

The first Civil War battle in Mississippi occurred at Ship Island. In July 1861 a small detachment of Confederate soldiers was stationed at Ship Island to prevent it from being taken by the Union navy. While they were building fortifications, a federal ship, the *Massachusetts*, bombarded the island but could not force the Confederates to evacuate it. A few months later, in September, a stronger force of Union troops captured Ship Island and built Fort Massachusetts. From this island stronghold Union naval and land forces launched assaults against the Gulf Coast at Biloxi, Pass Christian, and New Orleans. Later in the war Fort Massachusetts and Ship Island were used as a Union prison camp.

Control of the Mississippi River

In a very complex campaign designed to capture and control the Mississippi River, Union land and naval forces launched a coordinated attack against New Orleans and Confederate forts on the Mississippi River north of Memphis. While these naval engagements were taking place, a massive troop movement was also underway. Union forces under General Ulysses S. Grant marched southwestward through Tennessee on their way to Vicksburg, their ultimate destination. As these Union forces approached Corinth, Confederate officials became alarmed. Corinth was a very important railroad center and Confederate

173

commanders were ordered to defend the railroads against a Union attack.

Shiloh, April 6–7, 1862

In early April 1862, Confederate troops intercepted General Grant's army just northeast of Corinth at Shiloh, Tennessee. On Sunday morning, April 6, Generals P. G. T. Beauregard and Albert Sidney Johnston led about 40,000 Confederate troops into battle against General Grant who had about 45,000 men. It was one of the bloodiest battles of the Civil War. The fighting lasted into the late afternoon. During the night General Don Carlos Buell brought reinforcements to General Grant. On the next day, April 7, the battle turned against the Confederates who had to pull back to Corinth. During the battle General Johnston was killed. The Confederates lost 11,000 men and the Union lost 13,000.

Battle of Corinth, October 3–4, 1862

Following the battle of Shiloh the Confederate army returned to Corinth with Union forces in pursuit. Realizing that his vastly outnumbered army was in great danger, General Beauregard gave up the city of Corinth and retired southward to Tupelo on May 29, 1862. Generals William S. Rosecrans and Henry W. Halleck fortified Corinth which became a Union base for operations in north Mississippi and Tennessee. A Confederate force under General Earl Van Dorn attempted to regain Corinth in a fierce battle on October 3–4, 1862, but was unsuccessful.

Bombardment of Vicksburg

In the meantime a federal assault against Confederate forts on the Mississippi River was underway. Since the establishment of the Confederacy, commerce between the Midwestern farm states and the port of New Orleans had been cut off. It was essential to the Union economy that Mississippi River trade be reopened to Midwestern states. Vicksburg's strategic location on the high bluffs above a sharp bend in the Mississippi River gave its shore batteries control over the traffic up and down the great river. Consequently, the capture of Vicksburg was given high military priority.

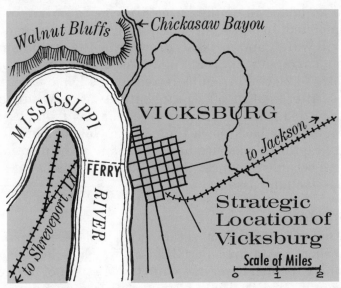

Admiral David Farragut began the federal assault from the south and captured New Orleans on May 1, 1862. He then sailed his large fleet up the Mississippi River. Natchez surrendered on May 12, and on May 18 Admiral Farragut began a bombardment of Vicksburg which lasted for almost two months. On June 28 Farragut fought his way up the river past Vicksburg where he met the federal gunboats which had sailed downstream after Memphis had surrendered on June 6, 1862. These combined forces attacked the city.

When Admiral Farragut realized that he could not capture the city, he attempted to dig a canal across the bend to divert river traffic around Vicksburg. When this effort failed, Farragut began fighting his way back downstream past Vicksburg.

The Arkansas

On his way downriver, Farragut's fleet was attacked on July 15, 1862, by the **Arkansas**, a Rebel ironclad. The **Arkansas** was under construction at Memphis when the Union fleet at-

175

tacked that city. When it became apparent that the Union would capture Memphis, the **Arkansas** was towed down the Mississippi River and then up the Yazoo River to Yazoo City where it was completed. In one of the most daring naval engagements of the Civil War, Captain Isaac Brown ran the **Arkansas** past Admiral Farragut's gunboats and took up a position south of Vicksburg to block Farragut's retreat to his home base in New Orleans. After fighting off repeated attacks, the **Arkansas** was finally scuttled when its engines failed. Farragut was then able to make his way back down the river to New Orleans. His attempt to capture Vicksburg had failed, and the Union military command became convinced that Vicksburg could be taken only by a massive land assault.

The Bridge

On August 6, 1862, Confederate forces under General John C. Breckinridge recaptured Port Hudson which is located at the point where the Red River flows into the Mississippi River. After the recapture of Port Hudson, the Confederates controlled the Mississippi River along the 240 mile stretch from the Red River to Vicksburg. This "bridge" across the Mississippi River enabled the Confederate States of America to transport goods from the western territories down the Red River, up the Mississippi to Vicksburg, and then by rail into the heartland of the Confederacy.

After this "bridge" was established, Vicksburg was more important than ever to both the Confederacy and to the Union. Vicksburg could close off all Union commerce and traffic between the Ohio Valley and New Orleans and it could also serve as a pipeline for the Confederacy. It became imperative for the Union to capture Vicksburg. It became essential for the Confederacy to defend it.

The Vicksburg Campaign

In the fall of 1862 the Union military command began amassing an army that would eventually number almost 100,000 men. The capture of Vicksburg was the major objective for this army. Over the next six or eight months several different plans were proposed for the capture of Vicksburg. At last a daring and dangerous maneuver planned and executed by a forty year old general, Ulysses S. Grant, brought the fortress down, and with it the Confederacy.

On October 14, 1862, Confederate forces in Mississippi and Louisiana were placed under the command of General John C. Pemberton whose duty was clear and unmistakable—to hold Vicksburg at all costs. Pemberton faced an almost hopeless situation. Vicksburg was already cut off by naval forces north of the city and south of Port Hudson. And soon he would be confronted by Grant's Army of the Tennessee which began moving south from Grand Junction, Tennessee, in November 1862.

On November 12, General Grant moved into Holly Springs, Mississippi, forcing General Van Dorn to pull back south of the Tallahatchie River. When Van Dorn built his defenses to halt Grant's march against Vicksburg, Grant ordered Union troops stationed at Helena, Arkansas, to move in south of Van Dorn and destroy the bridges across the Yalobusha River to cut off Van Dorn's army from Vicksburg. Realizing this danger, Van Dorn hastily pulled back south of the Yalobusha on November 29 before the federals could block his retreat.

Grant's army was then bogged down between the Tallahatchie and Yocona Rivers. But by this time he had been joined by General Sherman who commanded the XV Corps of Grant's Army of the Tennessee. Sherman was ordered to move his army to Memphis and then down the Mississippi to the Yazoo River. Sherman was supposed to sail up the Yazoo River and occupy the high ground northeast of Vicksburg. This maneuver was designed to force Pemberton to order Van Dorn's army to attack Sherman and thus open Grant's line of march against Vicksburg.

However, Van Dorn was given a cavalry command with orders to circle around behind Grant to destroy his supply depot at Holly Springs. At the same time General Nathan Bedford Forrest was ordered to strike the rail lines between Grand Junction and Holly Springs to further disrupt Grant's supply lines. These two strikes were highly successful. On December 20, 1862, Van

Dorn caught the federals at Holly Springs completely off-guard and totally destroyed the supplies which Grant had accumulated there.

General Sherman was also having difficulty occupying the high ground northeast of Vicksburg. For several days in late December, Sherman met strong resistance from Pemberton's forces which had already occupied the high ground around Chickasaw Bayou. Unable to advance any further, Sherman retreated on January 3, 1863. With his 30,000 troops, Sherman made his way back to the Mississippi River. At Milliken's Bend Sherman met General John A. McLernard, Grant's XIII Corps Commander. They waited at Milliken's Bend for further orders from General Grant.

After Van Dorn's raid of Holly Springs, Grant was forced to revise his strategy. Since his approach to Vicksburg from the northeast was no longer possible because his supply line had been disrupted, Grant decided to go to Memphis and then down the river to join Sherman and McLernard at Milliken's Bend.

Having learned from Farragut that Vicksburg could not be taken from the river, Grant ordered Sherman to dig a canal connecting the two main channels of the river where it made a hairpin bend at Vicksburg. A canal would have enabled him to get part of his force safely past Vicksburg. He could then attack the city from the south. However, Sherman's attempt to dig a canal was not any more successful than Farragut's had been. And Grant was eventually forced to abandon the scheme.

While Grant was trying to get part of his army south of Vicksburg, he set in motion another movement to get part of his army in a position northeast of Vicksburg. Grant ordered his men to dynamite the levee at a place called Yazoo Pass (now known as Grant's Pass). A break in the levee at Yazoo Pass would divert enough water from the Mississippi River to flood an old channel connecting the Mississippi River with Moon Lake. Grant's troops could be transported from the Mississippi River by way of this old channel into Moon Lake, then down the Coldwater River into the Tallahatchie and eventually into the

Yazoo River. By way of this water route, Grant could get his men to the high ground northeast of Vicksburg. On February 3, 1863, the levee was broken. By March 10, Union forces reached the Tallahatchie River about 32 miles north of Greenwood.

Once again, however, General Pemberton deployed his troops in a manner to block Grant's advance toward Vicksburg from the northeast. Pemberton ordered General William W. Loring to Greenwood to construct breastworks across the narrow neck where the Tallahatchie flows into the Yazoo River. Loring also built Fort Pemberton and named it in honor of his commanding officer. The federals attacked Fort Pemberton on March 11 and 13, 1863, but were unable to take it. On March 14 Admiral David Porter began transporting men and supplies up the Yazoo River to reinforce the federal troops. He was almost captured while navigating a narrow, winding stream called Deer Creek. On March 19, Colonel Samuel W. Ferguson forced Porter to abandon his attempt to reinforce the federals on the Tallahatchie River.

After this move failed, Grant felt checkmated. The only other option open to the Union general was to march his men down the Louisiana side of the Mississippi River and then cross over into Mississippi somewhere south of Vicksburg. Unlike the low, swampy flatlands of the Delta north of Vicksburg, the terrain south of the city was much higher. On this higher ground Grant could better use his superior manpower in an overland attack. It would be extremely difficult, however, for Grant to get his huge army from the Louisiana side back across the river into Mississippi. Confederate control of Port Hudson prevented Admiral Farragut from bringing transport ships up from New Orleans to ferry Grant's army across the river. The only way Grant could get his army across the river was for Admiral David Porter to run his ships past Vicksburg and meet Grant south of the city.

This plan was so dangerous that General Pemberton did not anticipate it. It was dangerous, first of all, because by marching through Louisiana and crossing over into Mississippi Grant would completely cut off his army from its supply lines. Port Hudson blocked the river south of Grant and Vicksburg blocked

Admiral David Porter's fleet runs the guns at Vicksburg to take supplies to Grant's army at Bruinsburg.

his lines to the north. The plan was also dangerous because Admiral Porter could possibly lose his entire fleet while trying to pass the big guns of Vicksburg. As great as the risk was, the prize was even greater. If the Union army could take Vicksburg, the Confederacy would be cut in half and the flow of supplies into the Confederacy from the west would be halted. And equally as important, the river commerce would be opened to the Union. Perhaps only so great an incentive as the capture of Vicksburg would have caused Grant to take such a chance.

The grand maneuver was inaugurated on March 29, 1863, when General McLernard began opening the road over which Grant's army marched southward from Milliken's Bend. On the night of April 16, Admiral Porter's fleet of eight gunboats and two transports made it past the city. Grant then had the means to get his army across the river into Mississippi.

To cover himself as well as possible and to disguise his strategy, Grant devised several diversionary attacks. Sherman was ordered to attack Snyder's Bluff northeast of Vicksburg. Another Union force was ordered to strike at Pemberton's supply lines stretching from Vicksburg up into the Delta. The third and most important diversion was a cavalry raid which Colonel Benjamin Grierson conducted from LaGrange, Tennessee, down through Mississippi to Baton Rouge, Louisiana. The purpose of Colonel Grierson's raid, lasting from April 17 to May 2, was to destroy the railroad lines that connected Vicksburg with the eastern part of the Confederacy. While Pemberton's reserve forces were chasing Grierson, Grant was building up his army in preparation for the assault on Vicksburg.

On April 30 General Grant moved his army of 24,000 men and sixty cannons across the Mississippi River at Bruinsburg. Two days later, May 2, Grant captured Port Gibson, a small town

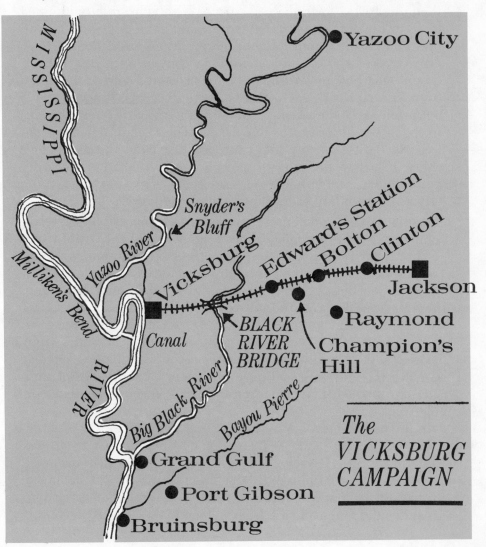

The VICKSBURG CAMPAIGN

twelve miles to the east. On May 8 Sherman's army joined Grant and the push toward Vicksburg began.

In anticipation of the Union assault against Vicksburg, President Jefferson Davis had ordered 10,000 Confederate troops to Mississippi to reinforce Pemberton. When Grant learned that General Joseph E. Johnston was bringing those Confederate reinforcements to Jackson, Grant did not march to Edwards and then pivot west toward Vicksburg as he had originally planned to do. If he had, General Johnston could have circled in behind him and Grant would have been caught between Pemberton's army at Vicksburg and Johnston's troops at Jackson. Instead, Grant marched toward Jackson to prevent General Johnston from linking his troops with Pemberton's forces. When General Johnston arrived at Jackson on May 13, 1863, he found the city in chaos. Governor Pettus had evacuated the capital upon learning that Grant's army had captured Raymond the day before (May 12). The prisoners had been released from the state penitentiary, and hundreds of former slaves had gathered in the city in anticipation of its capture by Union forces.

Realizing that a defense of the city was impossible, General Johnston set fire to Confederate supplies to prevent Grant from getting them and then retreated north toward Canton. On May 14 Grant's army walked into the evacuated capital. One of General Sherman's young sons was given the honor of raising the American flag over the state capitol building. This same boy, a favorite among Sherman's men, later contracted fever and died in the Mississippi swamps during the siege of Vicksburg. After burning several buildings housing Confederate supplies and destroying the railroad leading to Jackson, Generals Grant and Sherman turned their attention toward Vicksburg, their major objective.

In the meantime, on May 14, General Pemberton was ordered to move his army out of Vicksburg and march east to attack General Grant. However, a Union spy had informed Grant of Pemberton's intention. With this information Grant deployed his troops in a manner that would place General Pemberton at a great disadvantage and might even lead to the destruction of the

Confederate forces. Therefore, General Pemberton did not act upon his orders but instead struck at Grant's supply lines south of Raymond. On May 16, Pemberton was again ordered to concentrate his troops north of the railroad between Vicksburg and Jackson. As the Confederate troops were moving into this position, they encountered Grant's army marching west toward Vicksburg. On May 16 the two armies met at Champion's Hill, southwest of Bolton. In what has been called the decisive engagement of the Vicksburg Campaign, the crest of this hill changed hands three times between ten-thirty in the morning and five o'clock in the afternoon. Finally the Confederates were forced to pull back west across Baker's Creek. General Loring's division was cut off in the retreat and Pemberton lost a vital part of his army in the defense of Vicksburg.

The next day, May 17, Grant pursued the Confederates who were retreating to Vicksburg. The Union army caught up with the Confederates as they were crossing a bridge over the Big Black River. The Confederates turned to meet the pursuing federals, but one Rebel brigade panicked and pulled back across the bridge. This action left an opening in the Confederate lines and exposed the retreating Confederates to the pursuit of Union soldiers. After the Battle of the Big Black Bridge on May 17, 1863, General Pemberton withdrew his weary army into the protective redoubts of Vicksburg.

The people of Vicksburg lived in caves like this one while their city was under siege.

When Pemberton withdrew his army into the city, he made a fatal mistake. General Grant concentrated his forces on the outskirts of the city. With his troops encircling the city, Grant placed Vicksburg under siege on May 19. He cut off all supplies to the city and simply waited for the soldiers and citizens of Vicksburg to exhaust their resources. They would have to surrender or starve. The siege of Vicksburg lasted forty-seven days.

Grant and Pemberton discuss the terms of surrender.

Surrender of Vicksburg

The story of the people and soldiers of Vicksburg is one of the heroic episodes in the Civil War. Not only were they cut off from their supplies but they were constantly bombarded by federal cannons. On several occasions they beat back assaults of federal troops. To shield themselves from the shelling, they dug caves in the hillsides. To feed themselves, they ate horse meat and eventually mule meat. Some even ate rats. The soldiers grew weak and weary. The citizens were racked with disease. The reinforcements which were to be supplied by General Joseph E. Johnston were blocked by the position of General Grant's army. Facing a desperate situation in the city and a hopeless military disadvantage, General Pemberton considered his alternatives.

Finally on July 3, 1863, General Pemberton met with General Grant and asked the Union commander what surrender terms he would demand. At first Grant demanded unconditional surrender, adding however: "Men who have shown so much endurance and courage as those now in Vicksburg will always challenge the respect of an adversary, and I assure you, will be treated with all the respect due them as prisoners of war." General Pemberton refused the terms of unconditional surrender. General Grant then assembled his corps commanders and other subordinates. After discussing the situation, Grant advised Pemberton that his commanders had recommended more favorable surrender terms. It was agreed that all the Confederate troops would be paroled upon signing an oath that they would not fight again until they were formally exchanged for Union prisoners. Officers were allowed to keep their side-arms, a horse, and their personal property. All other military weapons, stores, and supplies were to be surrendered. General Pemberton accepted these terms. On July 4, 1863, Vicksburg was formally surrendered to General Grant.

In the surrender of Vicksburg the Confederate States of America lost not only the city and control over the Mississippi River but also 40,000 fighting men, 260 cannons, 60,000 rifles and other small arms and over 7,000,000 rounds of ammunition. In addition to the loss of military supplies, there was also a great psychological loss. Vicksburg had become the focal point of the war. The Rebels considered it an impregnable fortress, the "Gibraltar of the Confederacy." They had come to believe that the survival of the Confederacy depended upon holding Vicksburg. When it fell to the enemy, the South suffered a severe blow to its morale.

Making the shock of the fall of Vicksburg even more disheartening was the news of the Confederate defeat at Gettysburg on July 3, 1863. Long considered an invincible commander, General Robert E. Lee had suffered a devastating defeat and had almost lost his entire Army of Northern Virginia. The impregnable fortress and the invincible general had fallen within a day's time.

Capture of Port Hudson

After the surrender of Vicksburg the only remaining Confederate military force on the Mississippi River was the garrison which held Port Hudson, about two hundred miles south of Vicksburg. By controlling Port Hudson the Confederates could still block the traffic on the river. But Port Hudson was no Vicksburg, and the small Rebel force there surrendered on July 9, 1863. The Union was now in control of the Mississippi River, and the Confederacy was split in half.

Sherman Occupies Jackson Again

After the surrender of Vicksburg General Grant and most of his army marched out of Mississippi to link up with other Union forces in east Tennessee. General Sherman remained in Mississippi to engage General Johnston who was between Vicksburg and Jackson. As Sherman directed his forces against him, Johnston withdrew into the fortifications around Jackson. Sherman then moved into a position to bombard the city. Realizing that he might suffer the same fate Pemberton had suffered if he allowed his army to be encircled, Johnston withdrew from Jackson on July 16 and moved east toward Morton. Governor Pettus and most of the town's citizens also withdrew from the capital during the early stages of the bombardment. On July 17, Sherman again occupied Jackson. During this second occupation, which followed several days of shelling, Jackson suffered additional property damage.

Sherman set up his headquarters in the Governor's Mansion and directed his troops to destroy military supplies, railroads, and private property that might be used by the Confederate army. However, before leaving Jackson on July 19, General Sherman provided Mayor C. H. Manship with 200 barrels of flour and 100 barrels of pork to be distributed among the citizens. He also supplied provisions to several other nearby towns. Sherman's army then returned by river to Memphis and by rail to Chattanooga. For the remainder of 1863 Confederate cavalry units in northeast Mississippi made hit-and-run raids against Sherman's army as it advanced across east Tennessee. The famous Union general was almost captured on one occasion by a cavalry unit under General James R. Chalmers.

Sherman's March Through Mississippi

Union military leaders realized that Confederate forces in Mississippi were still a threat to their troops in Tennessee. Therefore, General Sherman was ordered back to Mississippi and instructed to destroy the railroad extending from Vicksburg to Meridian and to disrupt other Confederate supply lines. On February 3, 1864, with 20,000 troops Sherman began his march across Mississippi. By February 14 Sherman had cut his way to Meridian, destroying rails and property all along the way. By March 4 his army, part of which had returned by way of Philadelphia, Louisville, Kosciusko, and Canton, was back in Vicksburg. Other Union forces from Memphis under General William Sooy Smith were conducting a similar march through north Mississippi. The purpose of these raids was to destroy the resources which enabled the Confederacy to maintain and supply its army. When Sherman had completed this task, he returned to Chattanooga and afterwards made his famous march through Georgia.

Cavalry Raids

After Sherman left Mississippi several Confederate cavalry units in north Mississippi under the command of General Stephen D. Lee, General Nathan Bedford Forrest, and General Wirt Adams continued to attack federal supply lines in Tennessee. On several occasions federal troops were sent to capture or destroy those units. The engagements in north Mississippi were of little consequence to the more important military operations taking place in the region around Richmond, Virginia, and the south Atlantic states. Nevertheless, the Mississippi battles in 1864 showed that the Confederate forces in this area were far from giving up. The most important of these engagements included Brice's Cross Roads (near Tupelo) on June 10, 1864; the Battle of Hurricane Creek (near Oxford) on August 13, 1864; and the Battle of Harrisburg (near Tupelo) on July 14, 1864, which was the last major engagement in Mississippi.

Mississippi Black Troops

As Union forces penetrated into Mississippi in the fall of 1862, agricultural operations were almost totally disrupted, and thousands of slaves were out of work. They soon began following the federal troops who provided them with food and clothing. Over 17,000 former Mississippi slaves joined the Union army. Among the units formed by these black Mississippians who fought for their freedom was the 3rd United States Colored Cavalry. This unit was attached to General John McArthur's division and fought several engagements against General Wirt Adams' Confederate forces along the Mississippi Central Railroad between Canton and Vaughn in May, 1864.

The Day of Jubilee

On January 1, 1863, President Abraham Lincoln issued the Emancipation Proclamation freeing all the slaves in those states in rebellion against the United States of America. Although many slaves in remote parts of Mississippi did not learn of their emancipation until the war was over, those who heard of the Proclamation greeted the news of their freedom with jubilation and excitement. It was a Day of Jubilee, a celebration of freedom.

The Emancipation Proclamation was made more formal and permanent in 1865 when the Fifteenth Amendment was added to the Constitution abolishing slavery everywhere in the United States and its territories and possessions. For the 436,631 blacks in Mississippi emancipation meant a new life, new opportunities, and new challenges. The long road to freedom had been a rugged one. They would later find that freedom itself was fraught with problems and difficulties that they had not anticipated. But for a while yet, they celebrated in the Day of Jubilee.

The War Ends

By the spring of 1865, the vastly superior military might of the Union had taken its toll against the Confederacy. In the summer of 1863, after the fall of Vicksburg, many Southern leaders called for an end to the war. But the Southern peace movement, which was very strong in Mississippi, did not prevail. The war continued for two more years at a frightful cost to the South's manpower, industry, and agriculture. After the Confederate capital of Richmond was evacuated on April 3, 1865, the collapse of the Confederacy accelerated. General Robert E. Lee surrendered his army to Grant on April 9; General Joseph E. Johnston surrendered to General Sherman on April 26; and General Richard Taylor surrendered the Confederate armies in Mississippi and Louisiana to General Edward R. S. Canby on May 4, 1865.

Capture and Imprisonment of President Davis

Even after most of his armies had surrendered, President Jefferson Davis hoped to make his way across the Mississippi River to rally his troops in the west and continue the fight. But President Davis was captured at Irwinville, Georgia, on May 10, 1865. He remained a prisoner for two years. Some Union authorities believed Davis and other Confederate leaders were

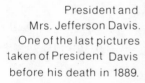

President and Mrs. Jefferson Davis. One of the last pictures taken of President Davis before his death in 1889.

189

guilty of treason because they made war against the United States. But other federal officials disagreed and called for the release of President Davis and a general amnesty for the ex-Confederates. When it was finally decided that the Southern leaders should not be tried for treason, President Davis was released from prison.

The Home Front

During the Civil War, Mississippi's citizens, both black and white, suffered great losses. The state lost almost half of the 78,000 men who served in the Confederate military forces. Roads, bridges, buildings, railroads, plantations, crops, and livestock were destroyed or damaged. Shortages of food, clothing, medicine, salt, and other commodities forced prices up beyond the means of most citizens. Many people were forced to do without these necessities for long periods of time.

During the early stages of the Vicksburg campaign, the state capital was temporarily moved from Jackson to Enterprise. After the fall of Vicksburg, the capital was moved to Meridian, then to Macon, then to Columbus, and finally back to Macon. In some areas of the state the war had completely disrupted civil government, and several counties operated without any elected officials.

When Governor Pettus' term expired in 1863, an election was held to select a new governor, the state legislature, and local officials. In this election during the fall of 1863, General Charles Clark was elected governor. Many people including former Governor Albert G. Brown and William Sharkey called upon Governor Clark to support the peace movement, but he favored continuing the war effort.

The Free State of Jones

When the state seceded from the Union in 1861, Mississippians in some areas of the state strongly objected to that action and refused to participate in the war on the Confederate side. In the Northeast Hills and in Choctaw County, for example, the opposition to secession was very strong, and some whites in

The three Capitols of Mississippi during the Civil War: (1) Courthouse, Columbus, (2) Calhoun Institute, Macon, (3) Church, Columbus.

those areas joined the Union army. The number of white Mississippians who served in various Union military units, mostly cavalry, was approximately 1,000. The most famous pocket of resistance to the Confederate cause was the legendary "Free State of Jones." It is difficult to separate fact from fiction in regard to the refusal of Jones County to support the Confederacy.

According to some sources Jones County residents tried to secede from Mississippi. There are stories and legends about Captain Newton Knight who deserted the Confederate army to lead a band of night-riders against Rebel forces and private citizens loyal to the southern cause. It was said that he assembled his men by sounding a large black horn which he always wore around his neck. When the echo of this black horn broke the stillness of night, it was a warning that old Newt and his gang would ride that very night.

Although it is a fact that Newton Knight did lead a band of night-riders and that there was some opposition to the Confederacy in Jones County, it is fiction that Jones County tried to secede from Mississippi. To correct this rumor and to display their support for the "lost cause," citizens of Jones County petitioned the state legislature in 1865 to rename the county for ex-President Jefferson Davis and to change the name of the county seat from Ellisville to Leesville in honor of General Robert E. Lee.

The tale of the "Free State of Jones" is an example of how legends and folklore, handed down from generation to generation, can become so familiar and well-known that they are accepted as fact and history.

Mississippi Blacks During Wartime

Wartime conditions presented Mississippi slaves with an opportunity to revolt against their white masters. In some areas in the state, blacks took advantage of this opportunity to gain their freedom. In several counties along the Mississippi River and in Amite, Lafayette, and Marshall counties, blacks took control of plantations and farms. Especially after the Emancipation Proclamation in 1863 large numbers of blacks left their plantations and congregated in towns and cities under federal control. Vicksburg was a favorite gathering place for the "freedmen," as the former slaves were called after 1863.

Slaves in the Confederate Army

Despite these examples of slave uprisings, which were rarely accomplished by violence, the great majority of Mississippi's black population remained peaceful during the war and displayed a remarkable loyalty to their former white owners. Diaries and letters and other statements of white Mississippians give high praise to Mississippi blacks during wartime. Many slaves even assisted the Confederate army in a great number of ways. When the Confederate ranks were almost depleted in the late stages of the war, the Confederate Congress passed a law authorizing the enlistment of Southern black slaves in the Confederate army. The promise of freedom was extended to black recruits **if** the South gained its independence. But when this law was passed, in March, 1865, it was too late. The war ended a month later.

Freedom Farms

When Mississippi was invaded by Union troops, many planters and farmers abandoned their land and farms. This meant not only that the white landowners would lose a crop, but that the freedmen and their families were without any means of making a living or gaining food, clothing, and shelter. In the early years of the war, the freedmen followed the Union army for food and other supplies. But after the surrender of Vicksburg, the federal government established the Freedmen's Bureau which took possession of the land which had been abandoned by whites and divided it among the freedmen who worked the land and shared the profit. One of the most important of these "Freedom Farms" was at Davis Bend, the home of President Jefferson Davis. This experiment was very successful and the Freedmen's Bureau later expanded the program. In 1865, 5,000 acres of land around Vicksburg was divided among 1,800 freedmen into 181 farming units. The profit from the cotton crop produced by the freedmen was estimated at $16,000. However, soon after the war was over, most of this land was restored to its former owners, and the freedmen found themselves again working a white man's land.

When Johnny Came Marching Home

Four years after it began amid singing and shouts of hurrah, the war ended in defeat, devastation, and bitterness. When "Johnny Reb" came home, he found a desolate land. Many old familiar landmarks had gone up in smoke. The Southern way of life, for which he had fought and for which many had died, was now only a memory. The post-war years were times of terrible adjustment. Former slaves would soon be law makers. Economic and physical recovery would be complicated by social and racial readjustments which Mississippi whites had never dreamed possible.

The decade following the Civil War is called Reconstruction. Those ten years were more difficult in some ways than were the four years of war. Mississippi whites were not prepared psychologically and emotionally for the change in the black man's status from slavery to citizenship. Among white Mississippians, resistance to that change was often expressed by acts of violence. We will examine this ten year period of Reconstruction in the next chapter.

A. KEY TERMS—Explain the following terms. If necessary, use a dictionary or encyclopedia.

1. John J. McRae
2. William Barksdale
3. Southern nationalism
4. Kansas-Nebraska Bill
5. Republican Party
6. Bleeding Kansas
7. John C. Fremont
8. John Brown's Raid
9. John J. Pettus
10. Election of 1860
11. Secession Convention of 1861
12. *Bonnie Blue Flag*
13. Union Military Strategy
14. blockade
15. Battle of Shiloh
16. Battle of Corinth
17. Admiral David Farragut
18. General Earl Van Dorn
19. The Bridge
20. General John C. Pemberton
21. General Ulysses S. Grant
22. General William T. Sherman
23. General Nathan Bedford Forrest
24. Siege of Vicksburg
25. General Joseph E. Johnston
26. Mayor C. H. Manship
27. Sherman's march through Mississippi
28. Free State of Jones
29. "freedom farms"

B. MATCHING EXERCISE

1. "fire-eaters"
2. Dred Scott Decision
3. John C. Breckinridge
4. Abraham Lincoln
5. L. Q. C. Lamar
6. Jefferson Davis
7. Vicksburg
8. *Arkansas*
9. Battle of Champion's Hill
10. Day of Jubilee

a. Southern candidate for president in 1860
b. a Rebel ironclad
c. drafted Ordinance of Secession
d. Gibraltar of the Confederacy
e. decisive battle of Vicksburg Campaign
f. favored secession
g. ruled that slaves could be taken anywhere
h. freeing of the slaves
i. President of the Confederate States of America
j. elected president in 1860

195

C. **MAKING A TIME LINE**—Arrange the following events in the correct order in which they took place:
    Battle of Shiloh
    Dred Scott Decision
    Election of Abraham Lincoln, President of U.S.A.
    Election of Jefferson Davis, President of C.S.A.
    Establishment of Republican Party
    John Brown's Raid
    Kansas-Nebraska Bill
    Secession of Mississippi

D. **MAP EXERCISE**
    Locate the major battles in Mississippi and trace the movements of General Ulysses S. Grant's army during the long Vicksburg Campaign.

E. **BATTLES AND LEADERS**
    Select several battles and leaders which interest you in particular and write brief reports about them.

F. **WRITE A DIARY**
    1. Suppose you were living in Vicksburg during the siege. Write a diary with daily entries for the week of June 29 through July 4 explaining conditions in the city.
    2. Suppose you were a freedman living in Mississippi in 1863. Write a diary with daily entries for your first week of freedom following the Emancipation Proclamation of January 1, 1863.

CHAPTER VIII

Reconstruction and Reform, 1865–1876

On May 6, 1865, two days after the Confederate troops in Mississippi surrendered, Governor Charles Clark ordered all state officials to return to Jackson and to bring with them the state records and other archives in their possession. The Governor also called a special session of the legislature for May 18. By the time the lawmakers finally assembled in Jackson on May 20, the capital city had again been occupied by federal troops.

General E. D. Osband, the Union commander in Jackson, advised Governor Clark that he had been ordered to arrest the state officials. When the legislators heard that orders had been issued for their arrest, they hastily adjourned and left Jackson. Governor Clark formally surrendered the state archives to General Osband at nine o'clock a.m. on May 22, 1865. Although Governor Clark was allowed to return to his home in Macon, he was arrested on June 6 and was imprisoned for a short period at Pulaski, Georgia. The state of Mississippi was then under martial law and the Reconstruction period began.

Presidential Reconstruction, 1865–1867

There were two separate phases of Reconstruction in Mississippi. The first period lasted only two years. It is known as Presidential Reconstruction because the policies and procedures by which Mississippi would be restored to its proper relations with the Union were under the control of the President. President Abraham Lincoln had started this plan in 1863. The Presidential Plan was very lenient and was designed to allow the Southern states a major role in their reconstruction. After President Lincoln was assassinated, his vice-president continued these policies when he was elevated to the presidency.

President Andrew Johnson

The death of Lincoln in April 1865 caused a strange turn of events in America. His vice-president was Andrew Johnson, a Tennessee Democrat. Johnson had opposed secession in 1861 and was the only Southern senator who did not resign his seat when his state seceded. At the time Johnson became President, the Congress was under the control of the Republican Party. The fact that he was a Southern Democrat hurt his relations with Congress and complicated his Reconstruction policy. The first indication of how President Johnson planned to deal with the South came on May 29, 1865. On that day he issued a proclamation of amnesty or pardon for all ex-Confederates who would swear an oath of allegiance to the United States of America and agree to abide by the terms of the Emancipation Proclamation.

Governor William Sharkey

President Johnson wanted to restore Mississippi and other Southern states to the Union as quickly and as easily as possible. On June 16, 1865, President Johnson appointed William L. Sharkey as provisional governor of the state. Governor Sharkey, a former Whig, had opposed secession and had been arrested during the Civil War for flying an American flag in his yard. At the time of his appointment, Governor Sharkey was also instructed to call a constitutional convention in Jackson. The purpose of the convention was to nullify the Ordinance of Secession and to abolish slavery in Mississippi. The Thirteenth Amendment to the United States Constitution had not been passed.

The convention met on August 14, 1865, and followed the instructions of President Johnson and Governor Sharkey. There was, however, one important exception. President Johnson sent Sharkey a telegram advising him that some Republican members of Congress wanted to extend all the rights and privileges of full citizenship to the freedmen immediately. These rights included, Johnson said, the right to vote. The President did not believe that all blacks were ready for full citizenship. He did, however, believe that blacks who could read and write and who owned property should be allowed to vote. President Johnson urged the Mississippi convention to give this class of blacks the right to vote. He explained to Governor Sharkey that his action would convince the Republican congressmen and the people in the North that Mississippians were willing to accept the results of the war and the emancipation of their slaves. It would also show the nation that the Southerners could be trusted to work out the problems of Reconstruction without force or intervention by federal authorities. President Johnson, however, was disappointed because the convention did not take any action on black voting rights. Instead the convention left the entire question of civil rights for the freedmen to the legislature which convened in October.

Restoration of Civil Government

Under the terms of President Johnson's amnesty an election was held on October 2, 1865. Since blacks did not yet have the right to vote, only white Mississippians took part in this election. Benjamin G. Humphreys, an ex-Confederate general and large slave owner, was elected governor. Governor Humphreys had opposed secession in 1861 but like most other Mississippians he had supported the Confederacy when it was established.

An all white legislature, most of whom were Confederate veterans, was also elected on October 2, 1865. Because the Mississippi legislature was the first Southern legislature to convene after the war, its actions were closely observed by federal officials and Northern newspapers. The entire nation awaited the Mississippi legislature's response to the dramatic changes brought about by the war.

Public Buildings in Jackson

Within a few days after the legislature convened on October 16, 1865, a special committee was appointed to study the condition of all public buildings in the capital city. The committee later reported that only one public building had been destroyed. Other buildings needed only minor repair before they could be used. The penitentiary which had been damaged, but not destroyed, was already in use. The state capitol, the Governor's Mansion, the City Hall, and several other buildings were soon repaired and put back in use. Although it was rumored throughout Mississippi that Jackson had been almost totally destroyed during the war, the lawmakers were relieved to find that these rumors, typical of wartime hysteria, had been greatly exaggerated.

Defense of President Davis

The state legislature appropriated a large sum of money and selected three of Mississippi's outstanding lawyers to defend President Jefferson Davis in case the United States formally charged him with treason. No trial was ever held and President Davis was eventually released and returned to Mississippi. He spent most of the remainder of his life writing a history of the Confederacy and making speeches throughout the South. When Jefferson Davis died in 1889, he had not asked for nor had he received a presidential pardon for his participation in the rebellion. In 1979, President Jimmy Carter issued a proclamation granting a full pardon to the Confederacy's only president.

The Black Codes

The problems facing the Mississippi legislature in 1865 were enormous. In addition to economic and physical recovery, they also had to deal with the fact that Mississippi's 436,631 slaves were now free. The exact status of the freedmen in American society, however, had not been determined. They were free. But were they citizens entitled to the same rights, privileges, and responsibilities as white citizens? In several Northern states free blacks were not granted the rights of full citizenship. If Mississippi's freedmen were not citizens, then what was their status? These were questions the Mississippi lawmakers had to answer.

As you might expect, there were no simple solutions. But there were a variety of opinions. Some lawmakers believed that blacks were inferior, intellectually and morally, to white people and should not be granted any of the rights of citizenship. Others believed that blacks were entitled to citizenship, but not immediately. Some Mississippi legislators believed that the former slaves should first be educated and then gradually allowed to exercise the rights of citizenship. Hardly any legislators favored extending full citizenship to the freedmen immediately. But

A school for Freedmen at Vicksburg just after the war.

something had to be done. The role of the blacks in Mississippi society had to be defined. So the legislature set itself to the task of determining the status of the freedmen in Mississippi.

After much discussion, debate, controversy, and compromise, the Black Codes were passed. These were laws that regulated and governed the lives of freedmen in Mississippi. Under the Black Codes, blacks would be allowed to testify in court, but only if blacks were a party involved in the case being tried. Blacks were not allowed to vote or to hold public office. Blacks could own property only within towns and cities and could carry firearms or other weapons only with special permission from local authorities. Blacks could not waste their time or money by gambling or drinking alcoholic beverages. If found guilty of such activities, blacks were subject to arrest, fine, and imprisonment.

The Black Codes also required all black adult males to enter into labor contracts before January 1, 1866. If adult males were not employed by that date, they were to be charged with vagrancy and fined or imprisoned. If convicted under this vagrancy law, they were to be hired or leased to any white man who paid their fine. This was an early form of the convict lease system that would become very controversial in the 1880's and 1890's. There were heavy fines for blacks who broke their contracts and even heavier fines for whites who encouraged them to do so. Freedmen under eighteen years of age who were not living with their parents were assigned to white men as apprentices.

Other provisions of the Black Codes legalized marriages between blacks and provided for the legitimacy of children born of black parents while they were in slavery. The legislature also declared that all the old slave codes that had been in force before the war would remain in effect unless nullified by the Emancipation Proclamation or by federal and state laws.

In addition to passing the Black Codes the Mississippi legislature took several other steps that attracted national attention. For one thing, the lawmakers refused to ratify the Thirteenth Amendment to the United States Constitution. They claimed that slavery had already been abolished by the state constitution and there was no need for a federal amendment abolishing slavery. Several lawmakers wore their Confederate uniforms, and on one occasion there was a debate over whether or not to fly the American flag over the state house. And finally, the legislature appropriated several thousand dollars to enlarge and rearm the state militia. Although this law was needed to suppress crime and violence throughout the state, many people in the North saw the rearming of the Mississippi militia as an attempt to revive the war.

To say the least, these actions of the Mississippi legislature were controversial. Realizing that the Black Codes would be taken in the North as an attempt to re-establish slavery in a modified form, many Mississippi newspapers were very critical of the legislature. Some of the state's leaders also realized that the Black Codes would undermine President Johnson's plan to let the Southern states control their own Reconstruction policies. The Vicksburg **Daily Journal** criticized the Black Codes and claimed that they did not reflect the opinions of most white Mississippians. The editor wrote:

> Have they [the legislature] as the representatives of the people complied with the conditions laid down by Mr. Johnson? and is their action a true exponent of public sentiment in this state? A thousand times NO! We protest their proceedings being given to the world as the sentiment of our people.

The editor of the **Vicksburg Herald** anticipated how Congress would react to the Codes: "We confess," he wrote, "with Mississippi's recent legislation . . . we have faint hopes of impressing Congress favorably toward us." And finally, a newspaper in Coahoma County claimed that

> the mass of the Southern people want peace and restoration and if allowed to act for themselves [they] will give such guarantees to our friends in the United States Congress, that will enable them to gain it for us.

This editor said the legislature had played into the hands of Radical Republicans in Congress which he predicted would soon pass laws as unpopular in the South as the Black Codes were in the North.

The Black Codes were very unpopular in the North. The **Chicago Tribune** wrote:

> We tell the white men of Mississippi that the men of the North will convert the state of Mississippi into a frog pond before they will allow any such laws to disgrace one foot of soil in which the bones of our soldiers sleep and over which the flag of freedom waves.

Some Democratic congressmen were also critical of the Mississippi legislature's actions. Samuel S. Cox, a Democratic congressman from Ohio wrote:

> It is surprising that the intelligent men of Mississippi could have persuaded themselves, after the terrible experiences through which they had passed that (the North) would for a moment tolerate this new slave code.

General O. O. Howard, Commissioner of the Freedmen's Bureau, argued that if the Black Codes were enforced "slavery would be restored in a far worse form than it was before." Henry Wilson, a Radical Republican, agreed with General Howard. Wilson said that the Black Codes made the freedmen "slaves of society and it is far better to be a slave of one man than to be the slave" of society in general.

The Failure of Presidential Reconstruction

By the end of December 1865 many congressmen, Northern newspaper editors, and other leaders who had originally supported President Johnson's Reconstruction policies began to have serious doubts. They began to question the idea of allowing Southern states to formulate their own reconstruction. But most Northerners were not ready to abandon Presidential Reconstruction entirely. What they wanted instead, was some kind of guarantee that slavery would never be revived in any shape or form whatsoever. They also wanted some guarantee that the civil rights of blacks would be protected in the South. Many if not most of these people believed that only an amendment to the United States Constitution could provide such a guarantee.

Consequently, the Fourteenth Amendment was passed by Congress and submitted to the states for ratification in the early fall of 1866. The two basic provisions of the Fourteenth Amendment were: (1) Blacks were awarded full citizenship and were protected from any state laws that discriminated against them; (2) Confederate veterans who had previously sworn an oath to the United States Constitution and later participated in the "rebellion" were not allowed to hold public office. Although the Southern states were not represented in the Congress that drafted this amendment, they were asked to ratify it as a measure of their willingness to accept and abide by its provisions.

President Johnson publicly opposed the ratification of this amendment and made many speeches against it. The Mississippi legislature refused to ratify it. When other Southern states also rejected the amendment, it failed to gain the required three-fourths of the states necessary for its ratification.

The failure of the Fourteenth Amendment spelled the doom of Presidential Reconstruction. Supporters of the amendment felt that it was fair and just to expect the South to protect the rights of blacks. On the other hand, Mississippians considered the Fourteenth Amendment a means of punishing the state's leaders, almost all of whom would be excluded from public office.

Using the rejection of the amendment as a major campaign issue in the fall elections of 1866, Radical Republicans gained a large majority in the Congress and passed a new plan for the Reconstruction of the Southern states. Under this plan, called Congressional Reconstruction, the federal government took control of Reconstruction in the South.

Congressional Reconstruction, 1867–1875

After the Radical Republicans gained control of the Congress, they passed several laws called the Reconstruction Acts. These laws divided the South into five military districts, each of which was placed under a military governor. Mississippi and Arkansas comprised the Fourth Military District. Headquarters for the Fourth District were originally established in Vicksburg, but were later moved to Jackson.

There were two basic differences between the congressional plan of Reconstruction and Presidential Reconstruction. Under the congressional plan, which was designed to carry out the provisions of the Fourteenth Amendment, blacks were guaranteed basic civil rights including the right to vote and the right to hold public office. The Presidential plan did not include these guarantees. And secondly, the congressional plan of Reconstruction prohibited ex-Confederate officials from holding public office if they had taken an oath to defend the United States Constitution prior to the rebellion. There were approximately 2,000 Mississippians excluded from office by this provision. However, Congress could and often did grant individual amnesty to this class of men and thereby make them eligible for office.

Congressional Reconstruction in Mississippi was complicated by the fact that **two different** governmental systems were functioning at the same time. Governor Benjamin Humphreys and other public officials were ordered to remain in office and to continue to perform their civil duties. But at the same time the military governor and other military officials were delegated certain powers and responsibilities. Even though the military government was established primarily to enforce the Reconstruction Acts, some of the powers and duties of the civil and military governors overlapped.

The first duty of the military governor was to replace those officials who were not eligible to hold office under the terms of the Reconstruction Acts. When he removed those officials, he was to appoint only men who were known to be loyal to the Union. There were three categories of loyal men in Mississippi.

Scalawags

One of the three groups of loyal men in Mississippi were native whites who joined the Republican Party after the war and supported Congressional Reconstruction. Native white Republicans were called scalawags by other Mississippians who opposed Congressional Reconstruction. Scalawags favored granting the full rights of citizenship to blacks: the right to vote, to hold office, to bear arms, to testify in courts, to serve on juries, and to own property.

Coined under the emotional stress of military defeat and during a great social revolution, the word "scalawag" was a term full of hate and bitterness which was used in anger and frustration. It is almost impossible to describe the enormous social changes in post-war Mississippi. In any society dramatic and unexpected changes will always arouse deep emotions. Nevertheless, Mississippi scalawags endured the criticism of their neighbors and life-long friends for what they believed was right and necessary. Among Mississippi's most famous scalawags were James Lusk Alcorn, one of the wealthiest planters in the state and a former Confederate general; Reuben W. Millsaps, a banker and philanthropist who endowed Millsaps College; Jehu Amaziah Orr, a delegate to the Secession Convention of 1861 and later a Confederate congressman from Mississippi; and Robert W. Flournoy, a planter and former slave owner. During Reconstruction, Flournoy edited a newspaper called **Equal Rights.** Flournoy was one of the few scalawags who advocated integration of the public schools, including the University of Mississippi, and social equality among the races. There were a few scalawags who took advantage of post-war conditions to enrich themselves and to gain public office. But the great majority of scalawags were reformers or realists who were trying to help their state adjust to the new circumstances brought on by the war and emancipation.

Carpetbaggers

A second category of loyal men who were eligible for appointment to office in Mississippi were Northerners who remained in the South or moved to the South after the war. It was said that these "Carpetbaggers" had so few possessions that they could keep everything they owned in a suitcase, which in those days would have been made of a carpet material rather than leather or plastic.

Mississippians opposed to Congressional Reconstruction and civil rights for blacks accused carpetbaggers of being "outside agitators" who came to the state to plunder and steal and to stir up hatred among the blacks. Again, these accusations were based more on emotion than on fact. Like some scalawags, some carpetbaggers were dishonest and crooked, but most of them were decent men who tried to help the state through a difficult period in its history. Some of the most influential carpetbaggers in Mississippi were Ridgely C. Powers, George C. McKee, G. Wiley Wells, Henry R. Pease, and Adelbert Ames.

Blacks

The third category of loyal men were Mississippi blacks. It was very difficult for most Mississippians to accept the idea that their former slaves should hold public office so soon after freedom. Obviously, some black officials who had been prevented from learning to read and write as slaves were illiterate, and were not capable of properly exercising their official duties. Mississippi however was fortunate in having very few black officials of this kind. Most black officials were conscientious and diligent in the performance of their duties. However, their jobs were made even more difficult by whites who often refused to cooperate with black officials.

It is only natural that people who have been taught to believe something all their lives would find it extremely difficult, if not impossible, to change their views over night. Many Mississippians believed that blacks were inferior to whites and that simply because they were no longer slaves did not mean that blacks should be immediately raised to the level of the ruling class. A good indication of the dramatic change in the status of blacks can be seen in the following letter from Ambrose Henderson to Governor James L. Alcorn:

House of Representatives
Jackson, Mississippi
March 26, 1870

To His Excellency Governor James L. Alcorn:

Governor, I was a slave of Col. W. G. Henderson. Boys together as we were, he is the center of the tenderest associations of my life. Arrived at manhood's estate, I was still intimately connected with him . . . When he was wounded at Upperville, . . . he languished in the valley of Virginia . . . until it was my privilege to take him away, secretly, through the lines to his own people.

My friend and loving master is a candidate for . . . Circuit Judge . . . and a good republican.

Now, Governor, I by the mysterious providence of God, am a member of the Legislature . . . and I now place . . . my earnest prayer that you appoint to the Judgeship of the First District the playmate of my boyhood, the companion of my manhood, the generous friend of my whole life—my former master, Col. Henderson.

/s/ Ambrose Henderson

The Constitution of 1868

The Reconstruction Acts authorized the military governor of Mississippi to conduct a voter registration in the summer of 1867. When General E. O. C. Ord, the military governor of Mississippi, completed the registration there were 79,176 blacks and 58,385 whites registered to vote. The Reconstruction Acts also called for the election of delegates to a constitutional convention. This election was held in the fall of 1867, and for the first time in Mississippi's history blacks voted and were elected to public office. The election of eighteen blacks to this convention caused several newspapers to call it the "Black and Tan Convention." The 1868 convention also included scalawags, carpetbaggers, and about seventeen conservatives who opposed Congressional Reconstruction.

The constitutional convention assembled at Jackson on January 7, 1868. After more than four months of controversy, the convention finally finished its work on May 18, 1868. The new constitution included many safeguards for black citizens, but it also disfranchised many ex-Confederates and disqualified many white Mississippians from holding public office. Because of these restrictive provisions, the constitution was rejected by the people in the summer of 1868. A general election was held at the same time, but results of that election were voided by the defeat of the constitution. Mississippi's political situation was in a state of complete confusion, and military rule was extended for another year.

The Election of 1869

During the months following the defeat of the constitution, James L. Alcorn took the lead in organizing support for the congressional plan of Reconstruction. Alcorn advised the people that the restoration of civil government and Mississippi's readmission to the Union could be accomplished only under the terms of the Reconstruction Acts. Even as unpopular as those terms were, Alcorn advised that they were better than continued military government. Large numbers of whites agreed with Alcorn and joined the Republican Party.

During the general election in the fall of 1869 the constitution was resubmitted to the people. The provisions which disfranchised ex-Confederates were separated from the main body of the document and were voted on separately. At the same time another state election was also held. The results of the 1869 election were very different from those of the 1868 election. The constitution was approved, but the disfranchising clauses were defeated.

In that election James L. Alcorn was elected governor. The legislature, which included approximately thirty-six blacks, and other public officials were also chosen. * Mississippi was at last ready to fulfill the requirements for readmission as outlined in the Reconstruction Acts. The state legislature convened on January 11, 1870, and quickly ratified the Fourteenth and Fifteenth Amendments. The legislature also appointed the state's two senators.

*The race of twelve Republican members of the House has not been determined.

Hiram Revels and Blanche K. Bruce.

Hiram R. Revels

One of Mississippi's senators was Hiram R. Revels, the first black man to serve in the United States Senate. As a young man, Revels, who had been born free in North Carolina, served as a minister in the African Methodist Episcopal Church. After receiving a college and seminary education, he became a popular lecturer and preacher. When the Civil War started, Revels became a recruiter for black regiments and eventually came to Vicksburg to work with the Freedmen's Bureau. Revels moved to Natchez after the war to serve as pastor of a large A. M. E. Church. When his senate term expired in 1871 Revels returned to Mississippi and became the first president of Alcorn University.

Adelbert Ames

The other United States senator was General Adelbert Ames who was the military governor of Mississippi at the time of his appointment. General Ames had won the Congressional Medal of Honor at the second Battle of Manassas and was very popular among Mississippi blacks. In 1873 Ames resigned his seat in the United States senate after he was elected governor of Mississippi.

Blanche K. Bruce

After the resignation of Senator Ames, the Mississippi legislature appointed Blanche K. Bruce to fill that vacancy. Bruce was the first black man to serve a full six-year term in the United States senate. Born a slave in Prince Edward County, Virginia, Bruce ran away when the Civil War began. He spent most of the war years in Missouri teaching in a school for freedmen. In 1868 Bruce moved to Bolivar County. He was elected sheriff in 1871. After his senate term expired in 1881, Bruce held several positions in the federal government including the Registrar of the United States Treasury Department.

Re-admission of Mississippi

The Reconstruction Acts did not empower the legislature to act beyond ratifying the Fourteenth and Fifteenth Amendments and appointing the state's two senators. After fulfilling these requirements the legislature recessed until the United States Congress officially re-admitted Mississippi to the Union and authorized the inauguration of Governor-elect Alcorn.

After extended debate the United States Congress passed a joint resolution re-admitting Mississippi and seating its congressional delegation. President Ulysses S. Grant signed the resolution on February 23, 1870, thereby restoring Mississippi to its proper relations within the Union of states.

Administration of James L. Alcorn, 1870–1871

As soon as Mississippi was re-admitted to the Union, the legislature reconvened to prepare for the inauguration of Governor Alcorn. After Alcorn took office on March 10, 1870, civil government was gradually restored throughout the state. After political restoration was completed, state officials turned their attention toward economic recovery. Roads and bridges, railroads, factories, courthouses, school buildings, and other public property that had been damaged during the war had to be repaired or replaced.

Taxation

All of these projects required the expenditure of public funds. The only way the state could get the necessary funds for these projects was through taxation. Taxes are never popular with people, especially in hard times such as those in Mississippi following the war. The legislature of 1870 adopted a new tax system that placed a much higher tax on land than had been the custom before the war. This property tax was the basic source of funds for the new state school system. But since few blacks owned land, this method of financing schools for blacks was opposed by many white Mississippians. High taxes remained a major issue throughout the Reconstruction period.

Mississippi School System

One of the major contributions of the Republican legislature of 1870 was the establishment of a state-wide system of public education. Every county was authorized to build school houses both in the towns and in rural neighborhoods where the demand was sufficient to justify a school. The response to the school system among blacks was tremendous, and almost overnight new school houses appeared throughout the state. In addition to the cost of the new system, some whites objected to the teachers who were employed in the black schools. Since very few local whites were willing to teach in the black schools and even fewer blacks were qualified, most teachers in the black schools were white Northerners. This fact led to the criticism that the schools were being used to indoctrinate the blacks in Republican politics rather than to educate them in reading, writing, and arithmetic.

Ku Klux Klan

As the opposition to black schools intensified, several organizations were formed among white Mississippians to discourage blacks from attending the schools and to intimidate the Northern whites who taught in them. The most famous of these groups was the Ku Klux Klan. The Klan was a secret organization with special handshakes, passwords, and disguises which protected their identity. At first, hooded Klansmen rode through the countryside at night shouting and hollering. They warned blacks not to send their children to schools and demanded that Northern teachers leave town. When these scare tactics did not prove effective, a criminal element took over the Klan and resorted to violence. Black schools and churches were often burned; teachers and blacks who sent their children to school were beaten and sometimes even killed by Klansmen.

To stop the spread of Klan violence, both the state and federal governments passed laws making it illegal for night riders to wear disguises or to deprive citizens of their civil rights. The legislature provided Governor Alcorn with a special fund of $50,000 to be used in suppressing the Klan. In 1872 several Klan leaders were prosecuted and imprisoned. After these trials Klan activity subsided until the election of 1875 when violence again became wide-spread.

Economic Development

The Republican Party's economic policies were very popular, especially in the early years of Congressional Reconstruction. In an effort to attract industry into Mississippi the state legislature

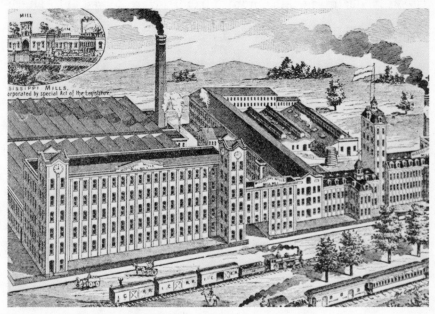

Mississippi Mills, located at Wesson.

passed a law granting tax exemptions to new manufacturing firms locating in the state. The legislature also authorized towns and counties to pass bond issues in order to subsidize railroads. Republican leaders like Alcorn, J. M. Wesson, and Reuben Millsaps encouraged Mississippians to diversify their crops rather than depending solely upon cotton. Alston Mygatt, a scalawag from Vicksburg, encouraged young men to learn new skills and trades to become mechanics and craftsmen.

Because of these policies, Mississippi experienced some industrial expansion during the next twenty years. Most of these gains resulted from timber, cotton, and woolen production. By 1890 there were sixteen cotton and woolen mills in the state, employing 7,226 workers. Railroad construction also showed significant gains.

But in spite of these advancements the great majority of Mississippians—both black and white—remained tied to the land and to cotton. Immediately after the war the value of land was so low that thousands of acres were lost because people could not even pay the taxes on their property. Gradually land values began to rise. But at the same time the price of cotton was steadily declining, and many farmers were forced into sharecropping.

Administration of Ridgely C. Powers, 1871–1874

After serving two years of his four-year term, Governor Alcorn resigned to accept appointment to the United States Senate. The lieutenant governor was Ridgely C. Powers, a carpetbagger. Powers had served in the Union Army and settled in Mississippi after the war. He was respected and well-liked by most white Mississippians. His two years as governor passed without any major scandal and with very little criticism from the Democrats. Many Democrats endorsed his candidacy for re-election to a full term in 1873. However, many Republicans, especially blacks, favored Adelbert Ames as the party's nominee in 1873.

Election of 1873

Perhaps the turning point of Reconstruction in Mississippi was the election of 1873. A split developed in the Republican Party between Senator Alcorn who endorsed the nomination of Powers in 1873 and Senator Ames, the choice of the more radical wing of the party. This conflict between the scalawag Alcorn and the carpetbagger Ames climaxed when Ames was nominated for governor in 1873. After Ames' nomination, Alcorn organized a second Republican Party and was chosen as its candidate. Ames was more radical than Alcorn and received the support of a majority of black Republicans. Alcorn, on the other hand, was supported by the conservative Republicans and by many white Democrats.

The most critical aspect of this election was the tendency of Mississippians to consider Ames as a black man's candidate and Alcorn as the white man's candidate. The state was almost to the point of drawing the "color line" in politics. To prevent this, several prominent white Democrats supported Ames because they opposed the color line in Mississippi politics. The best known of these Democrats who supported Ames were John Marshall Stone, Hiram Cassedy, and Francis Fitzgerald. But on Alcorn's side were such well-known Democrats as L. Q. C. Lamar and Ethelbert Barksdale, the editor of the **Jackson Clarion.**

There were two main results of the 1873 campaign. First Ames was elected. His election meant that the state government would be more radical than it had been under Alcorn and Powers. Secondly, the number of black officials increased after 1873. A black presided over both the Senate and the House of Representatives.

Administration of Adelbert Ames, 1874–1876

Ames' administration began with substantial support from whites who had not previously supported the Republican Party. But his administration ended abruptly during the bitterness and violence that characterized the election of 1875. Ames had campaigned in 1873 on a moderate platform. He pledged to reduce

215

Governor Adelbert Ames, a former Union general and winner of The Congressional Medal of Honor for gallantry during the second battle of Bull Run.

taxes on land and also promised to do everything possible to reduce racial tension in Mississippi. Unfortunately, circumstances beyond his control prevented Ames from accomplishing either of these goals.

Land Sales

In 1874 the legislature passed a new tax law which was designed to relieve the state's taxpayers. But Democratic leaders claimed that those new taxes were so high that thousands of people lost their land. What the legislature actually did was to authorize anyone who had lost their land for non-payment of taxes to reclaim that land by paying only the tax for 1874. Land owners did not have to pay the other back taxes; they only had to pay for the one year—1874. The law further provided that only original land owners would be permitted to regain the land under this privilege. Any land that was not re-claimed by the original land owner before 1875 would then be available to anyone who paid all the back taxes. In 1875 millions of acres of land that had not been claimed by the original owners was advertised for public sale by the state. Many Democratic politicians and newspapers insinuated that the sale of this land was caused by high taxes passed by the Republican legislature. But, most of the land put up for sale in 1875, about five million acres, had been forfeited several years earlier and was being advertised for sale because the original owners had not redeemed it. Democratic politicians were correct in saying that the land was being sold for taxes, but they did not point out all the facts of the situation.

The Vicksburg Riot

Perhaps Ames' greatest challenge was to fulfill his promise of easing racial tensions in the state. His effort was certainly not helped by the situation in Vicksburg and Warren County where corruption and graft were extensive. In the summer of 1874, during the city elections in Vicksburg, racial disturbances were frequent and eventually culminated in full scale riot.

The Vicksburg riot occurred after a predominantly black grand jury indicted the black sheriff, Peter Crosby, and several other county officials. Following Crosby's indictment a group of whites, including Democrats and Republicans, took over the Warren County Courthouse. The purpose of this takeover was to preserve the county records which contained the evidence necessary to convict Crosby and the other officials. Governor Ames advised Crosby to regain possession of the Courthouse even if he had to use force. When Crosby tried to occupy the Courthouse on December 7, 1874, a riot broke out. Two whites and twenty-nine blacks were killed.

News of the riot, which was highly exaggerated, swept the state. Perhaps the most important result of the riot was that white Democrats lost their confidence in Governor Ames. Hiram Revels and several other conservative Republicans also publicly criticized Governor Ames for his handling of the Vicksburg Riot. This dissension within the Republican Party was naturally exploited by the Democrats. For the first time since 1868, Democrats decided to wage a state-wide political campaign in 1875.

The Revolution of 1875

Because of the extensive violence which occurred during that campaign, the election of 1875 has been called the "Revolution of 1875." One Democratic campaign official held the title of "Director of Military Operations." When riots broke out in Clinton, Yazoo City, and other parts of the state, Governor Ames acti-

217

vated several companies of the state militia to maintain law and order. However, since most of the militia companies were composed of blacks, this action intensified racial discord rather than calmed it. The state was on the brink of massive violence. To avoid further bloodshed, Governor Ames agreed to disband the militia and Democratic leaders promised to restrain party members from further violence. But the violence and intimidation of black voters did not subside.

The Assassination of Charles Caldwell

During the "Revolution of 1875" several blacks were murdered. One of them was Charles Caldwell. Caldwell was born in slavery but rose to a position of power and leadership in the Mississippi Republican Party during Reconstruction. He was a delegate to the state convention of 1868 and later represented Hinds County in the state legislature. As an officer in the state militia, Caldwell became known among whites as a defiant and dangerous black leader. After marching his militia unit through Hinds County in an effort to restore order following the Clinton riot in September, Caldwell became a marked man. On Christmas night, 1875, Caldwell was assassinated.

Ethelbert Barksdale, editor of the JACKSON CLARION, was one of the major forces behind the Democratic victory in 1875.

The Mississippi Plan

After the militia had been disbanded by Governor Ames, Democratic officials were free to devise a campaign plan that would virtually guarantee victory in the fall elections. Several years later, W. Calvin Wells, secretary of the Hinds County Democratic Committee, explained the tactics employed by Democratic officials during the election of 1875. This strategy, which was known as the "Mississippi Plan," was outlined by Wells as follows: (1) organize a solidly Democratic front; (2) intimidate Negroes if persuasion fails; (3) stuff the ballot box with Democratic ballots; (4) destroy Republican ballots; (5) substitute Democratic for Republican ballots for illiterate Negroes; (6) if those plans do not work, then count out the Republicans and count in the Democrats. This plan was an overwhelming success and the Democratic Party swept the fall elections in all but about a dozen counties. The Democratic Party gained over a two-thirds majority in the state Senate and a majority in the House of Representatives.

Impeachment of Republican Officials

The two-thirds majority in the senate was especially significant. The Democrats had the votes necessary to impeach Republican officials they considered to be corrupt or incompetent. When the Democratic legislature convened on January 4, 1876, impeachment proceedings were initiated against Lieutenant Governor Alexander K. Davis, Superintendent of Education Thomas Cardoza, both of whom were black, and Governor Adelbert Ames.

The evidence presented against Thomas Cardoza was very damaging and appeared to substantiate the charges that he had misappropriated state funds. Cardoza was already under several indictments which had been returned by a Vicksburg grand jury in 1874. In the case against Alexander K. Davis, who was accused of making illegal appointments and granting illegal pardons, the evidence was not quite so clear-cut, but was sufficient to convince the Democratic legislature that he was guilty.

In the case of Governor Ames there were no charges of actual fraud or corruption or misappropriation of funds. Rather, the charges were largely political in nature. Many years later R. H. Thompson, who served as the President of the Mississippi Historical Society in 1929, recalled his role in the impeachment of Governor Ames:

> I am the sole survivor of the 1876 State Senate to which articles of impeachment against Ames were presented by the House Of Representatives . . . I was then a very young man but had imbibed to some extent the prejudice against Governor Ames then prevalent in a large majority of white people of this state. Looking backwards, it appears to me that the charges made against Governor Ames, in the newspapers of the state and in political harangues of that day, must have been exaggerated to a considerable extent.

When it became certain that the Senate would impeach him, Governor Ames submitted his resignation on March 28, 1876. The Senate then dropped the charges, and Governor Ames left Mississippi.

John Marshall Stone, served twelve years as Governor of Mississippi, longer than any other in the state's history.

John Marshall Stone

Since the lieutenant governor had already been removed, the president **pro tempore** of the senate, John Marshall Stone of Tishomingo County, became governor. Stone was the first Democrat to hold the office of governor since 1868.

The End of Reconstruction

After the Revolution of 1875 the Democratic Party controlled all state-wide offices and local governments except in a few counties. Blacks continued to hold one congressional seat and some minor offices in predominantly black counties until the mid-1890's. For example, in 1876 John Roy Lynch was elected to Congress from the "shoe-string district" which included the predominantly black counties bordering on the Mississippi River. Other black officials included George W. Gayles who represented Bolivar County in the state legislature from 1892 to 1894, J. E. Ousby who served as Circuit Clerk of Bolivar County from 1880 to 1895, and Isaiah T. Montgomery who represented Bolivar County in the Constitutional Convention of 1890—the only black member of that convention. In several other counties such as Coahoma, Adams, Hinds, Lowndes, Issaquena, Noxubee, and Madison local Republican organizations survived the Revolution of 1875 and continued to exercise political influence over the next twenty years. The Mississippi Constitution of 1890, however, eliminated the base of Republican strength—the black voter. The voting requirements of that constitution were designed specifically to make it difficult, if not impossible, for blacks to vote.

Black Leaders

The Reconstruction period provided the first real opportunity for Mississippi blacks to develop a leadership class in the true sense of the word and the only opportunity they had ever had to exercise both the rights and responsibilities of citizenship. If these opportunities had come at any other time or under any other circumstances, the results might have been very different. These opportunities came to blacks as a result of military defeat, economic ruin, and social revolution—a terrible cost to their white neighbors and their former owners. These opportunities also came with such dazzling speed that it caught both blacks and whites unprepared and off guard.

Neither blacks nor whites were ready for the consequences of the defeat of the Confederacy. In the confusion and chaos that

SHOESTRING
DISTRICT
1876

followed the war, Mississippi blacks were caught up in a political struggle between white Republicans and white Democrats,
between white Southerners and white Northerners. Nevertheless, they exercised as best they knew how the responsibilities of
citizenship with which they had had no previous experience.
Blacks did not try to "lord over" their former masters. In fact,
the black vote was largely responsible for defeating the Constitution of 1868 which would have disfranchised most white

John Roy Lynch, one of Mississippi's most distinguished and successful black statesmen.

Mississippians. Black leaders tried to cooperate with white leaders on a basis of uneasy and awkward equality. It is a tribute to Mississippi blacks that they achieved as much as they did before they were deprived of the full rights of citizenship—almost as suddenly and as unexpectedly as those rights had come to them.

Redemption of Mississippi

The Democratic leaders who planned and directed the campaign of 1875 were called "Redeemers" by Democratic newspapers because they had saved the state from Republican corruption and black domination. The campaign strategy the "Redeemers" used in the election was to make the Republican Party appear to be a black man's party and the Democratic Party a white man's party. They drew the "color line" in Mississippi politics and established a one-party system which has dominated Mississippi for the last one hundred years. The first quarter of that Democratic century is called the Bourbon Era. In the next chapter we will study that important period in Mississippi's history.

A. KEY TERMS—Explain the following terms. If necessary, use a dictionary or encyclopedia.

1. Governor Charles Clark
2. General E. D. Osband
3. Presidential Reconstruction, 1865–1867
4. President Andrew Johnson
5. amnesty
6. oath of allegiance
7. nullify
8. Governor Benjamin G. Humphreys
9. Black Codes
10. citizenship
11. Radical Republicans
12. Congressional Reconstruction, 1867–1875
13. Reconstruction Acts
14. scalawags
15. carpetbaggers
16. General E.O.C. Ord
17. Constitution of 1868
18. James L. Alcorn
19. Adelbert Ames
20. Blanche K. Bruce
21. Ku Klux Klan
22. Ridgely C. Powers
23. Election of 1873
24. Vicksburg Riot, 1874
25. Revolution of 1875
26. impeachment
27. The Mississippi Plan
28. Thomas Cardoza
29. Alexander K. Davis
30. Peter Crosby
31. John Roy Lynch
32. Redeemers

B. MATCHING EXERCISE

1. General O. O. Howard
2. Thirteenth Amendment
3. Fourteenth Amendment
4. Fifteenth Amendment
5. Robert W. Flournoy
6. Ambrose Henderson
7. Hiram Revels
8. Charles Caldwell
9. Ethelbert Barksdale
10. John Marshall Stone

a. granted full citizenship to blacks
b. editor of newspaper, *Equal Rights*
c. a black legislator
d. editor of newspaper, *Clarion*
e. a black leader who was assassinated
f. Commissioner of Freedmen's Bureau
g. gave black males right to vote
h. succeeded Ames as governor
i. first black U.S. Senator
j. abolished slavery

C. WRITING EXERCISE

1. Suppose you were a newspaper correspondent sent to Mississippi by the **New York Times** in 1865, and that you remained here until 1875. Write a one or two paragraph dispatch to your paper on the following topics:

    a. The freedom farms near Vicksburg
    b. The Black Codes
    c. The Ku Klux Klan
    d. Economic Recovery
    e. Race Relations
    f. Election of 1869
    g. Election of 1873
    h. Revolution of 1875
    i. Vicksburg Riot
    j. Impeachment of Republican officials
    k. The Mississippi Plan
    l. Black leaders in Mississippi

2. If you were an adult in Mississippi during Reconstruction, would you have joined the Republican Party? Explain your answer.

3. Do you believe Reconstruction was a success or failure? Explain your answer.

CHAPTER IX

The Bourbon Period, 1876–1900

In many ways the Bourbon Period is the most difficult part of our history to understand. Even the term—Bourbon—has several meanings. The word appeared in the Mississippi political vocabulary shortly after the Civil War and was used, at first, in reference to those Southern leaders who refused to accept the changes brought about by war and Reconstruction. These Mississippi leaders were compared to the French ruling family of the House of Bourbon which was restored to power after the French Revolution. It was said that the Bourbon family had learned nothing from the great upheaval that caused the French Revolution. The Bourbon rulers wanted to re-establish the social and political system that had existed in France before the Revolution. Mississippi Bourbons were accused by their opponents of wanting to do the same thing in Mississippi.

But this is not the whole truth. Some leaders who were called Bourbons did not want Mississippi to remain a cotton state. These Bourbons promoted the development of industry, railroads, vegetable farming, and timber in addition to cotton production. These Bourbons were sometimes called "New Departure Democrats," a term which suggests that they wanted Mississippi to take a new direction, or new departure, toward its future. They favored a "New South" and a "New Mississippi" based on economic diversification rather than the Old South which was based on a cotton economy. As you can see, these Bourbons had very little in common with those Bourbons who favored the re-establishment of the old cotton plantation system.

While some Mississippians did look to the future, others kept glancing back over their shoulder at the Old South. During the 1880's and 1890's nostalgia for the Old South, the love for the "Lost Cause" and its fallen heroes, kept many white Mississippians from letting go of their past as they struggled to build their future. It was also during this period that black Mississippians found themselves increasingly isolated from the councils of state government and were unable to influence the important decisions that affected their lives and the future of their children.

Politics During the Bourbon Era

One Party System

One of the most significant developments of the Bourbon period was the establishment of the one-party system. The politicians who gained control of state government after the defeat of the Republican Party in 1875 formed a political machine that dominated the state until the election of Governor James K. Vardaman in 1903. This power elite controlled the Democratic Party and defeated all attempts to revive the Republican Party. The Democratic leaders also put down several efforts to organize new parties in Mississippi. They were very popular and powerful men. Because most of them had been high ranking Confederate military officers, those Democratic officials were often called the "Brigadiers." Their strategy to maintain political power was both very clever and very effective. There were two basic points in that strategy.

Fear of Republican Rule

First, Democratic officials, who were strongly supported by most Mississippi newspapers, constantly talked about how bad Republican rule had been and especially how burdensome taxes had been during Reconstruction. They told the people that corruption and waste in state government had left the citizens with an enormous public debt. They accused Republican officials of all sorts of things that were really not true. Newspapers echoed those accusations and added some of their own. The end result of this political propaganda was to create in the minds of the people a great fear and dread of all Republicans. The people believed and trusted their leaders.

Whenever the Republican Party ran candidates for office, the Democrats repeated the horror stories of Reconstruction and the people voted solidly Democratic. When other parties were organized, such as the Greenback and Populist parties, Democratic officials told the people that these parties were nothing but Republicans in disguise. For about one hundred years the state of Mississippi remained almost totally Democratic. Only recently has the Republican Party been able to gain any significant support among Mississippi's white population.

Color Line Politics

The second method that Democratic officials used to maintain their control over state government was to establish a color line in Mississippi politics. The chief architect of this strategy was L. Q. C. Lamar. As a senator and Secretary of the Interior, Lamar had great influence on political appointments in Mississippi. He used this influence to get several minor appointments for black Republicans, but he almost never appointed white Republicans. By not appointing whites, Lamar kept blacks in control of the Mississippi Republican Party. Since whites could not get appointments through the Republican Party, most of them drifted back into the Democratic Party. From the 1880's until the 1950's, the Mississippi Republican Party remained almost entirely a black man's party. Through fraud, violence, and intimidation of black voters the size of the Republican Party was gradually reduced during the Bourbon Period. Eventually, by the suffrage provision of the new state constitution drafted in 1890, blacks were almost totally disfranchised. After the elimination of blacks from politics, which we will discuss more fully later in this chapter, the Republican Party virtually disappeared in Mississippi. The Democrats then held total sway over the destiny of Mississippi and its people.

Politics of Personality

Whenever one party controls the politics of a state and there is no other party to offer the people a choice, factions or cliques will inevitably develop within the ruling party. Sometimes these factions develop around a particular issue, but more often they will form around a strong political personality. Consequently, in a one-party state elections are not usually decided on important issues but on the basis of the personality of the various candidates. This is the primary reason that Mississippi has produced so many dramatic and charismatic politicians. If candidates do not differ on the issues, or if they are afraid to inject new and controversial issues into their campaigns, they must resort to some other means of attracting the attention of the people and gaining publicity for their candidacy.

During the Bourbon Period the most successful Mississippi politicians were those who could "cuss" the Republicans the loudest and were the most effective in promising to keep the blacks "in their place." Economic development, improvements in education, levee construction, highways, and agricultural issues were given a back seat to the issue of race and Republicanism.

However, a few Mississippians did challenge the Democratic Party leadership from time to time. But when these challenges came, the power structure bargained and traded with local Democratic leaders to put down these challenges. The ruling elite exercised almost total control over the Democratic Party. Election to public office could be accomplished only through the Democratic Party and those who disagreed with party leaders usually found themselves labeled as "trouble makers" and "agitators." Such people were not given any consideration for jobs or offices by the party bosses. The Democratic leaders who controlled the party thought they were acting in Mississippi's best interest. They were strong personalities who were motivated by ideals and theories which they, like most other whites, believed to be true. The Democratic rulers were unyielding and unwilling to share their power with anyone that did not agree with them, not only on matters of race, but on economic issues as well. We will see, later in this chapter, that the conditions of poverty in which most Mississippi farmers lived during the 1880's gave rise to a new group of leaders who eventually toppled the Bourbons from power.

The Mississippi Triumvirate

Probably the three most powerful and influential men in Mississippi during the Bourbon period were James Z. George, Edward C. Walthall, and L. Q. C. Lamar. All three of these men served in the United States Senate. Walthall, a former Confederate general, was elected to the Senate by the legislature in 1885 and served until 1894 when he resigned because of ill health. Senator George, also a Confederate general, served his state in many capacities during his distinguished public career. He was the state Democratic campaign manager and director of the "Revolution of 1875." Later, he was elected to the Senate where he served from 1881 until his death in 1897. During his senate term George returned to Mississippi to serve in the Constitutional Convention of 1890. Senator George was chairman of the committee that drafted the article apportioning the seats in the state legislature to the various counties.

L.Q.C. Lamar, James Z. George and Edward C. Walthall, the Mississippi Triumvirate.

The third member of this triumvirate was L. Q. C. Lamar, perhaps Mississippi's most distinguished statesman. A native of Georgia, Lamar moved to Oxford in 1849 and was appointed professor of mathematics at the University of Mississippi in 1850. During the early years of the Civil War, Lamar served as a Confederate ambassador in Europe. After the war Lamar returned to the University of Mississippi to teach law. While serving in the United States Congress in 1874, Lamar attracted national attention and won the acclaim of his fellow congressmen by his stirring eulogy of Senator Charles Sumner. Senator Sumner of Massachusetts was a Radical Republican who had advocated a stern policy of Reconstruction for the South. When Sumner died, Lamar used that occasion to plead for national reconciliation and a spirit of peace between the North and the South. Lamar's fame and reputation as a peacemaker between the states of the Union and the states of the Confederacy continued to grow over the years. In 1877 he helped work out a compromise which settled the disputed presidential election of 1876.

In 1878 Senator Lamar was criticized by the state legislature for voting against a bill to increase the circulation of silver money. This bill was supported by Mississippi farmers who favored putting more money in circulation to relieve the depression which farmers were experiencing at that time. The state legislature criticized Lamar for his vote and even called for him to resign. But Lamar was too strong and popular with the people, and not even this disappointment could bring the powerful senator down. When President Grover Cleveland was elected in 1884, Lamar was appointed Secretary of the Interior. His long distinguished career was capped by his appointment to the United States Supreme Court where he served from 1888 until his death in 1893.

Governor John Marshall Stone

No public figure in Mississippi better illustrates the results of a one-party system than John M. Stone. Between 1876 and 1900 Stone served as governor for twelve of those twenty-four years. After assuming the governorship upon the resignation of Adelbert Ames in 1876, Stone was elected for a full term in 1877 by the astounding vote of 97,729 to 47. In 1889, Stone was elected for another term by a vote of 84,929 to 16. Governor Stone has the distinction of serving as governor longer than any other man in Mississippi history.

Governors Robert Lowry and Anselm J. McLaurin

Mississippi's other two governors during the Bourbon Period were Robert Lowry and Anselm J. McLaurin. Both Lowry and McLaurin were ex-Confederate officers, and both were active in the Democratic victory in 1875. During Lowry's administration, 1882–1890, strong emphasis was placed on railroad construction. Governor Lowry boasted that more track was laid during his eight years in office than in all the preceding years combined. As beneficial as railroad development may have been to some people in the state, farmers frequently complained about the high freight rates. Farmers also accused political leaders of promoting industry to the neglect of agriculture. Their protests against that policy became more vocal in the late 1880's and 1890's.

By the time Governor McLaurin was elected in 1895, Lamar had already died. Senators George and Walthall would also soon pass from the Mississippi political scene. The passing of these Democratic leaders intensified factionalism within the Party. McLaurin put together a political organization which was called the "McLaurin Clan." However, this organization, which included several of McLaurin's brothers, did not have the popular support that Lamar, Stone, George, and Walthall had enjoyed. New leaders representing the discontented farmers openly challenged the "McLaurin Clan." Governor McLaurin personally survived those challenges and after his term expired in 1900, he was elected to the United States Senate where he served until his death in 1909. As we will see in the next chapter, the McLaurin Clan and the old political machine did not survive.

Reduction of Government Expenditures

During the Revolution of 1875, Democratic leaders accused the Republican Party of waste and extravagance and pledged to reduce government expenditures when they gained control of the state. After their successful campaign, Democratic leaders kept those promises. Government positions which were not considered necessary were abolished and the salaries of many other officials were reduced.

Shortly after he was inaugurated in 1876, Governor Stone received a letter from L. Q. C. Lamar who made several suggestions for cutting state expenses. One of his suggestions was to sell the Governor's Mansion in order to save the state the costly up-keep and repairs on the executive residence. Even the governor's salary was affected by the Bourbon's cost-cutting policies. In 1881 the annual salary of Mississippi's chief executive was reduced from $4,000 to $3,000.

Other areas of state government were affected also. The number of judicial districts were reduced by combining smaller districts into one large district. This consolidation not only reduced the number of judges, but also eliminated other costs for conducting court.

Convicts provided labor during construction of the Mississippi levee system.

Convict Lease System

The most controversial cost-cutting scheme initiated by the Bourbons was the convict lease system. In order to eliminate the expense of maintaining a state penitentiary, the state legislature authorized the Board of Public Works to lease the penitentiary to private citizens. These leasees in turn leased, or hired out, the convicts to railroad companies, manufacturers, or plantation owners for $50.00 a year plus food, clothing, and housing.

The convict lease system soon became a public scandal because the convicts were abused, overworked, underfed, ill-clothed, and ill-housed by the people to whom they were leased. An early historian of Mississippi gave this description of the system:

> The barbarism of the system continued to arouse public resentment, which culminated in the winter of 1884 when . . . [a] squad of eighteen convicts were shipped through Vicksburg from a Delta plantation on their way to the prison hospital at Jackson. Their half-naked bodies showed signs of cruel torture, their fingers and toes were frost-bitten and they were hardly able to walk.

The physical condition of the convicts was not the only thing that provoked public resentment. In 1887 several public officials, including the attorney general and the governor, were accused of falsifying state records to show that one of the major leasees had reimbursed the state for the number of convicts under his control. These accusations led to a grand jury investigation and an investigation by a special legislative committee. Although no criminal charges were brought against any public officials, both investigative bodies recommended that the convict lease system be abolished.

During the constitutional convention of 1890 a special committee was appointed to draft an article abolishing the system. But the provision included in the new constitution did not actually abolish the system. Under the provisions of the new constitution the Penitentiary Board was authorized to employ convicts on land that was leased from private individuals. However, the individual leasing the land to the state was usually employed to supervise the convict labor and many of the abuses of the old system continued. Although the state profited much more from the new system, the convicts experienced no real improvement in their conditions.

When James K. Vardaman was elected governor in 1903, he vowed to bring an end to this shameful system that enriched a few individuals at the expense of many. We will discuss Vardaman's efforts more fully in the following chapter.

Public Education

The efforts of Bourbon leaders to economize extended to almost every aspect of government services, including public education. The bitterness of whites concerning the high cost of educating blacks continued to hamper the state school system, and during most of the Bourbon period there was a declining enrollment in black schools. In 1890 less than half of the black school-age children attended school at all. Teachers' salaries and expenditures for both white and black schools also declined during the same period. In 1872 the legislature appropriated approximately $1,137,000 for public education in Mississippi. Ten years later, although public school enrollment had increased from 148,000 students to 237,000, the legislature appropriated only $758,000.

In spite of these discouraging figures, however, the public school system was gaining more acceptance among the people of Mississippi. By the end of the nineteenth century state appropriations for public schools were increasing. The people realized that an educated citizenry was essential for the economic and social development of the state.

GROWTH OF TOWNS, 1860-1890
POPULATION

TOWN	1860	1870	1880	1890
COLUMBUS	*	*	3,955	4,559
GREENVILLE	*	*	2,191	6,658
JACKSON	2,107	4,234	5,204	5,920
MERIDIAN	*	2,709	4,008	10,624
NATCHEZ	4,272	9,057	7,058	10,101
VICKSBURG	3,158	12,443	11,814	13,373

* NOT ESTABLISHED UNTIL LATER

Higher Education

During the Bourbon period institutions of higher learning received much greater support than did the elementary and secondary schools. In the first few years after the war several colleges and universities were established. Most of these institutions were founded by religious denominations but three new colleges were established by the state of Mississippi.

Mississippi Agricultural and Mechanical College

In 1862 the United States Congress passed the Morrill Act which granted to each state a large area of federal land to be used in support of an agricultural and mechanical college. Originally, the land grant was made available to the University of Mississippi at Oxford which began offering agricultural courses in 1872. However, since very few students enrolled in those courses, the need for college training in scientific agriculture and industrial technology was not being met. Consequently, in 1878

235

the state legislature chartered Mississippi Agricultural and Mechanical College and located the state's white land grant college at Starkville. Over the years this institution has made an enormous contribution to the economic development of the state of Mississippi. In 1935 the name of the school was changed to the Mississippi State College and in 1958 to Mississippi State University.

Irwin Russell

Sherwood Bonner

Two of Mississippi's most important writers during this period were Sherwood Bonner of Holly Springs, and Irwin Russell of Natchez. Russell's poem, CHRISTMAS NIGHT IN THE QUARTERS, is considered a classic example of the literary use of black dialect.

Alcorn Agricultural and Mechanical College

In the same year that Mississippi A. & M. was established, the charter of Alcorn University was modified. Alcorn was changed from a liberal arts university to an agricultural and mechanical college. For many years Alcorn was the only state-supported institution of higher learning for blacks in Mississippi. In recent years liberal arts and education courses have been added to Alcorn's curriculum and enrollment in these areas has increased more rapidly than enrollment in the agricultural and mechanical programs. In 1974 Alcorn A. & M. College was renamed Alcorn State University.

Annie Peyton, one of the state's leading advocates for the establishment of the Industrial Institute for Women, was also one of the college's first women teachers.

Mississippi State College For Women

For several years after the war, there was strong support among Mississippi leaders for the establishment of a training institute for the young white women of the state. Although the University of Mississippi began admitting women students in 1882, the movement for a separate woman's college continued to gain support. In 1884 the state legislature established the Mississippi Industrial Institute and College for white women in Columbus. The Industrial Institute was later renamed Mississippi State College for Women and Mississippi University for Women in 1974.

Private Colleges

In the post-Civil War period blacks were eager to get an education and within a few years after the emancipation several black private colleges were established in Mississippi. Jackson College was founded at Natchez in 1877 by the Baptist denomination. The school was moved to Jackson in 1883 and in 1940 Jackson College became a state-supported institution. In 1974 the name of the college was changed to Jackson State University. Campbell College was established in 1887 with branches in Vicksburg and Friars Point. In 1898 the two branches were combined and transferred to Jackson. Campbell College, which

237

was originally established by the African Methodist Episcopal Church, eventually merged with Jackson State University.

Shaw University was established at Holly Springs by the Mississippi Conference of the Methodist Episcopal Church in 1866. Although Shaw University faced great financial difficulty, it survived and in 1890 its name was changed to Rust College. Tougaloo College was established by the American Missionary Association at Jackson in 1869. Tougaloo was given some financial assistance by the state until 1891. Since that time, Tougaloo has operated as a privately endowed college.

The Methodist denomination established two colleges for white women, the Port Gibson Institute (1869) and Grenada College (1882). This denomination had already established Whitworth College for Women in Brookhaven just prior to the war in 1858. Blue Mountain (1869) and Belhaven (1883) were also women's colleges and were supported by the Baptists and Presbyterians. Millsaps College for men in Jackson was originally founded in 1888 by a gift from Reuben W. Millsaps, but in later years Millsaps became affiliated with the Methodist Church.

Economic Development During the Bourbon Period

The greatest loss sustained by Mississippi and the nation during the Civil War was the 600,000 men who died during that four year period. The second greatest loss, especially to Mississippi, was the disruption of the economy. For several years large cotton fields lay vacant. Grass, weeds, bushes, and sage covered the southern landscape.

During the Civil War, Mississippi banks and other businesses were required by law to accept Confederate money in payment for goods and services. After the defeat of the Confederacy, this money was worthless. In May 1866, the state treasurer burned $341,000 worth of Confederate paper money in a brief ceremony in front of the state capitol. Called "cotton money" because it was backed up by cotton rather than gold or silver, this money was literally not worth the paper it was printed on.

The state also suffered great losses from the destruction of railroads, factories, livestock, bridges, and buildings. Economic

Coca-Cola was sold and distributed in bottles for the first time by the Biedenharn Candy Company of Vicksburg in the early 1890s. The original Biedenharn building is now a museum.

recovery had been a major goal of the Republican administration during Reconstruction. But economic development was hampered by the political and racial discord that characterized the first decade following the Civil War. When the Bourbon Democrats came to power in 1876, they were not distracted by those problems as the Republicans had been. So under the Bourbons, the state embarked upon the long and difficult road to economic recovery.

Timber Production

In 1865 over two-thirds of the land area of Mississippi was in timber. Those virgin forests were a valuable natural resource which had not been developed during the antebellum period. After the war the state's timber resources were developed and lumber production provided jobs and income to thousands of Mississippians. By 1890 there were 338 sawmills providing employment to 4434 people. The total value of timber products had more than doubled in the twenty years between 1870 and 1890.

TIMBER PRODUCTION, 1870-1890

	1870	1880	1890
NO. OF ESTABLISHMENTS	265	295	338
CAPITAL INVESTMENT	1,153,917	922,595	4,433,229
NUMBER OF WORKERS	1,954	1,170	4,434
TOTAL WAGES	580,056	197,867	1,287,391
TOTAL VALUE OF PRODUCTS	2,160,667	1,920,335	5,670,774

Manufacturing

Since most of the state's factories had been destroyed during the war, industrial recovery was a slow and costly process. To aid in the recovery and to encourage the location of new factories within the state, the legislature awarded tax exemption to certain kinds of businesses in 1870. And again in 1882 new industries were given a ten-year tax exempt status.

These laws were successful in attracting new industries, especially textile mills, to Mississippi. By 1890, there were sixteen mills manufacturing both cotton and woolen products in Mississippi. The largest of these, the Mississippi Mills, was owned by J. M. Wesson and was located in the town that now bears his name. The sixteen mills provided 2,266 jobs. Most manufacturing establishments in Mississippi, which also included cottonseed oil mills and fertilizer plants, were directly related to agriculture.

COTTON MANUFACTURING, 1860-1890

	1860	1870	1880	1890
NUMBER OF MILLS	4	5	8	9
VALUATION OF MILLS	230,000	751,500	1,122,140	2,053,143
NUMBER OF SPINDLES	6,344	3,526	18,568	57,004
NUMBER OF WORKERS	215	265	722	1,184
TOTAL WAGES	36,264	61,833	133,214	290,981
VALUE OF PRODUCTS	176,328	234,445	679,093	1,333,398

WOOLEN MANUFACTURING, 1860-1890

	1860	1870	1880	1890
NO. OF ESTABLISHMENTS	4	11	8	7
CAPITAL	75,000	195,250	331,500	1,553,455
NUMBER OF WORKERS	235	116	218	1,082
SPINDLES	1000	344	3,734	9,196
WAGES	27,620	28,800	53,100	306,270
VALUE OF PRODUCTS	158,507	147,323	299,605	924,185

Railroad Boom

The most significant industrial development in post-war Mississippi was the railroad boom. In 1860 there were only 872 miles of track in Mississippi. Since much of this track had been destroyed during the war, Mississippi's entire rail system had to be reorganized and rebuilt. One of the major factors stimulating railroad construction during the Bourbon Period was the large scale timber operations which used the railroad as the primary means of transportation. Another factor was the development of vegetable farming in Copiah, Lincoln, and Lawrence Counties. Vegetable producers shipped their products by rail to large cities such as New Orleans, Memphis, St. Louis, and Chicago. Still another factor in railroad expansion was the decline of water transportation in the interior region of the state. Many of the small navigable rivers used during the pre-war period could no longer accommodate steamboats. Railroads provided an alternative and soon replaced water transportation on all but the largest rivers.

The growth of Mississippi's railway system during the 1880's was spectacular. During that decade the railroad mileage increased from 1,118 to 2,366, an increase of over 110%. In the single year of 1883, more track was laid in Mississippi than in any other state. The expansion of the railroad network was of great benefit to the state in many ways. It provided the state with a transportation system that was essential for the growth and development of both manufacturing and agriculture.

There were, however, serious problems connected with railroad expansion. Basically, the problems stemmed from the fact that railroad companies were not regulated by the state government. Railroading in those days was a cutthroat business. The larger lines did everything possible to drive the smaller lines out of business. In this way a few companies were able to develop a monopoly over rail service in certain parts of the state.

Without competition from other lines, these few lines were free to raise their rates for shipping goods and for carrying pas-

RAILROAD MILEAGE IN MISSISSIPPI, JUNE 30, 1891

RAILROADS	MILES
ILLINOIS CENTRAL	636.06
LOUISVILLE, NEW ORLEANS AND TEXAS	626.36
MOBILE AND OHIO	306.00
GEORGIA PACIFIC	241.31
NEW ORLEANS AND NORTHEASTERN	153.04
ALABAMA AND VICKSBURG	143.49
KANSAS CITY, MEMPHIS AND BIRMINGHAM	142.89
LOUISVILLE AND NASHVILLE	73.83
GULF AND CHICAGO (NARROW GAUGE)	57.00
MEMPHIS AND CHARLESTON	33.40
ALABAMA GREAT SOUTHERN	18.78
EAST TENNESSEE, VIRGINIA AND GEORGIA	7.73
GULF AND SHIP ISLAND	7.00
NEW ORLEANS AND NORTHWESTERN	2.66
MERIDIAN, BROOKHAVEN AND NATCHEZ	7.00

TOTAL ... 2,456.45

sengers. Some companies used a "flat rate" system to increase their profits. Under this system a minimum charge, or flat rate, was established for the shipment of goods up to one hundred pounds. In other words, if a customer shipped a package weighing only twenty pounds, he paid the same fee that he would have paid for the shipment of one hundred pounds.

Mississippi farmers were also caught in the middle of a rate war between several of the larger lines. For example, if two companies were competing for business between Chicago and New Orleans, the companies might reduce their rates for this "long haul" to the barest minimum in order to attract shippers to their lines. In the rural sections of Mississippi these companies were not in competition with each other because there was usually only one line serving these sparsely populated areas. Therefore, to make up for the losses it might sustain in competing for the long haul business, a company would charge high rates to its short haul customers. Because of this long haul and short haul rate system, it cost a farmer more to ship his goods from Clinton to Vicksburg than it did to ship his goods from Vicksburg to St. Louis. As you might expect, farmers became very angry with this situation.

Farmers began to demand that the legislature pass laws to regulate freight rates and to restrict the merger of small companies with the larger lines. Eventually the legislature did pass a law that included both of these provisions but Governor Stone, who had been a railroad agent before the war, vetoed the bill. A couple of years later the legislature passed another law establishing a Railroad Commission with the power to regulate railroads. That law was also vetoed, this time by Governor Lowry. After the legislature yielded to Governor Lowry's demand that the Commission members be appointed by the governor rather than the state legislature, a Railroad Commission was finally established in 1884. Governor Lowry's first appointment to the Commission was John M. Stone. Stone's appointment convinced agrarian leaders that the Commission would not be sympathetic to their complaints and agrarian discontent intensified.

Agricultural Conditions

Mississippi farmers suffered from a wide variety of problems throughout the Bourbon era and they frequently complained that state government was doing nothing to improve their conditions. In addition to high freight rates and interest rates, farmers were also troubled by an unstable labor supply.

Black Exodus

Within two or three years after Reconstruction, blacks began to leave Mississippi in such large numbers that this population shift was called the "Black Exodus." These people, most of whom were farm workers, were being lured to Kansas and other Midwestern states by promises of high-paying jobs. The black migrants were recruited by fast-talking labor agents who told them that they would make such good wages that they would soon be able to buy their own land.

These promises were greatly exaggerated and the 6,000 Mississippi blacks who moved to Kansas in 1879 found only poverty and exploitation. One Mississippian wrote to his friends back home: "Negroes are not any more respected in Kansas than they are in Mississippi." Another wrote to his friends and family: "You had better stay where you are." Most Mississippians who moved to Kansas during this exodus gradually returned. There was another important outmigration of Mississippi blacks during the 1920's and 1930's. We will study that population shift in a later chapter.

Chinese Immigrants

Many white planters and political leaders believed that the Black Exodus would create a critical labor shortage in the state. To offset this possible shortage, Mississippi leaders made an effort to attract Chinese and European immigrants to Mississippi. Brochures and pamphlets describing Mississippi were published in several foreign languages and distributed in Denmark, Norway, and other European countries. These attempts were not very successful and only a few European immigrants came to Mississippi before the early 1900's.

The effort to attract Chinese laborers to Mississippi was only slightly more successful. Delta planters hired labor agents to recruit Chinese families on the West Coast and provided transportation for those who migrated to Mississippi. Although several Chinese families moved to the Delta and initially worked as farm laborers, most of them soon became small merchants. The failure to attract a significant number of European and Chinese immigrants meant that blacks would continue to supply the labor for Mississippi's large plantations.

Sharecropping

The emancipation of Mississippi's black population and the disruption of Mississippi's banking system during the war, meant that a new credit arrangement had to be designed to finance agricultural operations. Farmers, large or small, almost never operate on their own money. They borrow money as they need it through the growing season and then pay it back when they harvest their crops. But, when a Mississippi planter went to a banker right after the Civil War to borrow money to make a crop, the banker was hesitant about lending him the money. For one thing, the banker was doubtful that the planter could find enough laborers who would remain on the plantation long enough to make a crop. Also, the banker would probably prefer to invest in a textile mill or a new railroad company. Investment in manufacturing or railroads seemed more promising to the banker than investment in cotton production.

Sometimes a planter was able to establish credit with a banker. But if he could not, he had to look for another source of credit. About the only other credit source available to a planter was a local merchant. Within a few years after the Civil War, local merchants became a key figure in Mississippi's agricultural operations. A local merchant would extend credit to a planter throughout the growing season under an agreement that the account be paid in full when the crop was harvested. Under this arrangement the planter resolved his credit problem. He could then turn to his second problem—finding laborers to make the crop.

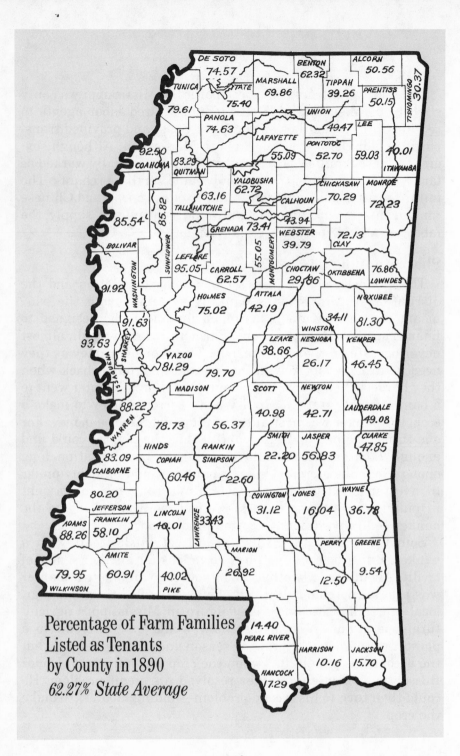

Percentage of Farm Families
Listed as Tenants
by County in 1890
62.27% State Average

In post-war Mississippi there was a temporary shortage of labor. The shortage was not caused by the Black Exodus, but by the fact that black men removed their wives and children from the labor force. Under slavery, fathers had no control over when their children started working or whether or not their wives worked. But in freedom the father controlled his family, and most black men refused to allow their wives and children to work in the fields. Initially this labor shortage worked to the advantage of Mississippi blacks. They could bargain from a position of strength because their labor was in great demand.

When a planter offered a black man a contract to work his land the laborer could negotiate the terms of that contract. In most cases the planter offered cash wages, but the black man usually suggested that the land be worked on shares. For the first time, blacks were in a position to demand a share of the fruits of their labor, a share of the land's bounty. Rather than working for fixed wages, blacks preferred and demanded a share of the crop they produced. Under this arrangement sharecroppers were supplied with the necessary "furnishings" by a planter during the growing season. When the crop was harvested, the cost of the furnishings were deducted from the worker's share of the crop and whatever remained from his share was paid in cash. This system, however, did not measure up to the sharecropper's expectations. Within a few years after the system began operating, the price of cotton began to decline. Sharecroppers soon found that the credit advances they received during the year amounted to more than their share of the crop. Within a few years, both the planters and the sharecroppers accumulated large debts to local merchants. The planters could settle their debts by deeding over some of their land to the merchant. But sharecroppers had no means of satisfying their debts. Consequently, the debts of the sharecroppers were carried over from one year to the next and they soon owed the merchant so much that they lost all hope of ever getting out of debt.

When a planter deeded some of his land to a merchant, he told the families working on that portion of his land that they would have to sign a new agreement with the merchant. Usually, the merchant would not allow his sharecroppers to raise cows, hogs, or vegetables. Instead, he insisted that they plant only cotton. The merchant preferred to sell the tenants those food items. Thus, he profited not only from the cotton his sharecroppers raised but also on their purchases of food supplies.

The sharecropping system, which blacks had initially favored, placed them in another kind of bondage to the planter-merchants. Sharecroppers were required by a state law, called a crop lien law, to remain on the land they were working until all their debts were paid in full. Since the price of cotton continued to decline throughout the 1880's and 1890's, sharecroppers were rarely ever able to free themselves from their debt bondage. And generations of black Mississippians lived out their lives in hopeless poverty.

Although the sharecropping system and the agricultural depression of the 1880's hit blacks the hardest, white farmers were suffering as well. Many white farmers eventually lost their land and were also reduced to sharecropping as a means of survival. The crop lien law applied to white sharecroppers as well as blacks. However, whites did have one advantage. They could vote and take part in the political process, and they could protest.

Farmers Protest

Because of the wretched conditions of agriculture in Mississippi during the Bourbon period, farmers organized in protest against the Democratic leaders who neglected their interests and refused to act swiftly on their complaints.

One of the earliest organizations of farmers was the Grange. More like a social or fraternal club than a political organization, the Granger movement could do little to improve the general conditions of Mississippi farmers. In the 1880's a new organization, the Farmers' Alliance, became very popular and thousands of Mississippi farmers, both black and white, joined it.

The Farmers' Alliance publicly supported political candidates who promised to work in the farmers' interests and opposed those candidates who did not make such a commitment. The new organization demanded state laws to regulate railroads. It also encouraged co-operative buying and selling among farmers as a means of raising the price of their crops and holding down the cost of goods they bought.

The most important demands of the Farmers' Alliance were political, rather than economic or social in nature. The white farmers demanded two things in particular. First, they wanted a new state constitution which would disfranchise blacks. They wanted this because every time white farmers tried to organize a new party or faction within the Democratic Party, the Democratic leaders accused them of splitting the white voters. If white voters divided on economic issues, party leaders warned, black voters would then hold the balance of power and could restore the Republican Party to power. For several years the party leaders used this tactic to maintain their control of the Democratic Party. The frustrated and angry white farmers finally decided that the only solution to their problems was to eliminate black voting altogether. Then the whites could divide on economic issues without worrying about blacks controlling the balance of power. White farmers had come to this conclusion by the late 1880's.

The farmer's second demand was a new method of distributing the seats in the state legislature. Each county has a certain number of representatives in the legislature. That number of seats is determined by the number of people in each county. Under the 1868 constitution, each county was represented in the legislature on the basis of total county population—including blacks and whites. Under that legislative apportionment plan the heavily populated black counties along the Mississippi River had more seats in the legislature than the predominantly white counties in the Northeast Hills and the Piney Woods. Since very few blacks voted in the river counties, the small number of whites in those wealthy counties actually controlled the state legislature and the laws passed by that body. Poor white farmers in the hills and Piney Woods accused the lawmakers of passing only those laws which benefited the rich landowners, merchants, railroad companies, and bankers.

One other aspect of the legislative apportionment plan in use at that time was of special significance to the white farmers. Each county's representation in the state Democratic Convention was based on its representation in the state legislature. Since the Delta and river counties had more seats in the legislature, they also controlled the state Democratic Convention. In the 1880's Democratic candidates for governor and other state offices were nominated by the party's state convention. Party leaders controlled the state convention and hand-picked the party's candidates. Since there was only one party in the state, the candidates selected by the Democratic Party leaders were always elected.

The only way farmers from the small white counties could gain control of the party, and the power to nominate the candidates they favored was to change the method of apportionment in the state legislature. Farmers' Alliance leaders believed that this change could come only through a new state constitution which apportioned the legislature on the basis of white population rather than on **total** population. In the general election of 1889 Farmers' Alliance candidates campaigned in support of a new constitution which they promised would include provisions to disfranchise blacks and to reapportion the state legislature. They believed that these two constitutional provisions would give farmers control over state government. In that election, farmers demonstrated their political strength by electing a legislature and a governor who favored a new constitution.

The Constitution of 1890

On August 17, 1890, a constitutional convention assembled in Jackson to write a new constitution for Mississippi. Solomon S. Calhoon was elected chairman of the convention by one vote over R. C. Patty, the Farmers' Alliance candidate. Of the 134 delegates, 130 were Democrats, two were Republicans, one was a conservative, and the other delegate was a Greenbacker. Isaiah T. Montgomery, the founder of Mound Bayou, was the only black delegate. The most influential delegate at the convention was Senator James Z. George.

250

Isaiah T. Montgomery, a former slave, led the black exodus from Mississippi in the 1870s, but returned to found Mound Bayou, one of the first and most successful all-black communities in America.

The suffrage requirements written into the new constitution included a literacy test and a poll tax of two dollars. These two provisions which were specifically designed to make it difficult for Mississippi blacks to register eliminated blacks as a potential force in state politics. After the adoption of the new suffrage requirements, the numbers of black voters decreased from 142,000 in 1890 to 8,615 in 1892. The removal of blacks from politics paved the way for the farmers' final victory over the Bourbon leaders. With blacks no longer a factor in Mississippi politics, whites could then divide along economic issues.

However, the farmers did not achieve the kind of legislative apportionment they wanted. The apportionment method drafted by Senator James Z. George was not based exclusively on white population. Instead legislative apportionment was based on the total number of males over twenty-one years of age, black and white, in each county. This apportionment plan did not give the predominantly white counties control over the legislature or the state Democratic Convention. Consequently, the Democratic Party and the state legislature remained under Bourbon control for another twelve years. The farmers' revolt was not successful until 1902 when a new method of nominating political candidates was adopted.

Other Provisions of the Constitution of 1890

The public school system with a four months compulsory school term was continued under the 1890 constitution. However, after the 1954 Brown decision ordering desegregation of the public schools, the Mississippi compulsory school attendance law was repealed.

The four-year term of the governor was also continued, but the chief executive was not allowed to succeed himself. Several other state officials, including the treasurer, auditor, and county sheriffs were also prohibited from serving two terms in a row. State judges were appointed by the governor under the new constitution but in the early twentieth century, the constitution was amended to provide for the election of all judicial officials.

The Constitution of 1890 abolished the convict lease system and eliminated the special tax exemptions for businesses and corporations. Although it has been amended many times since its adoption, the Constitution of 1890 is still in effect today.

Frank Burkitt

The chief spokesman for Mississippi farmers at the Constitutional Convention in 1890 was Frank Burkitt of Chickasaw County. During the convention, Burkitt strongly objected to the requirement that voters must be able to read and write. He also objected to the poll tax provision. Burkitt argued that these provisions would eliminate about 50,000 white voters who could not read and write and who would be unwilling to pay two dollars for the privilege of voting. Burkitt's prediction of a drastic decrease in white registered voters came true. When the voter registration under the new constitution was completed, the total number of white registered voters had dropped from 120,000 in 1890 to 68,000 in 1892. Burkitt was so opposed to these voting requirements that he refused to sign and support the final adoption of the constitution. Burkitt realized that the farmers would not gain control of state government under the new constitution. He also realized that the old party bosses would continue to control the Democratic Party.

Populist Party

Just before the presidential election of 1892 the Populist Party was organized. Sometimes called the People's Party, this new

252

national political party received strong support in Mississippi. Frank Burkitt actively campaigned for the Populists throughout Mississippi. In an effort to break the control of the Democratic Party, Burkitt encouraged blacks to register and to vote for the Populist candidates. This attempt to recruit black voters, however, hurt the Populist Party in Mississippi where blacks had been disfranchised only two years earlier.

Unlike Burkitt, James K. Vardaman did not support the Populists but remained within the Democratic Party where he worked from the inside to gain control of the party. As later events proved, Vardaman's strategy was wiser because white farmers preferred to have only one party — a white man's party — but one which they controlled. The key to gaining that power was to devise a new means of nominating candidates for public office. As long as the candidates were chosen by the convention method, the small group of party bosses could continue to exclude those candidates who disagreed with them. What was needed was a system that would let the people, the voters, nominate the candidates for themselves. For several years such a system, known as a direct primary election, had been discussed by newspapers and agrarian leaders. But the direct primary had been opposed by the Democratic Party leaders who realized that the nomination of primary candidates by a popular election would mean the end of their power.

When a primary law was finally passed in 1902, Mississippi entered a new era — politically, economically, and socially. That new era, sometimes described as the "Revolt of the Rednecks," will be discussed in the next chapter.

A. KEY TERMS—Explain the following terms. If necessary, use a dictionary or encyclopedia.

1. Bourbon
2. French Revolution
3. "New South"
4. New Mississippi
5. New Departure Democrats
6. economic diversification
7. nostalgia
8. "Lost Cause"
9. color line politics
10. politics of personality
11. clique
12. power structure
13. triumvirate
14. L. Q. C. Lamar
15. Robert Lowry
16. John Marshall Stone
17. convict lease system
18. Morrill Act
19. "cotton money"
20. tax exempt status
21. flat rate system
22. rate war
23. Railroad Commission
24. Black Exodus
25. Chinese immigrants
26. furnishings
27. crop lien law
28. Farmers' Alliance
29. balance of power
30. legislative apportionment
31. Constitution of 1890
32. literacy test

B. MATCHING EXERCISE

1. Lamar, George, Walthall
2. McLaurin Clan
3. Mississippi A & M College
4. Alcorn University
5. Mississippi University for Women
6. Mississippi Mills
7. sharecropping
8. Isaiah T. Montgomery
9. poll tax
10. Frank Burkitt

a. a land grant college at Starkville
b. first state-supported college for women
c. farming someone else's land
d. campaigned for Populist Party
e. Mississippi Triumvirate
f. founder of Mound Bayou
g. designed to keep blacks from voting
h. supporters of Governor Anselm J. McLaurin
i. the state's largest cotton mill
j. first state-supported university for blacks

C. WRITING ASSIGNMENT

1. Suppose you are a newspaper or television reporter and you are sent to interview an elderly black person who grew up as a child of sharecroppers in Mississippi. Write out a series of questions you would like to ask that person and, from what you have learned about sharecropping, supply the answers to your questions.

2. Write a biographical sketch of the following Mississippians:
   John Marshall Stone
   L. Q. C. Lamar
   James Z. George
   Anselm J. McLaurin
   Isaiah T. Montgomery
   Frank Burkitt

3. Write essays on the following topics:
   a. Railroading in Mississippi During the late Nineteenth Century
   b. The Development of Higher Education in Mississippi After the Civil War
   c. Color Line Politics in Mississippi
   d. Farmer Unrest in Mississippi
   e. The Mississippi Constitution of 1890

4. Suppose you were a delegate to the Constitutional Convention of 1890. Which of the major provisions would you have voted *for* and *against*. Explain your reasons for each of your votes.

CHAPTER X

Revolt of the Rednecks, 1900–1932

The turning of a century is an exciting event to witness. Celebrations, ceremonies, and extravaganzas were held throughout America to welcome the twentieth century. Even then the new century was being hailed as a century of progress and change. But even the most imaginative Americans living in 1900 would probably be dazzled by the technology that modern Americans now accept as common place. Most of you reading this book will observe the turn of the next century. We can only wonder at the marvels the twenty-first century will bring.

A rural family in the early 1900s.

Administration of Andrew H. Longino, 1900–1904

It is significant that the first governor of this new century represented a major turning point in Mississippi history. Andrew H. Longino was the first governor elected after the Civil War who was not a Confederate veteran. He was also the last governor nominated by the convention system. In this respect, Longino represents the end of an era. He was the last governor to be hand-picked by that small group of party leaders who dominated the state Democratic Convention.

Industrial Expansion

Governor Longino anticipated the sweeping changes the twentieth century would bring to Mississippi and in his first speech as governor he warned the people to brace themselves for those changes. He advised Mississippians not to look back toward the past but ahead toward the future. Governor Longino believed that Mississippi's future economic prosperity depended upon industrial expansion, and he encouraged the legislature to pass laws that would attract new industries to Mississippi.

The governor told the lawmakers, "I confidently hope that no . . . prejudicial opposition to . . . corporate enterprises will find favor with this legislature." Instead, he recommended that the legislators offer tax exemptions to new industries locating in Mississippi. On the basis of the number of new industrial charters issued during his administration, Governor Longino was highly successful in attracting new industry to Mississippi. Between 1900 and 1904 the number of charters for new businesses rose to 1,312, substantially above the 365 issued during the previous four years. Perhaps Governor Longino's efforts may have eventually solved the economic problems of Mississippi's sharecroppers and day laborers had they been continued for a longer period of time. But the program of industrial expansion was abandoned by Governor Longino's successor, James K. Vardaman.

The Growth of Jackson

The impact of industrial expansion was especially evident in Jackson. In July of 1902, a local newspaper reported that over $2.1 million in new construction was in progress. Jackson is uniquely a city of the twentieth century. Before 1900 the state's capital city grew very slowly. But after the turn of the century,

Jackson experinced phenomenal growth as reflected in the following population figures:

1880-	5,204	1940-	62,107
1890-	5,920	1950-	98,271
1900-	7,866	1960-	144,422
1910-	21,262	1970-	153,968
1920-	22,817	1980-	200,338
1930-	48,282		

New Capitol

In addition to encouraging industrial expansion, Governor Longino also promoted the construction of a new state capitol building. The old capitol which had been in use for over sixty years was in need of extensive repair. In 1888 an architect who examined the building predicted that the capitol might collapse at anytime. After this report, a bill was introduced in the legislature authorizing the construction of a new capitol. But the bill was vetoed by Governor McLaurin who objected to both the size and the design of the new capitol building. Governor McLaurin said the new building would be too small and was more suitable for a county court house than a state house. No further action was taken until Governor Longino took office.

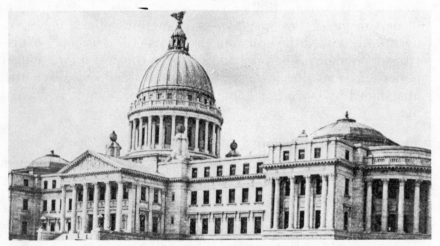

Mississippi's "new" Capitol as it appeared in 1903. The Capitol, now more than seventy-five years old, is undergoing complete repair and renovation. While it is being renovated the Legislature will meet in the old Central High School building in downtown Jackson.

In his inaugural address, given in the old dilapidated capitol, Governor Longino recommended a new building that all Mississippians could be proud of. The legislature reacted favorably to his suggestion and established the Capitol Commission. The new commission, of which the governor was a member, was authorized to select a design for a new state house and to proceed with its construction. Following ground-breaking ceremonies on January 1, 1901, construction of the capitol which cost one million dollars proceeded with few delays or difficulties. Two years later on June 3, 1903, Jefferson Davis' birthday, dedication ceremonies were held and state officials moved into their new quarters in September.

A "Teddy Bear" Story

In 1902 President Theodore "Teddy" Roosevelt came to Mississippi to assist in the settlement of a boundary dispute between Louisiana and Mississippi. While he was in the state, he went bear hunting in the Yazoo River swamps. He was accompanied on the hunt by a few local residents and a guide named Holt Collier. This black hunter and famous guide claimed to have served in the Confederate army as a fighting soldier and not merely as an orderly or cook as some other blacks had done.

Holt Collier

259

After a couple of days, the hunting party had not seen any bears and "Teddy" was getting ready to return to Washington. Shortly before the President left the hunt, a bear cub was spotted and the other hunters offered "Teddy" the first shot. However, the President refused to shoot the cub. One of the reporters who was traveling with the President wrote a story about "Teddy's" refusal to shoot the cub and soon a cartoon showing Roosevelt walking away from the cub appeared in newspapers throughout the country. After seeing the cartoon in a New York paper, a Brooklyn toy manufacturer designed a bear cub which he called a "Teddy bear" and began selling the stuffed animal. The teddy bear has remained the most popular toy in America over the last seventy-five years.

Direct Primary Law of 1902

During his administration, Governor Longino signed a law establishing the direct primary system. This new method of nominating candidates transformed Mississippi politics. A few men could no longer hand-pick the candidates for public office, because voters nominated the candidates in a popular election. Candidates for office made their appeals directly to the people rather than to a few party leaders.

As you have already learned, in a one-party system elections are not usually decided on the important issues, but upon the personality and style of the candidates. The primary system produced a new breed of flamboyant politicians who used gimmicks to attract attention to themselves. For example, James K. Vardaman often traveled around the state on a wagon drawn by several teams of oxen. Theodore G. Bilbo and several other candidates wore red neckties to emphasize their identification with rednecks.

The winners of the Democratic primaries which are held in August were assured of victory because they never had any opposition in the general election held in November. It was not until the revival of the Republican Party in the 1960's that Democratic candidates had any real opposition.

James K. Vardaman — On the campaign trail.

The Election of 1903

The first direct primary election was held in 1903. That campaign set the tone and style of Mississippi politics for many years. The three major candidates for governor were Frank A. Critz, James K. Vardaman, and Edmund F. Noel. Because blacks had been virtually disfranchised under the 1890 constitution and were prohibited by Democratic Party rules from participating in the Democratic primary, blacks could not influence the outcome of the election in any way. The state's white population was free to divide over economic issues and other pressing matters of importance. Candidates were free to discuss all shades of opinion.

In spite of black disfranchisement, however, race was the dominant issue in the 1903 campaign. Vardaman advocated the repeal of the Fourteenth and Fifteenth Amendments to the United States Constitution. He also accused blacks of being lazy, dishonest, and mentally unfit for the rights and responsibilities of full citizenship. He even went so far as to say that blacks were more prone to crime than whites were. Vardaman played on the fears and negative instincts of white Mississippians and excited the people on the issue of race. He promised that blacks would be kept in "their place" if he were elected governor.

261

Vardaman also advocated the abolition of black schools. Why deny the rights of citizenship to blacks, Vardaman asked, and then educate them to fulfill the responsibilities of that citizenship? However, something more than race was behind Vardaman's proposal to close the black schools. He accused the white leaders in the predominantly black counties of using the money appropriated to black schools for white schools in those counties. This misuse of school funds made the white schools in the Delta and river counties much better than the schools in the white hill counties and Piney Woods section. Vardaman argued that if all black schools were discontinued there would be more money for white schools throughout the state.

Vardaman's racial rhetoric was matched by his attacks on big business, banks, and railroads. The wealthy class, he warned, ran the world for their own selfish desires and possessed no conscience or pity for the poor. During the 1903 campaign, Vardaman called for tight regulation of big business and the abandonment of Mississippi's industrial expansion program. He even predicted that the government might have to take over ownership of railroads and other businesses if something was not done to curb the power of large corporations. Vardaman claimed that Governor Longino was controlled by a small group of businessmen and politicians in the state capital which Vardaman identified as the "Jackson ring." Because he was poor and had risen from a humble background, Vardaman declared that he was the only true representative of the people. This campaign style proved highly successful for Vardaman and other politicians for many years. Vardaman led the ticket in the first primary and then defeated Frank A. Critz in the run-off.

Governor Vardaman and Reform

Shortly before the Civil War, Vardaman's family had moved to Texas where he was born on July 26, 1861. His family returned to Mississippi and settled in Yalobusha County in 1868. After studying law with his cousin, Hernando DeSoto Money, Vardaman was admitted to the practice of law in 1882. For a short time he edited the Winona **Advance.** He later moved to

Greenwood. After failing as a planter, Vardaman began editing the Greenwood **Enterprise.**

Not long after moving to Greenwood, Vardaman was elected to the state legislature. As a legislator, Vardaman became known as a champion of the small farmers. In 1895 and 1899 he sought the Democratic Party's nomination for governor, but on both occasions he was rejected by the party leaders. After these two defeats, Vardaman was convinced that the only way he or any other agrarian leader could get the nomination was through the primary system which he began to support in 1900. In the first state-wide primary, the poor farmers and workers rallied to Vardaman's campaign and elected him to the state's highest office.

Administration of James K. Vardaman, 1904–1908

When Vardaman took the oath of office on January 19, 1904, he was the first governor to be inaugurated in the new capitol. In his inaugural address Vardaman outlined the aims of his administration which was characterized by reform and progress, at least for white Mississippians.

Blacks did not suffer as much as might be expected in view of Vardaman's racial theories. In fact, in two very important ways, living conditions for black people improved under the "Great White Chief," as Vardaman was sometimes called.

First, Vardaman led the fight to end the convict lease system which was still practiced in various forms even though it had been declared illegal under the 1890 constitution. He actually put his political career on the line in his stand against the use of convicts by private landowners. During his term in office a new system of penal farms owned and operated by the state was established. The largest of these farms was Parchman in Sunflower County which eventually became the state penitentiary. Since most of the convicts who had suffered abuses under the old system had been black prisoners, Vardaman's penal reforms worked more to the advantage of blacks than whites.

The second important way Vardaman helped blacks was his fight against "white capping." In southwest Mississippi black landowners aroused the anger of white farmers who were in competition with them for the sale of farm products. In an effort to reduce that competition, white farmers attacked black landowners and tried to drive them off their land. These white farmers were known as "white cappers," probably because they wore white hoods somewhat similar to the old Ku Klux Klan costumes. Vardaman publicly condemned the "white cappers" and sent agents to infiltrate their organization. The evidence these agents accumulated was turned over to local police, and Vardaman demanded that the guilty persons be arrested and brought to trial. The governor warned local officials that if they did not stop the terrorists from attacking the black farmers, he would order the attorney general to press charges against the "white cappers." Vardaman's efforts were very successful, and by the end of his administration the "white cappers" had ceased to exist.

Vardaman's racial actions were very different from his racial speeches. During the 1903 campaign, Vardaman had said that as a private citizen he would help lynch a black man accused or strongly suspected of raping a white woman. But he added that as governor he would do everything within his power to prevent a lynching. After his election, on two occasions Governor Vardaman sent the National Guard, once leading them personally, to rescue a black man from a lynch mob.

Most of Vardaman's administration was devoted to improving the economic conditions among poor white farmers and workers. Among the most important reform measures supported by Vardaman was a child labor law. In the early 1900's small children, eight to twelve years old, often worked ten or twelve hours a day in factories, mills, or on farms. Vardaman called for an immediate halt to this practice. Although he did not secure the passage of a law prohibiting the abuse of child laborers during his term, a child labor law was achieved by Vardaman's successor in 1908. Among the reform measures passed during Vardaman's administration were a school textbook commission, separate rural school districts, and a thirty percent teacher pay raise.

Other Reforms

In addition to the reforms he actually accomplished, Vardaman also endorsed many others which were enacted later. In his last address to the state legislature, he recommended legislative reapportionment, an elective judiciary, state depositories to reduce the power of banks, regulation of interest rates and railroad companies, a state charity hospital, a home for elderly women, an institution for the mentally retarded, and a teacher's college.

During Vardaman's four years in office practically no accusations of corruption or graft were leveled either at him personally or at his appointees. A northern journalist touring the South concluded that, apart from his negative attitudes on race relations, Vardaman had given the state its best administration up to that time.

Senatorial Election of 1907

In 1907, Vardaman campaigned for the senate seat held by his cousin, Hernando DeSoto Money, who had announced in 1905 that he would not seek re-election. Vardaman's opponent was John Sharp Williams who had represented Mississippi in the United States congress for several years. Mississippi's other senator at that time was Anselm J. McLaurin. Both Williams and Vardaman belonged to the anti-McLaurin faction of the Democratic Party. Some of the supporters of both men feared that a Vardaman-Williams contest for the senate would split the anti-McLaurin faction and wipe out the political gains they had won in the last few years. A heated contest between them did develop, but the campaign did not erupt into a personal clash between the two men nor did it disrupt the unity among the anti-McLaurin forces. In an extremely close race, Williams won the senate seat by a vote of 59,496 to 58,848. After Williams was elected, it was generally agreed that all anti-McLaurin forces would unite behind Vardaman who would challenge McLaurin for his seat in 1912. When his term as governor expired Vardaman edited the Jackson **Issue** and prepared for his campaign against McLaurin.

Secret Caucus of 1910

Vardaman's challenge of Senator McLaurin did not take place because McLaurin died in 1909. By the time the legislature convened in early January, 1910, to appoint someone to fill McLaurin's unexpired term, a bitter contest for that appointment had already developed. Former Governor Vardaman and Leroy Percy, a wealthy Delta planter were the front runners. Percy's supporters in the legislature secured the adoption of a resolution to conduct the vote by secret ballot. Vardaman's forces charged that this "secret caucus" would open the door to bribery and political deals among the various factions in the legislature. Wine and women and money were allegedly used to sway the vote of several legislators during the "secret caucus" which lasted over two months. Reckless accusations were made by both sides. State senator Theodore G. Bilbo later charged that a Percy supporter gave him a bribe of $645 to secure his vote. When the balloting finally took place, Leroy Percy was elected to fill the unexpired term.

The Campaign of 1911

Both Percy and Vardaman were the favorite candidates for the senatorial primary election in 1911. This primary election would decide who would fill the full Senate term beginning in 1912. Bilbo, who had been damaged by an investigation of his bribery charge that nearly resulted in his expulsion from the state senate, joined the Vardaman camp and announced his candidacy for lieutenant governor.

Vardaman, the somewhat crude and flamboyant stump orator, waged an unrelenting attack upon the aristocratic and soft-spoken Percy. Class antagonism was apparent in every aspect of this bitter campaign. It was in this campaign that the term "redneck" took a political meaning. During one of his speeches which was frequently interrupted by Vardaman supporters, Percy referred to demonstrators as a bunch of "rednecks." Vardaman followers quickly picked up the term and used it in their campaign speeches and literature. Vardaman was proud to be identified with white farmers and laborers who toiled in the

266

fields doing an honest day's work. In later campaigns Vardaman and Bilbo supporters wore red neckties as badges of their plain and humble backgrounds.

The 1911 election brought out more voters than any other campaign up to that time. Vardaman won the senatorial primary by gaining 79,000 votes to Percy's 21,000. Earl Leroy Brewer and Theodore G. Bilbo were elected governor and lieutenant governor respectively. In addition, Vardaman supporters won a majority of seats in the state legislature. Mississippi rednecks had taken control of state government from the Bourbon leaders and the McLaurin Clan. For the next few years Mississippi was controlled by a new political machine under the leadership of Vardaman. His machine was destined, however, for an early break-down and he was soon replaced by Bilbo as the state's most powerful and colorful political figure.

Edmund F. Noel's Administration, 1908–1912

Governor Edmund F. Noel, who succeeded Vardaman in 1908, continued the reform program begun by his predecessor. In 1908 a state-wide prohibition law replaced the local option law which had been in effect since 1886. Both a child labor law and a pure food law were enacted, and a state charity hospital was established. Several significant school measures were also passed. These measures included the establishment of a college board of trustees to supervise all senior colleges and the state university, a system of agricultural high schools which later became the state junior college system, consolidation of many small rural school districts, and public transportation for rural schools. In 1912 the Mississippi Normal School was established at Hattiesburg. It was later renamed Mississippi Southern College and then the University of Southern Mississippi. During Governor Noel's term, agricultural extension work at Mississippi A. & M. and Alcorn A. & M. was significantly increased.

Earl Brewer's Administration, 1912–1916

During Governor Brewer's administration, several changes in Mississippi's governmental system were enacted. Judicial of-

Governor Earl Leroy Brewer and his colonels in 1912. The governor's staff of colonels dressed in military uniforms for inaugural ceremonies until 1956 when Governor J.P. Coleman abolished the tradition. The colonels staff continued, however, for another twenty-four years until it was abolished by Governor William Winter in 1980.

ficials were made elective by constitutional amendments, and the initiative and referendum were adopted by the state legislature. Initiative is the means by which the people, through a petition signed by a certain percentage of qualified voters, can introduce bills in the state legislature. A referendum is a similar petition which can require the legislature to submit a particular bill to the voters for approval or disapproval.

Dr. Laurence Jones
— founder of Piney Woods School.

Theodore G. Bilbo and Mississippi Politics, 1907–1932

Theodore Gilmore Bilbo, often referred to as "The Man" by both his friends and enemies, was one of Mississippi's most illustrious and controversial politicians. His long career was punctuated by scandals and bribery, by victories and defeats. Probably no other Mississippi public figure could elicit such unqualified loyalty on the one hand and such bitter opposition on the other. For over forty years Bilbo strode across the Mississippi political scene, either urged on by his admirers who laid the garland of public office before him, or goaded by his enemies whose traps and intrigues seemed never to spring until he was safely past.

Early Life

Bilbo, the youngest of several children, was born at Juniper Grove in Pearl River County on October 13, 1877. His father was a typical small farmer who later became the president of a small town bank at Poplarville. Bilbo entered high school at fifteen and graduated four years later in 1896. Although he was "authorized" by the Baptist denomination to preach, as he often did, he decided not to become an ordained minister. After attending George Peabody College in Nashville, Tennessee, he taught school in south Mississippi.

His first political campaign was in 1903, when he ran for circuit clerk of Pearl River County against a one-armed Confederate veteran. When informed that he had lost the election by fifty-six votes he replied, "You know I could see that empty sleeve myself when I went into the booth to vote," and then added, "I started to vote for him myself." After this defeat Bilbo taught school for two years at a boarding school in Wiggins.

State Senate

In 1907 Bilbo returned to Poplarville to run for the state senate. After winning the election for senator, Bilbo took the bar examination and was admitted to the practice of law. When he entered the senate chamber for the first time, Bilbo told a friend, "This is my world, and [I am] going to conquer it." Bilbo was

Governor Bilbo, during his term in office. His dream house near Poplarville was completed during the 1930s.

unknown outside his senate district, but he was very ambitious, and within two years his name would become a household word throughout Mississippi.

During the "secret caucus" of 1910, Bilbo became as famous as the two men seeking the senatorial appointment. When he charged the Percy faction with paying him a $645 bribe, the state senate ordered a full investigation. However, the investigation did not turn out the way Bilbo had planned it. Instead of bringing charges against Percy and his supporters for offering the bribe, the senate formally charged Bilbo with accepting a bribe. A resolution to expel Bilbo from the senate fell one vote short of the two-thirds majority required for his expulsion from the senate. However, a resolution asking him to resign because he was "unfit to sit with honest, upright men" did pass by a vote of twenty-five to one. Claiming that he had been framed, Bilbo refused to resign and vowed to take his case directly to the people and let them decide his political future.

Lieutenant Governor

Following the humiliating investigation, Bilbo entered the race for lieutenant governor in 1911. Running as a martyred victim of the aristocracy which had tried to buy him, he campaigned with his characteristic fury. The 1911 campaign was one of the most exciting campaigns in Mississippi's stormy political history. Class antagonism was the keynote of the campaign. "The fight between the classes and the masses," Vardaman announced, "is on." Throughout the campaign Bilbo not only wore a red necktie, he also wore red suspenders. When asked why he wore both, Bilbo replied. "The red suspenders keep up my pants and the red necktie keeps up my courage."

On some occasions, the political struggle actually became a physical struggle. When U. B. Boddie, a Percy supporter, made some derogatory remarks about Bilbo, "The Man" leaped up on the platform and physically assaulted Boddie. In the tussle Boddie lost his wig, to the utter delight of the big crowd of Bilbo supporters. This incident was only one of several situations in which Bilbo was involved in a physical as well as a political confrontation.

Although Bilbo was a small man—only 5'2" tall—he was very bold and often ridiculed his opponents. In a speech in east Mississippi, Bilbo referred to Washington D. Gibbs of Yazoo City as "Old Wash Gibbs, a renegade Confederate soldier." Sometime later, when Bilbo spoke in Yazoo City, Gibbs walked up to Bilbo and without warning, hit "The Man" in the head with a walking stick. Known among his friends as the "War Horse of Yazoo,"

Gibbs hit Bilbo so hard that he broke the walking stick. Bilbo fell semi-conscious to the gutter. After lying there for a few minutes, "Bilbo deguttered himself and made a quick pass at Gibbs, missing the 'war horse' completely." Gibbs offered to continue the fight, but Bilbo declined, as he had a speaking engagement in Belzoni. When the election finally took place Bilbo won by 23,000 votes. As lieutenant governor, Bilbo became the presiding officer of the Mississippi senate which a year earlier had declared him unfit to sit among honest and upright men.

Bribery Charges

After taking office in 1912, Governor Earl Brewer established a detective agency to investigate corruption among state officials. He enlisted the State Librarian, Miss Mattie Plunkett, as an undercover agent. Miss Plunkett hid a recording machine in the Law Library in the state capitol. Bilbo and his law partner, G. A. Hobbs, were among the officials whose conversations were recorded by the unsuspected lady detective. On the evidence recorded by Miss Plunkett, they were later indicted and tried for accepting a $2,000 bribe from a businessman who enlisted their support for the creation of a new county in the Delta. Although both Bilbo and Hobbs were eventually acquitted, this episode led to Bilbo's determination to once again seek vindication from the people. He announced that he would run for governor in 1915.

Bilbo's First Administration, 1916–1920

Political factionalism and bitterness reached an all time high during the 1915 campaign. The editor of the Jackson **Daily News,** Fred Sullens, suggested that if Bilbo were elected governor, the eagle on the dome of the state capitol should be replaced by a buzzard. In spite of this opposition from one of the state's best known and most powerful editors, Bilbo defeated four other candidates in the first primary. Lee Russell, a Bilbo protégé, was elected lieutenant governor and succeeded Bilbo to the governorship in 1920. Bilbo was well on his way to building his own machine that would soon rival Vardaman for political supremacy in Mississippi.

Although outgoing Governor Brewer claimed a treasury surplus of over one million dollars, Bilbo discovered that the state was in fact over a million dollars in debt. Brewer's assertion of a treasury surplus may have been an attempt to discredit Bilbo, who would have to raise taxes to offset the deficit. Brewer and Bilbo were bitter political enemies. Governor Brewer even refused to ride with Bilbo in the inaugural parade or participate in the inaugural ceremonies.

Bilbo was undaunted, however, either by Brewer's bitterness or by a treasury deficit. During his first administration Bilbo proposed a tax measure to pay off the deficit. His proposal was to equalize property assessments. At that time, land, houses, and other buildings were assessed at only twenty-five or thirty percent of their real value. Bilbo recommended that all property be assessed at its actual value. Bilbo wanted the large property owners to pay higher taxes and the poor to pay lower taxes. This new tax plan, which was enacted by the legislature, was very successful although unpopular with the large land owners. Because of the increased revenue made possible by Bilbo's new tax structure, the state was able to balance its budget for the first time in many years.

Educational reforms would naturally be of interest to an ex-school teacher in the governor's office. Bilbo thought of the governor as the head of the public school system in the same way that he was head of the state militia. He took several educators on a tour of northern schools to find new methods which could be used to upgrade Mississippi's school system. Additional reforms accomplished during Bilbo's first term included a livestock dipping law, a board of pardons, a highway department, and an expanded public health program.

World War I

In 1917 Mississippi was preparing to celebrate its centennial of statehood. But America's entry into World War I caused the cancellation of that celebration. Although several military installations were established in Mississippi and approximately 56,700 Mississippians served in the armed forces, World War I had only a temporary impact on the state's economy. Most of the new jobs available to Mississippians during the war were discontinued after the armistice was signed on November 11, 1918. Perhaps the most direct impact the war had on Mississippi was the defeat of Senator Vardaman.

Most Mississippians supported America's participation in the war which President Woodrow Wilson called the "war to end all wars." One of Mississippi's United States senators, John Sharp Williams, voted for American involvement in the war and strongly supported President Wilson's wartime policies. James K. Vardaman, Mississippi's other senator, did not. Vardaman was one of six United States senators to vote against the declaration of war on April 6, 1917.

Vardaman Defeated

Senator Vardaman, who was up for re-election to the United States senate in 1918, was defeated primarily because he had opposed President Wilson's wartime policies. After first criticizing Wilson's domestic program, which he thought offered too little for the common man, Vardman became one of the most outspoken opponents of Wilson's policy of neutrality during the early stages of World War I. To Vardaman, Wilson's strategy to stay out of the European War was insincere and was only a cover-up of Wilson's sympathy for the Allies. Vardaman not only voted against the declaration of war, he later voted against the drafting of young Americans to be sent off to Europe. The Mississippi press which almost unanimously supported America's entry into the war referred to Vardaman as "Herr von Vardaman," and accused him of being worthy of the German Kaiser's Iron Cross.

During Vardaman's re-election campaign in 1918, President Wilson addressed a letter to the senator's opponents expressing his desire to see Vardaman defeated. President Wilson's letter was published in many Mississippi newspapers and helped Congressman Byron Patton Harrison defeat Vardaman by almost 13,000 votes.

Bilbo Defeated

In 1918 Governor Bilbo ran for the United States congress but lost to Paul B. Johnson, Sr. His defeat was not as crucial as Vardaman's however. Bilbo still had two years remaining in his term as governor and had time to recover most of his support before leaving office.

When Bilbo made his farewell address to the legislature in 1920 he recommended a comprehensive program for the improvement of the state's educational and charitable institutions. He also urged the lawmakers to pass a major highway construction program and the establishment of a state-owned power plant to provide electricity to public buildings in Jackson. His address embraced such a wide range of suggestions, that he left his successor, Lee Russell, with very little to say in his inaugural address.

Administration of Lee Russell, 1920–1924

During Governor Russell's administration, Mississippi suffered four consecutive years of agricultural depression. And as farm tenancy and rural poverty increased, racial violence showed a corresponding rise. The old Ku Klux Klan was revived during the 1920's. Public lynchings and burnings of blacks became a national disgrace. Racial brutality and mob violence was so widespread in Mississippi in the 1920's that a group of lawyers published a book entitled **Mississippi and the Mob.** The purpose of this book was to persuade all Mississippians that mob violence must be stopped. Lawyers, educators, doctors, politicians, and even school children were called upon to do what they could to discourage lynching. Law enforcement authorities were especially urged to arrest the individuals who participated in mob violence.

The Birkhead Suit

While the Klan terrorized the countryside, several new factions developed within the Democratic Party. The leaders of these various factions made crude and irresponsible accusations against each other. The culmination of this bitter factionalism was the $100,000 seduction and breach of promise suit filed by Francis Birkhead against Governor Russell. Governor Russell, who attributed the suit to his political enemies, was acquitted by a jury in a federal court trial at Oxford.

In spite of his acquittal, Governor Russell and the office of governor were ridiculed in the state press. The **Natchez Democrat**, proclaimed that it was "time for all Mississippians to get together, call "a halt on such horrible conditions," and bring the "ship of state back to the moorings of honor and common decency."

Bilbo in Jail

After leaving the governor's office in 1920, Bilbo began organizing his campaign for the 1922 election against Senator John Sharp Williams. However, his plans had to be cancelled when he became involved in the suit filed against Governor Russell. Miss Birkhead had called Bilbo to testify in the suit. When he refused to appear in court and testify, Bilbo was sentenced to thirty days in jail for contempt of court. He was confined in the Lafayette County jail. After serving a reduced sentence of only ten days, Bilbo announced that he would again take his case to the people and run for governor in 1923.

The 1922 and 1923 Elections

By 1923 the Bilbo-Vardaman faction had fallen apart. Vardaman was defeated for the United States Senate again in 1922, and Bilbo was defeated for governor in 1923.

In the senatorial race of 1922 Vardaman and Belle Kearney, the first woman to run for the United States Senate in Mississippi, faced Congressman Hubert D. Stephens of New Albany. John Sharp Williams, aging and ill, had decided not to seek re-election. In an effort to help his old ally, Bilbo stumped the state for Vardaman in the last few weeks of the campaign. Stephens won the election and Vardaman soon moved to Alabama, where he died in obscurity in 1930.

Bilbo's defeat for the governorship in 1923 by a former school teacher, Henry L. Whitfield, was again only a temporary set-

Mrs. Theodore G. Bilbo, Ms Belle Kearney, and Mrs. Nellie Nugent Somerville were among the first women in Mississippi to campaign and to gain election to public office.

back. Following the 1923 election, Bilbo remained in Jackson and edited the **Free Lance**. While editing his newspaper, Bilbo was also preparing for the 1927 gubernatorial campaign.

Henry L. Whitfield's Administration, 1924–1927

Henry L. Whitfield, a former state superintendent of education and president of MSCW, was slightly rotund and soft-spoken. On the campaign trail he presented quite a contrast to the bantam and bombastic Bilbo. Throughout the campaign, Whitfield addressed himself to the problems of rural unemployment and the alarming increase of racial violence. The people responded to his positive and constructive approach to these problems. In 1923 Mississippi women voted in a gubernatorial campaign for the first time. Their vote undoubtedly gave Whitfield his narrow margin of victory over Bilbo.

Once in office, Whitfield embraced a broad legislative program including better mental health care, the expansion of the state's vocational training, tax reform, and improvement of the quality of life for Mississippi blacks. Whitfield's position on race received a generally favorable response and even praise from some of the state's leading newspapers. In commending Whitfield for his pledge to be the governor of *all* the people, including Mississippi blacks, the **Jackson Daily News**, admitted, "We all know . . . that we have not been giving the Negro a square deal, and it is gratifying to know that we have a Governor endowed with

277

the courage to speak out and tell the truth about it." The Committee of One Hundred, an organization of prominent Mississippi blacks, also praised the governor for his concern. "Certainly," proclaimed a committee spokesman, "when the highest official of the commonwealth (the state of Mississippi) speaks thus, the Negro has another big reason for not losing faith."

Lumbering was big business along the Pearl River which winds its way through the Piney Woods forests to the Gulf Coast.

In two important areas Governor Whitfield was successful in improving the condition of blacks in Mississippi. During his three years in office there was a marked decline in racial violence and a substantial increase in state appropriations for the education of blacks.

Whitfield's achievements in race relations were only one facet of his efforts to reorder the state's priorities. In his inaugural address, Whitfield referred to the prejudice against business corporations and outside investment which had dominated the state's economic climate since the days of Vardaman. To counteract this prejudice and offset the state's declining personal income, Whitfield recommended a state-sponsored program to attract additional industry into Mississippi. New industry, Whitfield said, was the only means of providing employment to small farmers who were no longer able to make a living from their exhausted and eroded farms. Though his success was modest, a later administration would revive and expand upon Whitfield's initial efforts to balance agriculture with industry.

Governor Dennis Murphree, 1927–1928

On March 18, 1927, Governor Whitfield died following a long illness. He was succeeded by Lieutenant Governor Dennis Murphree. Governor Murphree had cooperated with Whitfield in the promotion of industrial expansion. Governor Murphree promoted industrial development through the activities of the "Know Mississippi Better" train. This specially equipped train carried displays of Mississippi products and natural resources throughout America, Canada, and Mexico. The purpose of the train and its displays was to attract new industries to Mississippi and to expand the market for Mississippi goods.

The Great Flood of 1927

On April 21, 1927, at 7:45 a.m., the levee broke at Mound Landing (near Scott) and the Mississippi River rushed through the break eventually flooding 2,722,000 acres of land. It was one of this nation's greatest natural disasters. Over 41,000 homes were flooded and more than 21,000 buildings were destroyed. More importantly, an entire crop year was lost in the Mississippi Delta and thousands of people depended on the Red Cross and other charitable organizations for food, clothing, and shelter. It took many years for the people to fully recover from the deluge.

Flooding in the Mississippi Delta made homeless refugees of thousands.

Bilbo's Second Administration, 1928–1932

In 1927 Bilbo made his third race for governor. His platform called for the establishment of a state owned printing press to supply free textbooks for public schools, a comprehensive highway program at a projected cost of $82,000,000, and the merger of Mississippi A. & M. and the University of Mississippi into one university to be located at Jackson.

Bilbo defeated Dennis Murphree by a majority of 16,500 votes in the runoff election. His free textbook proposal was not enacted, and his highway program was eventually abandoned during the great depression of the 1930's.

A Crisis in Higher Education

The most controversial aspect of Bilbo's second administration was the crisis involving the state institutions of higher learning. During the campaign of 1927, Bilbo's proposal for the consolidation of State and Ole Miss met strong opposition among the alumni and officials of those two schools. This idea for the consolidation of the two schools was not Bilbo's. It had been recommended in 1924 by an out-of-state team of educators who were invited by Governor Whitfield to study Mississippi's system of higher education. Nevertheless, many school administrators and faculty members campaigned against both Bilbo and this recommendation in 1927.

After he took office in 1928, Bilbo was finally convinced that he could not achieve his goal of merging the two colleges. He then decided to replace the administrators and faculty members who had opposed his recommendation. Within two years Governor Bilbo had persuaded the Boards of Trustees which governed the state's colleges and the university to replace four college presidents and approximately forty faculty members. Although many of these dismissals stemmed from the bitterness of political factionalism characteristic of a one-party system, the new presidents and faculty members were younger and in most cases better trained than those they replaced.

Bilbo's interference in the operation of the colleges caused the Southern Association of Colleges and Schools to revoke the accreditation of Mississippi's institutions of higher learning in 1930. The loss of accreditation meant that courses and degrees granted by Mississippi colleges would not be recognized or accepted by institutions of higher learning in other states. Political interference in the colleges had been a problem for many years. Bilbo was certainly not the first governor to try to control the colleges, but he went further than any of his predecessors.

When the colleges were expelled from the Southern Association, leaders of the various political factions finally realized that something must be done to take politics out of the school system. The three existing college boards were reorganized into one single Board of Trustees with authority over all the colleges. To further protect the new board from political influence, the nine members were appointed to staggered terms of twelve years. This arrangement, with only three members coming up for appointment every four years, would prevent future governors from appointing a majority of the Board members.

Because of this reorganization plan and Governor Martin S. Conner's pledge not to interfere with the operation of the colleges, the Southern Association of Colleges and Schools restored accreditation to Mississippi's institutions of higher learning in 1932. The crisis was over and the colleges, which were placed under a new Board of Trustees free from political control, were better off than they had been before.

Bilbo Rejected and Dejected

When Bilbo left office in 1932, he was disheartened. Many believed that his political career was at an end. The economic depression was at its depth in Mississippi and Bilbo had been unable to prevent the state's financial ruin. His wife had divorced him. His public had deserted him. The Mississippi press recorded his political demise and Fred Sullens printed this epitaph:

> Beneath this stone old Theo lies;
> Nobody laughs and nobody cries;
> Where he's gone, or how he fares,
> Nobody knows, and nobody cares.

Sullens held a contest and invited his readers to send in their own suggested epitaphs. The winner was:

> Here lies the body with Bilbo's name
> Of shame he had no terrors
> He was born a ham and died the same;
> No hits, no runs, many errors.

In 1933 Bilbo secured a job with the Agricultural Adjustment Administration, a federal agency in Washington, D.C. Although he gave his title as "Advisory Counselor of the A.A.A.," his duties actually consisted of clipping and pasting newspaper articles about the Department of Agriculture in a department scrapbook. Fred Sullens wrote that Bilbo had been appointed "The Paste-master General." Bilbo's career was at an ebb.

Bilbo Elected to the United States Senate

Like the sea which gives life and is unruly, Mississippi politics is also unpredictable. In 1934 Bilbo ran for the United States Senate against Hubert D. Stephens and was elected. Upon receiving the news of his victory he exclaimed, "Bilbo, Long, and Roosevelt, that isn't a bad line-up is it?" These references were to Senator Huey Long of Louisiana and President Franklin D. Roosevelt, two of the most popular and powerful men in America.

Bilbo was re-elected in 1940 and again in 1946. Most of his energy in the senate was expended in opposing civil rights bills, anti-lynching laws, and the Fair Employment Practices Commission. In 1947, the United States Senate took steps to deny Bilbo his seat on the grounds that large numbers of Mississippi blacks had been denied the right to vote in the senatorial election of that year.

There were other charges also pending against Bilbo. During World War II Bilbo had made some expensive repairs and improvements on his twenty-three room mansion at Poplarville. Much of the work had been done by government contractors who were building Keesler Air Force Base at nearby Biloxi. Several state newspapers reported that this work was done without charge and in violation of federal laws prohibiting public officials from doing personal business with wartime contractors. The United States Senate was already investigating these charges when the question of Bilbo's right to take office became an issue in 1947. He became ill, however, and the senate postponed any action until he could return to the senate to defend himself against these charges. Bilbo did not recover. He died in New Orleans on August 21, 1947.

The bells that tolled the death of Bilbo also sounded for the rednecks. He was the last of his kind, the end of an era. The redneck faction of the Democratic Party had already lost control to a new breed of Mississippi politicians. A new era had begun. We will study that new era in the following chapter.

A. KEY TERMS—Explain the following terms. If necessary, use a dictionary or encyclopedia.

1. Andrew H. Longino
2. industrial expansion
3. New Capitol
4. Edmund F. Noel
5. Holt Collier
6. Election of 1903
7. Frank A. Critz
8. "Jackson ring"
9. "white capping"
10. Leroy Percy
11. Secret Caucus of 1910
12. class antagonism
13. Washington D. Gibbs
14. Child labor law
15. Earl Leroy Brewer
16. initiative
17. referendum
18. Mattie Plunkett
19. G. A. Hobbs
20. Lee Russell
21. Paul Johnson, Sr.
22. *Mississippi and the Mob*
23. Francis Birkhead
24. Belle Kearney
25. Nellie Nugent Somerville
26. Hubert D. Stephens
27. Henry L. Whitfield
28. Dennis Murphree
29. Great Flood of 1927
30. Crisis in Higher Education

B. MATCHING EXERCISE

1. direct primary
2. James K. Vardaman
3. John Sharp Williams
4. Laurence Jones
5. Theodore G. Bilbo
6. Fred Sullens
7. "Know Mississippi Better" train
8. Byron Patton Harrison
9. Henry L. Whitfield
10. Board of Trustees

a. defeated Vardaman for U.S. Senate in 1907
b. editor of **Jackson Daily News**
c. defeated Vardaman for U.S. Senate in 1918
d. favored fair treatment of blacks
e. nomination of candidates by popular vote
f. "The Man"
g. established to keep politics out of colleges
h. promoted industrial development in Mississippi
i. founder of Piney Woods School
j. "Great White Chief"

284

C. WRITING ASSIGNMENT

1. During Governor James K. Vardaman's term in office, a northern journalist toured the state and then wrote an article. The writer stated that blacks were no worse off than they had been and in some ways their condition had improved under Vardaman. In what ways do you believe blacks were better off under Vardaman? Or, do you believe their condition was worse than before? Write an essay on "The Condition of Blacks Under Governor James K. Vardaman."

2. Write a political epitaph for the following Mississippians:
   a. Andrew H. Longino
   b. James K. Vardaman
   c. Edmund F. Noel
   d. Henry Whitfield
   e. Theodore G. Bilbo
   f. Laurence Jones

3. If you had been living in Mississippi in the early 1900's, would you have supported the policy of industrial expansion as favored by Governors Longino and Whitfield, or would you have supported Governor Vardaman's stand against industrial growth. Explain your reason for which ever position you take.

4. Write a biographical sketch of Governor Vardaman or Governor Bilbo. Include in your sketch your own opinion of the positive and negative contributions these men made to Mississippi.

CHAPTER XI

The New Politics, 1932–1952

Fred Sullens, editor of the **Jackson Daily News**, heralded the election of Martin S. Conner in 1931 as the beginning of a new era in Mississippi politics. Governor Conner was one of the state's new businessmen-politicians who were determined to improve Mississippi's national image and to develop a more balanced economy. Conner admitted that people in other parts of the country pictured Mississippi as a big swamp inhabited by alligators and mosquitos where malaria stalked and racial disorder ruled. During the governor's campaign of 1931, Conner told the people that the only way for Mississippi to change its image and for its people to improve their economic conditions was to elect men who would conduct the affairs of state in an honest and business-like manner. He further pointed out that poverty could be overcome only by the new jobs that industry could provide for the thousands of unemployed Mississippians. To understand the urgency in Governor Conner's remarks, we must examine economic conditions in Mississippi at the time of his election.

The inaugural parade of Governor Martin S. Conner.

The Great Depression of the 1930's

In October 1929, the New York Stock Exchange experienced a drastic and rapid fall in the price of stocks. This collapse is known as the Panic of 1929. Within a few weeks after this panic many large corporations began laying off workers in anticipation of a decline in their sales. By the beginning of 1930 the country was in a major depression. President Herbert Hoover and his economic advisors believed the depression was only a temporary decline and that the economy would soon recover. However, instead of getting better, the economy continued to decline and the nation experienced the worst depression in its history.

Perhaps nowhere in the country was the depression more severe than it was in Mississippi. It was not as sudden in Mississippi as it was in other parts of the country because the state's economy had been in a downward cycle throughout the 1920's. This decline was especially evident among farmers.

Boom, Bust, and Boll Weevils

At the end of World War I Mississippi farmers were more prosperous than at any other time since the 1850's. The wartime demand for staples, or raw material, had driven the price of cotton up and in 1919 there was some expectation that cotton would rise to a dollar a pound. But the end of the war brought a sharp decline in both the demand for and the price of cotton. From a high of 38.5 cents a pound in April of 1920, cotton prices fell steadily to 9.8 cents a pound in April of 1921. By 1931 the price had fallen to 6.16 cents. The wartime boom was over and the decline in cotton prices forced many farmers to sell their land to pay off their debts.

Low prices was not the only problem Mississippi farmers faced in the 1920's. The cotton crop was also short, that is, the total amount of cotton produced was less than it had been. In 1920 only 895,000 bales were harvested. This was the first time in many years that production had not exceeded one million bales. The average yield of lint also dropped to 148 pounds per acre in 1920. By 1923 the yield per acre averaged only 97 pounds. The total yield in 1923 dropped to only 604,000 bales.

Under normal circumstances a man and his wife with a team of mules and additional labor at the chopping and harvesting season, could cultivate about ten acres of cotton. In 1923, which was one of the good years during the 1920's, a ten acre crop produced 970 pounds of lint. The seasonal average price for cotton in that year was 31.12 cents a pound. From a ten acre crop, the farm family made $302 in 1923. The cost of seed, fertilizer, ginning, and the extra help was paid from the $302. Farmers simply could not maintain a decent standard of living on that income. The situation became even worse in the late 1920's and early 1930's.

There were two basic reasons for the decline of the total cotton production in Mississippi during the 1920's. The most serious problem was caused by the boll weevil, a small pest that migrated from Mexico, through Texas, Louisiana, and finally into Mississippi in 1907. The boll weevil lays its eggs in the young cotton boll which is consumed when the weevils hatch. By the 1920's the boll weevil had spread throughout Mississippi and destroyed thousands of acres of cotton.

You will remember at the beginning of this book, U. B. Philips was quoted as saying, "Let us begin by discussing the weather." Well, in discussing the various problems cotton farmers experienced in the 1920's, we must talk about the weather. In 1919 the rainfall in Mississippi exceeded the annual mean average by sixteen inches and in 1920 the rainfall was ten inches above normal. During those wet years the boll weevil multiplied rapidly. The measures which had been developed to control the weevil worked well in dry seasons but not in wet years. For four years in succession Mississippi farmers produced less than a million bales of cotton.

The wettest year on record, though not from rainfall, was 1927—the year of the great Mississippi River flood. As we saw in the previous chapter, that disaster cost the state an entire crop. During the 1920's Mississippi farmers were battling against great odds over which they had very little control.

Mule power gave way to tractor power over the years.

Tenants and Sharecroppers

Successive crop failures and falling prices during the 1920's forced many farmers to sell their land. Most of these farmers became tenants. Mississippi farmers in the 1920's may be classified in these four broad categories: land owners, renters, share tenants, and sharecroppers.

Land owners, who comprised about 35% of Mississippi farmers, were at the top of the agricultural system. Renters, who comprised about 5%, were farm families who rented a certain number of acres at a fixed price from the landowners. Renters were free to plant whatever crops they thought would make them the most money. They were entitled to keep the entire

A sharecropper's shack.

crop. Share tenants provided their own tools, seed, animals, and fertilizer. They worked the land for a certain share of the crop. The remainder of the crop went to the land owner. The sharecropper, who provided nothing but his labor, also worked the land on shares but for a much smaller share than the share tenant. The last two categories comprised about 60% of Mississippi farmers in the 1920's. In addition to these four categories of farmers, a fifth group of Mississippians also made their living from farming although they were not classified as farmers. This last group, which included about 21% of the white population and 37% of the black population, was classified as wage laborers. They were usually hired by land owners or renters during the chopping and harvesting seasons when additional temporary labor was needed.

Livestock and Dairying

As the price of cotton steadily declined in the 1920's small farmers turned to livestock and dairying as a means of livelihood. Livestock, especially before the Civil War, had been very important to the economy of south Mississippi. But its recovery had been very slow during the late nineteenth century and was hampered by the spread of cattle ticks in the early twentieth century. After the eradication of the ticks, livestock and dairy cattle was again providing income to a substantial number of Mississippi farmers. This increase in dairy farming led to the establishment of several creameries, condensaries, and cheese plants. The first condensary—a process for canning milk—was built at Starkville in 1926 by Gail Borden who later founded the Borden Company.

290

Canning Industry

Since the 1870's vegetable farming had provided a profitable alternative to cotton production in south Mississippi. Most of these products were shipped by rail to large cities in the north. In the 1920's an effort was made to develop a canning or processing industry which would provide additional jobs to Mississippians. But the growth of this industry was slow. By 1930 there were only seven canning plants in south Mississippi. The largest of these was a pickle factory located at Wiggins.

Masonite Corporation at Laurel. One of the largest plants of its kind in the world.

Lumber Products

By the 1920's Mississippi's large forest reserves were exhausted and about 40,000 lumbermen were seeking employment in other industries. Both Vardaman and Bilbo had warned that lumber companies were cutting Mississippi timber too fast and were not restoring this natural resource. Yet their warnings went unheeded.

291

Some lumber companies did realize the danger of exhausting Mississippi's hardwood timber reserves and developed allied industries which could utilize the faster growing pine trees. The Dantzler Company, a family-owned lumber corporation located at Pascagoula, established a paper mill at Moss Point in 1912. At Laurel, William H. Mason developed a process to make fiberboard or wood paneling. In 1926 he opened a processing plant and later established the famous Masonite Corporation. L. O. Crosby, Sr., of Picayune, also found a profitable use for the pine stumps left behind after the lumber boom had passed. He established a plant to extract the resin from the stumps and later expanded his operation to include a creosote plant and a furniture factory. The DuPont Company also established a plant at Hattiesburg to extract oil, turpentine, and resin from pine stumps. All of these operations provided employment opportunities in south Mississippi, but unfortunately, these plants were adversely affected by the depression of the early 1930's and had to lay off many workers.

Manufacturing

Following the election of Vardaman in 1903 manufacturing in Mississippi entered a period of decline. Neither Vardaman nor Bilbo promoted industrial development. Governor Whitfield did make an attempt to expand manufacturing during his administration, but his efforts were not very successful. By 1930 there were actually fewer manufacturing jobs in Mississippi than there had been in 1920.

The Land Boom

One of the most important economic developments during the 1920's, when the national economy was in a growth cycle, was the great land boom which was especially significant in California and Florida. The Mississippi Gulf Coast also felt the effects of that land boom. In the late 1920's beach property was selling for over $200 a front-foot. Millions of dollars were invested in land, hotels, restaurants, and other vacation facilities along Mississippi's Gulf Coast. However, during the depression of the

1930's people could not take expensive vacations and land values dropped on the coast as the tourist trade declined.

Economic Reform and Recovery

The condition of the state's economy was the most pressing issue during the governor's election in 1931. In January of 1931 the Mississippi treasury showed a cash balance of only $10,000 and a large deficit. The anticipated revenue for 1931 was less than half of the expenditures which had already been appropriated. Bilbo's attempts to issue revenue bonds had been unsuccessful and the state debt mounted. Martin Sennett Conner, pledging a program of rigid economy, a balanced budget, and industrial development, was elected governor in an intense and sometimes bitter campaign against Paul B. Johnson, Sr., and Hugh L. White.

Administration of Martin S. Conner, 1932–1936

"Mike" Conner, a graduate of Yale University's law school, was elected to the state legislature in 1915. He served as Speaker of the House for eight years. In 1923 and 1927 he was defeated in his first two campaigns for governor. In his third try for the governorship, Conner convinced the Mississippi voters that new and expanded industries were the only hope for the state's economic recovery.

Conner's administration inherited a $12,000,000 deficit—a legacy of Bilbo's depression-ridden second term. Governor Conner immediately enforced the rigid economy he promised during his campaign. Hundreds of public employees were dismissed and the salaries of many others were reduced. Conner also promoted the reorganization of county governments to reduce expenditures and he discarded the highway program started under Bilbo.

Sales Tax

The state still needed additional revenue even after cutting expenses everywhere possible. Conner proposed the enactment of a sales tax to bring in more revenue. Only a few states had

Mrs. Ellen Sullivan Woodward served in the state Legislature in 1926-1928, and later became the second ranking official in the Works Progress Administration (WPA) during the depression of the 1930s.

adopted a direct sales tax on food, clothing, homes, and other items purchased in the open market. Merchants, who would be responsible for collecting the tax, opposed the measure because they did not want to act as collection agents for state taxes. Private citizens also protested the tax which placed the same burden on the poor as it did on the rich. It was not fair, many argued, for a family with an annual income of $500 to pay the same tax on bread as a family with an income of $5,000.

Nevertheless, there was also strong support for the sales tax. Willard F. Bond, State Superintendent of Education, endorsed the sales tax as did most public school teachers. Their support was based on the belief that only the sales tax with its revenue potential could save the public school system. For months many teachers had either received no pay at all or had received state checks which could be cashed only at a reduced value. After a long and bitter controversy, a sales tax of two cents on a dollar was finally enacted by the legislature and Mississippi became one of the few states to employ this form of direct tax. The income derived from sales tax and the other cost-cutting measures taken by Governor Conner enabled the state to balance its budget.

The New Mississippi

By the time Conner left office in 1936, he had paid off the state's deficit of $12,000,000 and had accumulated $3,243,661 surplus in the state treasury. This was proof, he claimed, of what could be accomplished by a business-like administration. He also pointed to the large increase in the number of jobs which had been created by the industrial development which occurred during his four years in office. Small farmers and laborers, who only three decades earlier were convinced that industrial expansion would only benefit merchants and bankers, were easily convinced by the "new businessmen-politicians" that the factory, not the farm, offered them relief from their depressed condition.

Benjamin Robertson, shown here after his retirement, was one of many black teachers who taught in school rooms like this one throughout the state before World War Two.

Administration of Hugh L. White, 1936–1940

The saying that "advertising pays" is a well-established tradition among American businessmen. Mississippi's "businessmen-politicians" successfully applied that technique to state politics. In 1935, a wealthy industrialist, Hugh Lawson White, campaigned for governor on the promise that he would continue to promote industrial development in Mississippi. White admitted proudly that he was not a professional politician. As mayor of Columbia, White had saved his city from economic collapse during the early 1930's by implementing a businessman's administration of rigid economy and industrial expansion. On that record he campaigned and defeated Paul B. Johnson, Sr., in a runoff election in 1935.

Balance Agriculture With Industry

During the Vardaman-Bilbo era big business had been the "whipping boy" of politicians, and the people in Mississippi were generally suspicious of large corporations. However, the depression had convinced Mississippi voters that industrial development was their only means of economic recovery. In 1935 they gave Hugh White a mandate to inaugurate a "Balance Agriculture With Industry" program. In 1936 the legislature passed the Industrial Act which established the goal of a balanced economy as official state policy. Two new agencies, the Industrial Commission and the Advertising Commission, were created to implement the law. Under the BAWI program, new corporations were granted tax exemptions. As an additional incentive to move to Mississippi, factory buildings financed and built through local bond issues were made available to new industries. The abundance of raw materials and the availability of low wage labor, in addition to tax exemptions, made Mississippi very attractive to northern industries seeking new locations for additional plants.

Ingalls

The most important industry attracted to Mississippi under the BAWI program was the Ingalls shipyards located at Pascagoula. Other than Ingalls, which is considered a heavy industry, most of the plants which located in the state were light industry which pays lower wages than heavy industry. Nevertheless, many small towns continue to benefit from the new industrial plants attracted to Mississippi under the BAWI program.

Several of the nation's atomic submarines were built at Ingalls Shipyards.

Highway Program

During Governor White's first administration the state's highway system was given high priority and a construction program was begun which successive administrations continued. Always a political issue, highway construction in Mississippi has not been conducted according to a long-range master plan. Instead, highways have usually been built according to the interest of a particular governor and state legislature.

Administration of Paul B. Johnson, Sr., 1940–1943

By 1939 Mississippi had made some progress toward economic recovery, but not nearly enough to satisfy the voters. The two businessmen-politicians, Conner and White, had opposed the New Deal policies of President Franklin D. Roosevelt. And, in the view of many Mississippians, they had failed to relieve the depression in Mississippi. Consequently, in his third try for governor, Paul B. Johnson was elected over Martin S. Conner in 1939. Johnson styled himself as the "Champion of the People," and pledged to inaugurate New Deal measures on a state basis. In supporting government programs to aid the farmers, sharecroppers, laborers, and the elderly, Johnson declared that he was trying to give the poor people their fair share of the nation's wealth.

Governor Johnson was skeptical of the BAWI program and took steps to curtail industrial development in Mississippi. Instead, he emphasized measures designed to increase the purchasing power of the poorer classes by more direct and speedier means. One of the major achievements of Johnson's administration was the adoption of a free textbook law which made textbooks available to Mississippi school children without charge. Johnson also secured legislation which increased the pensions for the elderly.

Throughout most of his term, Governor Johnson was ill. On the day after Christmas, 1943, Governor Johnson died at his home in Hattiesburg. For the second time in less than twenty years, Lieutenant Governor Dennis Murphree was elevated to the office of governor. Governor Murphree served the remaining twenty-one days of Johnson's unexpired term.

Administration of Thomas L. Bailey, 1944–1946

In the 1943 gubernatorial campaign Thomas L. Bailey, a school teacher and lawyer from Webster County, defeated former governor Martin S. Conner. As Speaker of the House for twelve years, Bailey had consistently opposed many of Bilbo's economic and social reforms and had often criticized his personal conduct. Governor Bailey, who was identified with the businessman faction of the Democratic Party, revived the BAWI program and took full advantage of the wartime boom to attract industry into Mississippi. During Governor Bailey's term the Agricultural and Industrial Board was established to promote and coordinate industrial development. The Mississippi Marketing Commission, an advisory agency to the A. & I. Board, was also established to assist Mississippi farmers in selling their products. Governor Bailey also promoted a system of "farm to market" roads and a reforestation program.

Bailey had inherited a surplus of $20,000,000 from Governor Paul Johnson's administration. This surplus, plus increased wartime revenue, enabled the state to grant salary increases to public school teachers and larger old age pensions to Mississippi's elderly citizens.

Mrs. Thomas L. Bailey, the first woman elected to a state-wide office in Mississippi. She was elected State Tax Collector in 1947, and re-elected in 1951 and 1955.

Presidential Elections Since 1944

When President Franklin D. Roosevelt ran for his fourth consecutive term, Mississippi voters gave him a large majority. The 1944 election, however, was the last time Mississippi voted for the winning presidential candidate until 1972 when Mississippians voted overwhelmingly for Richard M. Nixon. In 1948 Mississippi voted for J. Strom Thurmond of South Carolina; in 1952 and 1956 Mississippi voted for Adlai Stevenson; in 1960 for a slate of unpledged electors who later voted for Harry F. Byrd of

Virginia; in 1964 for Barry Goldwater; and in 1968 for George Wallace. In 1976 Mississippi voted for a native southerner, Jimmy Carter of Georgia.

Administration of Fielding L. Wright, 1946–1952

In 1946, when Governor Bailey died, Lieutenant Governor Fielding L. Wright succeeded him and later was elected to a full term beginning in January of 1948. Governor Wright, a highly successful corporation lawyer, was sophisticated and aloof and was often criticized for his aristocratic bearing. Some of his political opponents accused him of being a tool of the big oil companies.

Governor Wright supported the continuation of the BAWI program and promoted the development of community hospitals and additional old age benefits. During his administration the University of Mississippi Medical Center was established in Jackson. The University Medical School was transferred from the Oxford campus to the new facility at Jackson.

World War II

It would be difficult to overstate the impact of World War II on Mississippi. The economic boom generated by the war ended the depression in Mississippi and restored full prosperity to both the state and the nation.

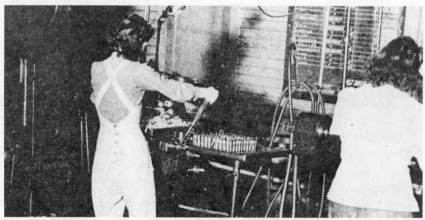

Mississippi women supported the war effort in many ways — one important way was through the manufacturing of arms at the munitions plant in Hattiesburg.

Military Installations

Mississippi's mild climate made the state an ideal location for military installations, especially air fields and training camps. Two of the nation's largest military bases, Camp Shelby and Keesler Air Force Base, were located at Hattiesburg and Biloxi. Smaller bases were also established at Columbus, Greenville, Clarksdale, Meridian, Laurel, Grenada, and other towns.

In addition to these bases, a flight training school for Dutch pilots was established at Jackson and several prisoner of war camps were maintained in various cities in Mississippi. Camp Shelby and the air bases at Columbus and Biloxi were maintained after the war and continued to promote the state's economic growth long after the war was over.

German prisoners of war provided some of the manpower to construct a scale model of the Mississippi River near Clinton.

Urbanization

The growth of Mississippi's towns and cities was accelerated by the wartime demand for manufactured products. Ingalls shipyards became the major industrial employer in the state and Pascagoula's population increased rapidly. Many other defense plants were built in Mississippi to produce the material necessary to support America's war effort. The large number of new industrial jobs drew thousands of people into towns and cities from the surrounding rural areas. When the war was over, many of the 237,000 men and women who had served in the armed forces settled in towns and cities rather than returning to the farms.

The Effects of the War on Blacks

The trend toward urbanization both improved economic conditions and altered the social customs of Mississippi. Mississippi's black servicemen and women who returned home after the war were not willing to resume a status of second class citizenship. They had fought for their country and many had died in defense of democracy. Mississippi's black population claimed the full rights of citizenship and in the years immediately following the war they pressed their demands for equal opportunity and social justice.

Fair Employment Practices

During the war, President Roosevelt issued an executive order establishing the Fair Employment Practices Commission. This order prohibited all business firms doing business with the federal government from discriminating against blacks or other minorities in hiring practices. This order made it possible for blacks to secure employment in job areas that had never been available to them before. In the first few years after the war, civil rights groups attempted to secure the establishment of a permanent Fair Employment Practices Commission. However, it took almost twenty years to establish the principle of fair employment as a guaranteed right in America.

The "Dixiecrats"

World War II had given a new impetus to the civil rights movement in the United States. President Harry S. Truman supported a Fair Employment Practices law and had ordered the desegregation of the armed forces. The southern reaction to both

President Truman and the increase in civil rights activity culminated in the "Dixiecrat" movement in 1948. Southern Democrats bolted the national Democratic Party in 1948 and nominated J. Strom Thurmond of South Carolina for President and Fielding L. Wright of Mississippi for Vice-President on a third party "Dixiecrat" ticket. Although the "Dixiecrats" carried only the four states of South Carolina, Alabama, Louisiana, and Mississippi, the movement was an indication that the South would oppose any significant change in the region's racial traditions.

The Taft-Hartley Law

In 1947 the United States Congress passed the Taft-Hartley Law. This law prohibited an all-union shop unless a majority of the workers employed at a factory voted to restrict employment to union members only. One provision of the bill that was particularly controversial was the requirement that all union leaders take an oath stating that they were not communists. During the 1950's many states passed "right to work" laws which exempted workers even in "union shops" from the requirement of union membership. Mississippi passed a right to work law in 1960. Union leaders charge that the right to work law is used by employers to maintain low-level wages.

The Revival of Race in Mississippi Politics

During the 1920's the Ku Klux Klan was reorganized and established units in most states throughout America. In the Midwest and other areas of the country the Klan added anti-Semitism, anti-communism, anti-Catholicism, and xenophobia (fear of foreigners) to its traditional anti-black philosophy. During the depression of the 1930's and during World War II, race was not a significant political issue. Mississippi's political leadership during those years did exploit race for political purposes. Businessmen were convinced that economic development could occur only under stable and tranquil social conditions. Post-war conditions, however, revived the race issue. As Southern blacks increasingly demanded the political, social, and economic benefits of full citizenship, a corresponding resistance among southern whites revived the old racial animosities and rhetoric. Mississippi's political leaders were aware of the growing unrest among blacks and instituted a crash program to upgrade black schools in the state. But they were too late.

Even though Hugh White was re-elected on a businessman's platform in 1951, there were many signs that race would soon replace economic development as the dominant theme in Mississippi politics. The decade of the 1950's, not unlike the decade of the 1850's, was characterized by racial disturbances that often led to violence. The 1954 school desegregation decision was no less controversial than the Dred Scott decision of 1857. The decade of the 1950's was capped by the Presidential election of John F. Kennedy in 1960. President Kennedy was as committed to the goals of the civil rights movement as Abraham Lincoln was committed to the prevention of slave expansion into the west. In the 1860's a violent confrontation between federal and state authorities occurred over the "peculiar institution" of slavery. The 1960's witnessed a dramatic re-enactment of that confrontation at the University of Mississippi where James Howard Meredith challenged the "peculiar institution" of racial segregation. After the Meredith crisis of 1962, Mississippi continued to experience racial violence for a few more years. By the late 1960's and early 1970's most white Mississippians had realized that further resistance would only lead to more violence. In the following chapter we will study those dramatic events that changed the way Mississippians live today.

A. KEY TERMS—Explain the following terms. If necessary, use a dictionary or encyclopedia.

1. business-men politicians
2. stock market
3. Panic of 1929
4. depression
5. renters
6. share tenants
7. Gail Borden
8. William H. Mason
9. L. O. Crosby, Sr.
10. land boom
11. revenue bonds
12. balanced budget
13. deficit
14. sale tax
15. Willard F. Bond
16. BAWI
17. New Deal
18. Works Progress Administration (W.P.A.)
19. A. & I. Board
20. Mississippi Marketing Commission
21. Mrs. Thomas L. Bailey
22. Camp Shelby
23. Keesler Air Force Base
24. urbanization
25. Fair Employment Practices Law
26. Dixiecrats
27. Taft-Hartley Law
28. right to work law
29. union ship
30. xenophobia
31. anti-semitism

B. MATCHING EXERCISE

1. boll weevil
2. Martin S. Conner
3. Mrs. Ellen Sullivan Woodward
4. Hugh L. White
5. Ingalls shipyards
6. Paul B. Johnson, Sr.
7. Thomas L. Bailey
8. Fielding L. Wright
9. Mrs. Thomas L. Bailey
10. John F. Kennedy

a. second ranking official in the W.P.A.
b. elected governor in 1935
c. elected governor in 1943
d. first woman elected to a statewide office
e. a small animal that destroys cotton
f. elected President of U.S. in 1960
g. presidential nominee by Dixiecrats
h. elected governor in 1931
i. "Champion of the People," elected governor in 1939
j. an industry attracted to Mississippi under BAWI

C. WRITING ASSIGNMENT
1. Write brief answers (two or three sentences) to the following questions:
    1. What were the major causes for the drop of cotton prices in the 1920's?
    2. What were the four broad categories of farmers in Mississippi in the 1920's and how did each differ from the others?
    3. What new industries developed in Mississippi in the 1920's and 1930's?
    4. What impact did the depression have on Mississippi politics?
    5. What impact did World War II have on towns and cities in Mississippi?
    6. What impact did World War II have on Mississippi blacks?
    7. If you worked in a factory, would you join a union? Explain your answer.

INTERVIEW ASSIGNMENT—Either take notes of your interview, or with the permission of the person being interviewed, use a tape recorder.
1. Interview your parents or other people in your community who lived in Mississippi during the depression. Ask them to explain what life was like during those hard times.
2. Interview a veteran of World War II and ask that person what Mississippi was like when he or she returned home. Ask the veteran to discuss the major changes in Mississippi since World War II.
3. Interview an older black citizen of your community. Ask that person to discuss the changes in race relations in Mississippi during the last twenty-five years.

CHAPTER XII

Mississippi Politics, 1952–1980

In the governor's campaign of 1951 Hugh White was elected for a second term over a field of eight candidates, including Ross R. Barnett, who was making his first of four gubernatorial campaigns. Other candidates in that election were Sam Lumpkin, the incumbent lieutenant governor; Mary D. Cain, the fiery lady editor of the **Summit Sun** who received 24,756 votes for fifth place; and Paul B. Johnson, Jr., who won a runoff spot against White. In other important races Carroll Gartin was elected lieutenant governor and James P. Coleman was elected attorney general.

Administration of Hugh L. White, 1952–1956

Continuing his emphasis on industrial development initiated during his first administration, Governor White devoted much of his interest and energy to attracting new industry to Mississippi. Because of the success of White's industrial program, Mississippi experienced a decade of significant economic growth. During the 1950's total personal income rose 59% from $1,583 million to $2,595 million; retail sales increased from $1,008.3 million to $1,482 million; bank deposits from $816.9 to $1,361.3 million; and expenditures for new manufacturing plants and equipment rose from $27.7 million to $57.7 million. Throughout the decade, however, Mississippi's per capita and average income remained the lowest in the nation.

School Consolidation

Under Governor White the initial implementation of a new school consolidation program was begun. In some localities violence erupted as opposition to the consolidation plan was intensified by the actual closing of schools in small communities. Many parents objected to the busing of their children over long distances which sometimes amounted to twenty miles or more. In 1952 the state superintendent of education reported that busing had increased significantly in the last eight years. In 1944

One-room schools were eventually replaced by consolidated schools like the one on the right.

only 20% of the children were bused to school. By 1950 over 80% were bused. The number of school buses had increased from 637 in 1944 to 2,994 in 1950.

Improvement of Black Schools

In an effort to forestall federal court intervention in state schools, Governor White pushed for an extensive program of equalization of black and white schools. Coming as it did during a major consolidation of the state's school system, the effort to upgrade black schools further complicated the already unstable conditions in the public schools. It was impossible to build new black schools or repair old ones quickly enough to establish "separate but equal" facilities in Mississippi. Comparative statistics indicate a large gap in the appropriation of funds for black and white schools for the year 1952–1953:

CATEGORY	White	Black
School enrollment	272,549	271,856
Transportation	$4,476,753	$1,179,826
Instruction	$23,536,002	$8,816,670
Average Teacher Salaries	$2,109	$1,153

The Brown Decision of 1954

On Monday, May 17, 1954, the United States Supreme Court ruled unanimously that the "separate but equal" principle in American public schools violated the Constitution. One year later in the second Brown decision, the court declared that racial segregation in public schools should be discontinued with "all deliberate speed." The original desegregation ruling was issued in a school case originating in Topeka, Kansas. White Mississippians were "shocked and stunned" by the Brown decisions. Governor White and other state officials were determined to prevent its implementation in Mississippi by every legal and constitutional means possible.

Organization of the Citizens Council

In July 1954, a group of white citizens at Indianola organized the first Citizens Council in Mississippi. The Council soon spread to other parts of the state and South. Robert B. Patterson of Greenwood became the Executive Secretary of the Mississippi Association of Citizens Councils which claimed a membership of 80,000 by 1956.

Black Monday

Tom P. Brady, a Justice of the Mississippi Supreme Court, wrote a book entitled, **Black Monday,** which was published by the Citizens Council. Brady declared in his book that the Brown decision rendered by the United States Supreme Court was neither valid nor binding and he recommended that state authorities prevent its implementation in Mississippi. In December, 1954, Mississippi voters approved a constitutional amendment authorizing the legislature to abolish the public school system if necessary to prevent its desegregation.

Election of 1955

There were several important issues raised during the campaign of 1955, including school consolidation, a new state constitution, economic development, and race relations. But race was the dominant issue. Yet, a man known as a "racial moderate" was elected. His victory was even more unusual because he was making his first bid for the governorship in a state which normally expects at least two, and often three, campaigns before the candidate is considered a "serious" contender. In 1955 James P. Coleman of Ackerman defeated Paul B. Johnson, Jr., Ross Barnett, Mary D. Cain, and former governor Fielding L. Wright. Johnson was making his third campaign and Barnett his second.

Administration of James P. Coleman, 1956–1960

Governor Coleman had campaigned in support of a new constitution. He also had pledged to continue school consolidation and to maintain school segregation. Because political and social conditions were already unstable, he was unable to generate much support for a constitutional convention. Many Mississippians feared that a convention might open the door to additional disunity and disharmony among whites. The race issue had revived the ironclad law of white solidarity.

Governor J.P. Coleman kept a plow in his office as a reminder of his own rural origin and the agrarian traditions of Mississippi.

The Resolution of Interposition

In 1956 the state legislature passed a law interposing the sovereignty of Mississippi between the Supreme Court's ruling on school desegregation and the implementation of that ruling within the state. Additional legislation directed all public officials in Mississippi to "prohibit, by any lawful, peaceful, and constitutional means, the implementation of or the compliance with the integration decisions of the United States Supreme Court." The legislature also repealed Mississippi's compulsory education statute which required that all school-age children be enrolled and attend school.

State Sovereignty Commission

In 1956 the legislature also established a commission "to prevent encroachment upon the rights of this and other states by the Federal Government . . . and to resist usurpation of the rights and powers reserved to this state." The Sovereignty Commission members included the governor, lieutenant governor, attorney general, and speaker of the house. Additional members, usually prominent leaders in the Citizens Council, were appointed to the Commission. Some of the funds appropriated to the Sovereignty Commission were channeled to the Citizens Council.

Birth of the Tenn-Tom Project

On February 25, 1957, Governor James E. Folsom of Alabama and Governor Coleman, along with legislators from both states, met at the Governor's Mansion in Jackson to plan the Tombigbee River inland waterways project. Both governors and the legislative representatives present at that meeting agreed that the cost of the project, originally estimated at $234 million, should be federally funded. But they also agreed that the two states should pursue the project even if federal funds did not become available. The construction of the Tennessee-Tombigbee waterway, which ultimately will connect the Tennessee and Tombigbee Rivers to the Gulf of Mexico, is now underway. The largest earth-moving project in history, the Tenn-Tom waterway, will be paid for by federal funds at an estimated cost of two billion dollars. Parts of the waterway are now open and the entire project will be completed in the early 1980's.

A Yankee General in the State Capitol

During Governor Coleman's administration, one of Mississippi's most famous former governors again became the focus of controversy. A Jackson newspaper printed a feature article on Governor Adelbert Ames whose portrait hung in the Hall of Governors in the capitol building. After seeing the article, a "76-year-old unreconstructed Rebel" wrote a blistering letter to the secretary of state. He was "shocked beyond words" that

311

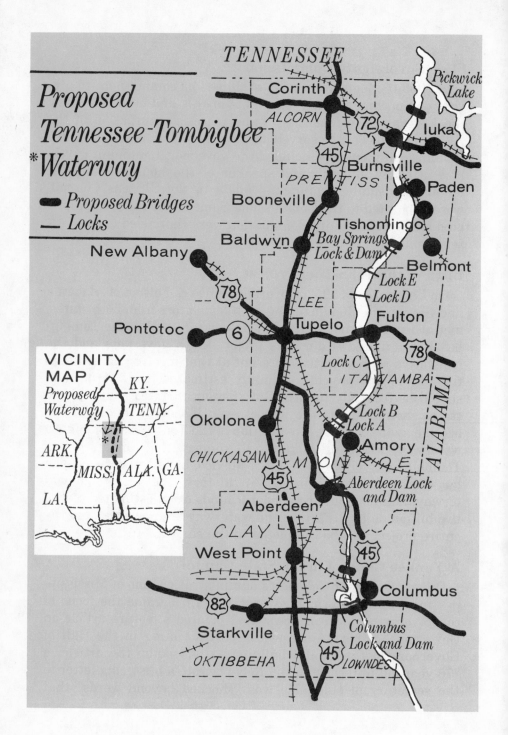

Proposed
Tennessee-Tombigbee
*Waterway

━━ *Proposed Bridges*
── *Locks*

VICINITY
MAP
*Proposed
Waterway*

312

the general's portrait decked in Union blue and adorned with medals "earned by the blood of Confederate soldier boys," was on public display. He demanded its removal. The old rebel was probably unaware that one of the decorations adorning General Ames' uniform was the Congressional Medal of Honor won for gallantry on the plain of Manassas.

When a local reporter called on the secretary of state for his comments, he found the office closed for a state holiday—it was Robert E. Lee's birthday. For several days, the press carried reports of the controversy. The state president of the United Daughters of the Confederacy, Helen Wamble, was interviewed. However, Mrs. Wamble provided little encouragement to the "unreconstructed rebel's" effort to have the portrait removed. In response to a question about the UDC's position on the matter, Mrs. Wamble replied that it was a historical fact that Adelbert Ames had been governor. Since the UDC was dedicated to the preservation of historical facts, she felt the picture should remain in the Hall of Governors.

When Governor Coleman was asked about the controversy at a press conference, he replied that there might be a number of people in Mississippi who would like to see the portraits of Vardaman and Bilbo removed. The Governor explained further that the Hall of Governors should not be confused with the Hall of Fame, which was located in the Department of Archives and History. The Hall of Fame contained the portraits of outstanding Mississippians who had made contributions to the state and the nation in law, politics, art, education, and business. The Hall of Governors included only the pictures of the state's chief executives who had served in that capacity since 1817.

Although this incident seems trivial and almost comical on the surface, the "unreconstructed rebel's" response at seeing a Yankee general's picture in the state capitol was not unlike Mississippi's reaction to the impending crisis of change. As Governor Coleman's term neared its end, plans were already underway to commemorate the centennial of the Civil War. Old and almost forgotten battlefields such as Brice's Crossroads, Baker's Creek, and Champion's Hill would be refurbished and revisited in the early 1960's. But there would also be new battlefields—like Oxford, Philadelphia, and Canton. Few people were aware that the Civil War centennial and the civil rights movement were on a collision course. It certainly did not seem that way during the gubernatorial campaign of 1959.

Administration of Ross R. Barnett, 1960–1964

In 1959 Ross R. Barnett was elected governor. The field of only four candidates included Carroll Gartin and Charles L. Sullivan, both making their first campaigns, and Robert "Blowtorch" Mason, a welder from Magee. In that same election, Paul B. Johnson, Jr., successfully campaigned for lieutenant governor and William Winter defeated ten other candidates in the tax collector's race.

Constitutional Amendments

The state legislature elected in 1959 almost unanimously endorsed Governor Barnett's campaign promises to maintain school segregation. The Mississippi voters further expressed their desire to maintain white supremacy by ratifying two constitutional amendments in December, 1960. The first amendment, in effect, empowered the governor to abolish any or all public schools in the state if necessary to prevent integration. The second amendment established an additional qualification to the voting requirements. According to the new requirement all qualified voters "shall be of good moral character." It was generally understood that this broad and vague requirement would be used to prevent significant numbers of blacks from registering to vote.

Presidential Election of 1960

On the same day that the two amendments mentioned above were ratified in Mississippi, America also elected a President. Mississippians, faced with the choice of either John F. Kennedy or Richard M. Nixon, chose neither of them. Instead, they cast their votes for a slate of unpledged electors who later voted for Senator Harry F. Byrd of Virginia. John F. Kennedy was

314

elected. Kennedy's outspoken support for the civil rights movement bred optimism among Mississippi blacks. Shortly after his
election, a young black man, enrolled at Jackson State University, initiated a plan that would eventually lead to the integration of the University of Mississippi in 1962.

The Meredith Crisis

On March 28, 1961, Governor Barnett, dressed in a Confederate uniform and standing in front of Mississippi's antebellum
Governor's Mansion, reviewed 6,000 Confederate-clad marchers
in a re-enactment of a typical Civil War parade of troops. The
two-hour parade drew thousands of excited and cheering onlook-
ers. In the midst of the most serious and dramatic challenge to
the state's racial and social customs since the 1860's, many Mississippians paused to recall the glories of former times.

Only the day before and just a block away from this parade,
there had been another parade. But in the language of the sixties it was called a demonstration. A group of Jackson State
University students were demonstrating against the jailing of
several black Tougaloo students who had been arrested for at-
tempting to use the Jackson public library. Among the students
then enrolled at Jackson State was James Howard Meredith.
Two months after Governor Barnett "reviewed the troops,"
Meredith filed suit in federal court seeking admission to the
University of Mississippi.

James Howard Meredith
— broke the color barrier in Mississippi.

315

James H. Meredith was born in Kosciusko, Mississippi, on June 25, 1933. When he was sixteen years old, he moved to St. Petersburg, Florida. After graduating from high school in 1951, he enlisted in the United States Air Force and served until 1960. In September 1960, Meredith returned to his native state. He enrolled at Jackson State University and began making plans for his applying to the University of Mississippi. Meredith's purpose in applying to Ole Miss can be best understood by letting Meredith speak for himself:

> To understand the events that occurred during my three years in Mississippi, one must always remember that I returned to my home state to fight a war . . . I had returned to Mississippi because I had developed a master plan to replace what I considered the Negro's worst enemy: The principles and doctrines of "White Supremacy." I have no desire to destroy the customs and systems of the South; instead, I intend to build a better system and to replace the old unsuitable customs with more desirable ones.

After his application for admission to the University of Mississippi was denied, Meredith filed suit on May 31, 1961, in the federal court at Meridian. Meredith's lawyer, Mrs. Constance Baker Motley, charged in the suit that Meredith had been denied admission to the University solely on the grounds of racial discrimination. For the next eighteen months the Meredith case was the subject of a major judicial confrontation between state and federal authorities.

After a long series of judicial delays and postponements, the United States Supreme Court issued a decree on September 10, 1962, ordering the University to admit James Meredith as a regular undergraduate student. Three days after the Supreme Court's order, Governor Barnett addressed the people of Mississippi on a state-wide television hook-up. In his speech Governor Barnett promised to go to jail before he would allow Meredith to be enrolled at Ole Miss and hinted that he might close the University if that was necessary to prevent its integration.

During the two weeks following this address, Governor Barnett was appointed registrar of the University and on two occasions, September 20 and September 25, the Governor personally and physically barred Meredith's enrollment. On one occasion, September 26, Lieutenant Governor Paul Johnson personally rejected Meredith's application.

By September 27 Mississippi officials had reached the limits of legal resistance. Emotion was running high in both the white and the black communities. In the black community support for Meredith and his cause was solid and undivided. But in the white community, support for continued resistance was eroding fast. Many educational and business leaders and some state officials realized that any further resistance might provoke widespread violence.

After both were charged with contempt of court for blocking the court-ordered admission of Meredith, Governor Barnett and Lieutenant Governor Johnson began looking for an alternative to a possible confrontation between federal troops and state law enforcement officials. A plan was finally devised by which Meredith would be brought to the University campus on Sunday afternoon, September 30. It was agreed that Meredith would register on Monday morning, October 1, 1962.

As these plans were set in motion large numbers of students and non-students gathered on the Ole Miss campus. Meredith came to the campus at about 5:30 Sunday afternoon and moved into the room which had been assigned to him in Baxter Hall. A few of the federal marshalls who had accompanied Meredith remained at Baxter Hall but most of the others surrounded the Lyceum where the registration would take place the next morning. The appearance of the marshals around the Lyceum attracted a large number of students and other individuals to the wooded area directly in front of the Lyceum. The crowd on the campus slowly and gradually turned into a mob. By eight p.m. a full scale riot was in progress. Tear gas was fired into the rioters and the sound of gun shots echoed across the campus. At eleven o'clock about sixty Mississippi national guardsmen were rushed to the campus to quell the riot. By two p.m. the first detachment of federal troops arrived on the campus just in time to reinforce the guardsmen who were in grave danger because their supply of tear gas was exhausted. At 6:15 a.m., Monday morning October 1, 1962, General Charles Billingslea, the commanding officer, advised President Kennedy that the riot was over and that the campus was secure.

Later that morning James Meredith was escorted by federal marshals to the Lyceum. At eight o'clock Meredith was registered. As Meredith came out of the Lyceum after being registered, a reporter asked him if he was happy. Standing on the Lyceum steps, Meredith looked around at the debris left over from a night of rioting and replied: "This is not a happy occasion." But the color barrier had been broken in Mississippi.

Meredith, who majored in public administration, completed the requirements for a bachelor's degree during the summer term of 1963. He graduated from the University of Mississippi on August 18, 1963.

Economic Development

During Governor Barnett's administration an expanded program of industrial development was enacted. As part of this program the state income tax was reduced from six percent to three percent. A series of amendments to the state workmen's compensation laws was passed to make Mississippi more attractive to industry by placing compensation rates in line with those of other Southern states. A "Right to Work Law" was also enacted.

Barnett's economic program also included the development of industrial parks on a state-wide basis. At these planned industrial sites, several different industries of a similar nature were built. The industrial parks improved the opportunities of local communities to attract new industries. A new state agency, the Youth Affairs Department, was established within the Agricultural and Industrial Board. This department promoted the development of specialized industrial programs to provide more employment opportunities for young Mississippians.

The economic policies of Governor Barnett and his predecessors were highly successful in providing new jobs to Mississippians. According to official figures, the number of industrial wage earners increased from 40,000 in 1936 to 140,000 in 1962.

During Governor Barnett's administration alone, almost 40,000 new industrial jobs were created. Agriculture, however, was not neglected during the early 1960's and agricultural workers still outnumbered industrial wage earners. The total number of Mississippians gainfully employed in agricultural occupations was 162,000 in 1964.

Port of Gulfport

In December of 1960 the state of Mississippi assumed ownership of the Port of Gulfport. The A. & I. Board instituted long-range plans to develop Gulfport into a major import-export facility in an effort to gain a greater share of Latin American commerce. A state port authority was established to administer and promote the use of Mississippi's only state-owned port. Since its establishment the port has become one of the major banana terminals along the Gulf Coast. The port was practically rebuilt after suffering heavy damage from Hurricane Camille in 1969. Future plans for the Port of Gulfport include the construction of a containerized cargo operation and the addition of bulk handling facilities. These new facilities will be adaptable to rail, truck, and waterborne transportation similar to those used in other major ports. Long-range plans also call for the development of interior waterways which will ultimately connect the inland counties with the ports at Gulfport and Pascagoula.

Election of 1963

The gubernatorial election of 1963 was the first time since Reconstruction that a Republican candidate for governor made a serious state-wide campaign. Although the election did not re-establish the two-party system, it did indicate that the potential number of Mississippi Republicans was much larger than commonly believed. Running in the Democratic primary were Lieutenant Governor Paul B. Johnson, Jr., making his fourth campaign; former Governor James P. Coleman; Robert F. Mason, in his second; and Charles L. Sullivan, making a strong second race. These Democrats competed for the right to meet Republican Rubel Phillips, a former Democratic Public Service

Commissioner, in the general election in November. Johnson, who had stood up to Meredith and the marshals at Oxford in 1962, campaigned on the slogan "Stand Tall With Paul." He won a hard fought runoff election against Coleman. In the race for lieutenant governor, Carroll Gartin won over one of Mississippi's most prominent women politicians, Evelyn Gandy. In the same election William Winter was elected state treasurer. In the November general election Paul Johnson defeated Rubel Phillips. However, the Republican candidate received 138,515 votes, 38.1 percent of the votes cast. Gartin won an easier victory in the lieutenant governor's race over Republican Stanford E. Morse, Jr., a Gulfport attorney.

Four famous southern governors review the inaugural parade with Paul B. Johnson, Jr. in 1964. Orval Faubus (Arkansas), Ross R. Barnett (Mississippi), Jimmie Davis (Louisiana), and George Wallace (Alabama).

Administration of Paul B. Johnson, Jr. 1964–1968

When Paul B. Johnson, Jr., took the oath of office on January 21, 1964, he became the only son of a former governor to succeed his father to the state's highest office. Johnson also became governor during some of Mississippi's most difficult years in the twentieth century. In his inaugural address Governor Johnson

320

told Mississippians, "You and I are part of this world whether we like it or not . . . We are Americans as well as Mississippians . . . While I am governor, hate, prejudice, and ignorance will not lead Mississippi." Johnson suggested an alternative. "If we must fight," he said, "it will not be a rear guard defense of yesterday. It will be an all out assault of our share of tomorrow." He concluded this remarkable address by saying, "God bless everyone of you, all Mississippians, black and white, here and away from home."

Governor Johnson's inaugural address won high praise from leaders throughout Mississippi and across the nation. The address set the tone of his administration. Although Mississippi experienced many difficult situations during the civil rights movement of the 1960's, Governor Johnson provided the state with constructive and positive leadership that enabled Mississippi to endure those turbulent years and adjust to a new era of race relations.

Balance of Agriculture with Industry Achieved

In March of 1965, Governor Paul Johnson held a brief ceremony in the Governor's office. In addition to representatives of the press and other state officials, former Governor Hugh L. White, who first instituted BAWI Program in 1936, attended the ceremony. The purpose of the meeting was to announce that Mississippi's effort to balance agriculture with industry had at last been achieved. Governor Johnson announced that non-agricultural employment in Mississippi exceeded agricultural employment for the first time in the state's history.

The Long Hot Summer

In the summer of 1964 civil rights activity increased dramatically as several hundred college students from throughout the nation came to Mississippi. Under the sponsorship of the Council of Federated Organizations (COFO) these students conducted "Freedom Schools" and voter registration drives. COFO was an organization composed of representatives from various civil rights groups such as the National Association for the Ad-

Medgar Evers — one of Mississippi's most influential black leaders. He was assassinated on June 12, 1963.

vancement of Colored People (NAACP), the Southern Christian Leadership Conference (SCLC), the Student Non-Violent Coordinating Committee (SNCC), and the Congress of Racial Equality (CORE).

The purpose of the "Freedom Schools" was to encourage blacks to exercise their rights as American citizens. Blacks were informed about the voter registration procedure. They were taught how to fill out the complicated forms and answer the tricky questions which had been designed to make it difficult for blacks to register.

Most white Mississippians considered these northern college students as "outside agitators" in much the same way Mississippians had reacted to the carpetbaggers during Reconstruction. Some newspapers referred to an "invasion" of Mississippi by a bunch of "long haired hippies" who were here only to stir up hatred and trouble.

The Ku Klux Klan reappeared and during the "long hot summer" of 1964 numerous acts of violence and church burnings occurred in various parts of the state. The most significant outbreak of violence occurred in Philadelphia, the county seat of Neshoba County. On the morning of June 21, 1964, three Meridian-based COFO workers, Michael Schwerner, James Chaney, and Andrew Goodman, drove up to Neshoba County to investigate reports that a black church had been burned. As they left Neshoba County later that afternoon, they were arrested and confined in the Philadelphia jail. Around midnight they were released and began driving back to Meridian. Somewhere between Philadelphia and Meridian they were overtaken by a group of Klansmen who took them out of their station wagon and murdered them. The three bodies were buried eighteen feet deep in an earthen dam which was being built for a cattle pond in Neshoba County. Although the most thorough search in the state's history was conducted, the bodies of the three civil rights workers were not found until an FBI informant led federal officials to the dam where the bodies were buried.

According to figures published in various magazines and newspapers, the casualties suffered by civil rights workers during the "long hot summer" included 3 murders, 80 beatings, 35 shootings, 1,000 arrests, 35 churches burned, and 31 homes or other buildings bombed. The northern college students and black Mississippians paid a heavy toll in the summer of 1964. Although their efforts did not produce any spectacular or immediate changes, they had set in motion a new force in Mississippi politics.

Freedom Democratic Party

In the spring of 1964 a group of civil rights leaders established the Freedom Democratic Party. The primary organizers of the Freedom Democratic Party were Lawrence Guyot, Aaron Henry, David Dennis, Ed King, Fannie Lou Hamer, and Robert Moses, a Harlem-born Harvard graduate who was considered one of the nation's most effective civil rights organizers. The Freedom Democratic Party challenged the all-white regular Mississippi

Mrs. Fannie Lou Hamer, the youngest of twenty children in a sharecropper's family — burst upon the national scene as a major civil rights figure with her remark "I'm sick and tired of being sick and tired." Until her death Mrs. Hamer was one of the nation's most admired and beloved civil rights activists.

323

Democratic Party delegation's right to represent Mississippi in the national democratic convention in August, 1964. The Freedom Democratic Party members claimed that they were loyal to the national party organization and that the regular Mississippi Democrats were not. The question of whether the "loyalists" or the "regulars" should represent Mississippi was debated on live television before a national audience. It was finally decided that both factions would be seated and jointly cast Mississippi's votes at the national convention. The "regulars" rejected this compromise and walked out of the convention. The 1964 challenge, and another one in 1968, eventually forced the Mississippi Democratic Party to accept blacks into the party, which it had not done since 1902. After the 1971 state election, the loyalists and the regular Democrats merged into one integrated state Democratic Party.

Civil Rights Legislation

The 1964 summer of violence convinced most white Mississippians that continued resistance was a greater danger to the welfare and safety of Mississippi than was peaceful acceptance of change. Do you remember Mississippi's experience during Reconstruction? It is difficult for people who have been taught to believe something all their lives to change those beliefs. But the vast majority of white Mississippians are law abiding and peaceful people. And many of them were willing to change their traditions and customs even if they did not change their beliefs, in the interest of peace and order.

In 1964 and 1965, the United States Congress passed several major civil rights laws. These laws made it illegal to discriminate against blacks in voting, hiring practices, housing, and in public restaurants, motels, swimming pools, and state parks. After the enactment of these laws, Governor Johnson advised Mississippians that the civil rights legislation was the law of the land, and whether we liked it or not, the law would be upheld. Governor Johnson's strong position in favor of law and order was endorsed by other public officials and the state's businessmen and professional leaders.

324

Within a decade, Mississippi's long-standing racial traditions were significantly modified. The changes continued to spark resistance and violence from those who could not or would not accept the inevitable changes that a new order brought. But on the whole, Mississippi adjusted to those changes with less difficulty than most people would have believed possible.

The Election of 1967

After the presidential election of 1964, John Bell Williams was stripped of his congressional seniority by the Democratic Party because he supported Barry Goldwater, the Republican candidate. Congressman Williams resigned his seat in Congress, which he had held for twenty years, and ran for governor in 1967. He faced six opponents in the Democratic primary. In that impressive field were former Governor Ross Barnett, Vernon E. Brown, C. L. McKinley, Jimmy Swan, William Waller, and State Treasurer William Winter. Williams and Winter won runoff berths as Swan, Barnett, Waller, Brown, and McKinley trailed in that order. In a heated runoff campaign, Williams defeated Winter. In the November general election Williams defeated Rubel Phillips who was making his second campaign. The 1967 lieutenant governor's race also attracted a formidable field of six candidates. In the runoff primary Charles Sullivan defeated Tupelo businessman, Roy Black, by almost 100,000 votes. Sullivan was unopposed in the general election.

The 1967 Democratic primary may have set some kind of record for the most candidates in a single election. There were seven candidates for governor, six for lieutenant governor, nine for land commissioner, and a host of others for district and local offices.

Blacks Elected to Office

Among the victorious candidates in this record setting election were 22 blacks. Most of these black officials were elected to local positions in predominantly black counties. The most significant black official elected in 1967 was Robert Clark of Holmes County who won a seat in the state legislature. Clark has been re-elected for three successive terms and presently serves as Chairman of the House Education Committee.

Administration of John Bell Williams, 1968–1972

Although Governor Williams was known as a champion of states' rights and of segregation, the most extensive integration in the state's history occurred during his administration. During the spring of 1969 and the fall of 1970, the state's dual system of public schools, one system for whites and one system for blacks, was abolished by a federal court order. There were times during those crucial months when the continuation of the public school program was in doubt. During the transition from the dual to the unified system, many white pupils withdrew from public schools and enrolled in the rapidly expanding private school system. However, enrollment figures for the 1970–71 school year indicated that the public school system would survive. Those figures showed that 92% of the students enrolled in public schools in 1969 had returned to the public schools in the fall of 1970.

Governor Williams, although he did not endorse the court ordered integration of the public school system, did not attempt to prevent its implementation. Most white Mississippians, the majority of whom had opposed the abolition of the dual system, also accepted it. There were only minor and isolated incidents of violence associated with the desegration of public schools reported during 1969 and 1970.

The Election of 1971

The 1971 governor's campaign was conducted in an atmosphere of excitement and enthusiasm that produced the largest voter turnout in the state's history. Charles Evers, the brother of the slain civil rights leader, Medgar Evers, ran as an independent candidate for governor. This was the first time in the state's history that a black candidate conducted a state-wide campaign for governor. Evers had run unsuccessfully for congress from Mississippi's fourth district in 1968, but had been elected mayor of Fayette in 1969. In the general election Evers faced

William Waller, the Democratic candidate. Waller was the district attorney who had prosecuted the man charged with the murder of Medgar Evers. The campaign of 1971 was remarkably free of the bitterness and racism which many had anticipated. The character of that election was a measure of the change Mississippi had achieved. Waller won the general election by a vote of 601,222 to 172,762.

Governor William L. Waller, shown above as a guest on a national television program, "Today". He did much during his administration to change Mississippi's national image and expand the opportunities for all Mississippians.

Administration of William L. Waller, 1972–1976

In the late 1960's and early 1970's a group of young and progressive Southern governors attracted national attention. Among this new breed of Southern politicians were Reubin Askew of Florida, Dale Bumpers of Arkansas, Jimmy Carter of Georgia and Bill Waller of Mississippi. These Southern governors assumed a leadership role at a very critical time in this nation's history. The civil rights crisis of the sixties had run its course and court-ordered changes had come to Mississippi and the South. Mississippi needed constructive and positive leadership to chart a new direction for the state.

Governor Waller had campaigned on a neo-Populist platform. He directed his campaign toward the small farmer, the blue collar worker, blacks, small businessmen, school teachers, and other workers. He identified himself with the working people rather than the large corporations, banks, and large agricultural associations. His most consistent promise during the campaign in 1971 was to break up the "Capitol Street gang." Waller identified the "Capitol Street gang" as a small group of powerful politicians and wealthy businessmen who had dominated state politics since the early 1950's.

Governmental Reorganization and Reform

For many years political and business leaders had favored governmental reorganization to reduce the unnecessary duplication of state agencies. In spite of Governor Waller's strong recommendations for a major reorganization of state government, only minor progress was made in this area during his administration. In some cases governmental reorganization resulted in the division of duties normally exercised by one officer. The officer of sheriff-and-tax collector was reorganized in 1972 by separating the law enforcement duties from the responsibility for the collection of taxes. In most counties the sheriff now deals only with law enforcement. And the tax collector, which is a separate office, deals only with tax matters.

Governor Waller also favored the reorganization of the state Highway Commission. The three highway commissioners, who are elected by districts, supervise the construction of all highways in the state. The Commission has almost always been embroiled in some controversy since its establishment in 1916. Governor Waller accused the three-member commission of acting too slowly in putting his new construction program into effect. Waller was unable, however, to achieve any significant modification in either the method of selecting commissioners or the procedure for establishing construction priorities.

Reapportionment

The issue of legislative apportionment had been one of the major factors in calling the 1890 constitution. As you remember the basic question about reapportionment in 1890 concerned black and white county representation in the legislature. When the number of representatives were assigned to each county in 1890 the population of the state was concentrated in the rural areas of north Mississippi. But in the seventy years from 1890 to 1960 a major population shift had occurred as urban areas throughout the state and south Mississippi especially showed significant population increases. During those seventy years the legislature was never reapportioned. The large counties with urban centers complained that they were under-represented in the state legislature. They also claimed that they paid a much larger share of state taxes than the rural counties but that representatives from rural areas determined how those taxes were being spent. The unfair apportionment of legislative representation in 1960 may be seen from the following comparison:

	1890 Population	Reps. in State Leg.
Noxubee Co.	27,338	3
Harrison Co.	12,481	1½
	1960 Population	Reps. in State Leg.
Noxubee Co.	16,826	3
Harrison Co.	119,489	1½

Residents of Harrison County, with support from other urban counties, filed a suit in federal court seeking an injunction to force legislative reapportionment in Mississippi. Harrison County won its suit in 1963 and a new legislative apportionment was conducted for the first time since 1890. Since 1963 two other apportionment plans have been ordered by the courts, one in 1972 and one in 1979. Legislative apportionment in 1890 was a racial issue. In 1960 the issue was a rural versus urban question. But in the late 1970's the matter of race was again made an issue in reapportionment. The 1979 reapportionment created several new legislative districts with black majorities. As a result of these new black districts, the number of black legislators increased following the election in 1979.

Black Officials

Early in his administration Governor Waller appointed several blacks to state boards, agencies, and commissions. They were the first blacks to hold state positions since the end of the nineteenth century. One of his first moves to bring blacks into public affairs, and many believe his most significant, was to integrate the state highway patrol. The real importance of this effort to bring blacks into state government was that the barrier had been broken. Governor Waller had made it much easier for his successors to extend the role of blacks in state government.

Loyalists and Regulars

A major indication of the new order of politics in Mississippi was the reconciliation and merger of the two wings of the Mississippi Democratic Party. Since the civil rights days of the sixties, the rivalry between the Loyalists and the Regulars had weakened the Democratic Party. Both factions realized that only by resolving their differences and merging the two organizations could they effectively meet the new challenges posed by the revival of the Republican Party. The two factions resolved most of the serious differences before the gubernatorial race of 1975.

Revival of the Republican Party

It is difficult to pinpoint a precise time when the Republican Party began its resurgence in Mississippi. After the National Democratic Party adopted a civil rights platform in 1948, many Southerners began to look for an alternative to the Democratic Party. Like the Southern Whigs in the 1850's, Southern Democrats in the 1950's saw their party being taken over by Northern, urban factions. In the 1850's the only real option open to the Whigs was the Republican Party. But that party was identified with anti-slavery. In the 1950's Southern Democrats who were unhappy with their national party also had only one option, the Republican Party. During the presidential election of 1952, some Mississippi Democrats formed an organization called "Democrats for Eisenhower" and supported the Republican nominee, General Dwight D. Eisenhower. From those early efforts the Republican Party gradually gained respectability and support in Mississippi.

The Presidential election of 1964 also had an impact on the revival of the Republican Party. In that year Senator Barry Goldwater of Arizona, the Republican candidate, ran against Lyndon Johnson who became President after John F. Kennedy's assassination. Goldwater, a staunch conservative, defeated Johnson in Mississippi by a vote of 356,512 to 52,616. Goldwater received 87% of the votes cast in Mississippi.

Goldwater's sweep of Mississippi also carried one Republican congressman into office. Prentiss Walker, running in the fourth congressional district, defeated Democratic congressman Arthur Winstead who had served in the House of Representatives since 1943. In 1966 Walker ran against Senator James O. Eastland. Although polling over 105,000 votes, Walker was defeated.

Rubel Phillips, regarded as one of the major figures in the revival of the Mississippi Republican Party, ran for Governor in 1963 and in 1967. On both occasions, this former Democratic office holder was often called a scalawag by Democratic politicians and newspapers. Phillips conducted strong state-wide campaigns and made the Republican Party a political force that the Democrats could no longer take for granted.

Another major figure in bringing the Republican Party back into power in Mississippi is Gil Carmichael, a Meridian businessman. In 1972 Carmichael ran a strong race against Senator James Eastland and in 1975 many political observers predicted that Carmichael would defeat Democratic gubernatorial candidate Cliff Finch in the general election. Carmichael did not defeat Finch though he ran a close second. In 1979 Carmichael ran for governor a second time, but was again defeated by the Democratic nominee. Although Carmichael has not won any office, he has made the Republican Party popular and respectable among the people.

If there was a specific turning point in the development of the Republican Party in Mississippi, it occurred during the presidential election of 1972. Richard Nixon, the Republican candidate, carried the state over the Democratic candidate George McGovern. In that election two Republican congressmen were also elected. Trent Lott was elected to the congressional seat in the fifth district which had been held by William Colmer since 1933. Thad Cochran was elected in the fourth district. Congressman Lott was re-elected in 1974, 1976, and in 1978. Cochran was re-elected in 1974 and 1976. In 1978 he was elected to the United States Senate. Cochran was the first Mississippi Republican to serve in the senate since Reconstruction. The fourth district congressional seat was retained by the Republican Party. Jon Hinson, a former Cochran aide, defeated Democrat John Hampton Stennis for that seat in 1978.

Before 1978 the Mississippi Republican Party concentrated on state or district races. But in 1979 hundreds of Republican candidates campaigned at state, county, and local levels. The surest indication that the Republican Party is now a major political organization is the fact that in several races, the most significant one being the governor's campaign, more than one Republican campaigned for the same office. Leon Bramlett, a former chairman of the Democratic State Executive Committee, challenged Gil Carmichael for the party's nomination for governor. Bramlett was narrowly defeated by Gil Carmichael in the Republican primary.

Administration of Cliff Finch, 1976–1980

After an unsuccessful campaign for lieutenant governor in 1971, Cliff Finch entered the Democratic primary for governor in 1975. William Winter, in his second try for governor, led the ticket in the first primary. Finch out-polled Maurice Dantin to get in the runoff election. In the runoff, Finch came from behind to win the Democratic nomination.

The combination of voters that swept Cliff Finch into the governor's office was a coalition of blacks and low-income whites. These rural whites and blacks, whose economic interest proved greater than their racial differences, were an unbeatable combination. During his administration Governor Finch continued many of the programs inaugurated by former Governor Waller, expanded some, and designed others of his own.

At no time since Reconstruction were blacks more active in governmental affairs than they were during the first two years of Governor Finch's administration. The governor appointed Charles Evers to the prestigious A. & I. Board and other blacks were also given prominent and highly visible positions in state government.

Governor Finch had campaigned on the promise of more jobs and economic development. However, national and international economic developments and energy problems complicated the state's economic progress and hampered Governor Finch's program. Some of Governor Finch's popular support began to wane after he decided to run for the United States Senate in 1978. Many of his former supporters favored his remaining on the job as governor until his term was completed. Many blacks also felt that Governor Finch had not fulfilled his promises of economic advancement for them.

Senate Campaign—1978

For the first time in over thirty years, Mississippi voters were given an opportunity to fill a senate vacancy. The vacancy was created in 1978 when Mississippi's senior senator, James O. Eastland retired after thirty-seven years in the senate. Senator Eastland had served as Chairman of the Judiciary Committee for many years and as President **pro tempore** during the last few years of his career.

The senatorial campaign attracted a large field of candidates from both the Democratic and Republican parties. The Democratic candidates included Governor Cliff Finch, former governor William Waller, former lieutenant governor Charles Sullivan, and Maurice Dantin, a candidate for governor in 1975. The two Republican candidates were Congressman Thad Cochran and state senator Charles Pickering. Governor Cliff Finch and Maurice Dantin won spots in the Democratic run-off primary Dantin defeated Governor Finch and faced Thad Cochran, the Republican primary winner, and two independent candidates in the general election on November 7, 1978. The two independent candidates were Charles Evers and Henry Kirksey.

Thad Cochran was elected to the senate seat and became the first Republican to serve in the United States Senate from Mississippi since Blanche K. Bruce, whose term expired in 1881.

Governor William F. Winter delivered his inaugural address in the historic Old Capitol on January 22, 1980.

Election of William Winter

In 1979 the Democratic candidates for governor included William Winter, making his third campaign; Lieutenant Governor Evelyn Gandy in her first race; John Arthur Eaves, in his second; veteran state representative Charles Deaton and Jim Herring both in their first campaign. Evelyn Gandy, Mississippi's most successful woman politician, led the ticket and faced William Winter in the runoff. Winter made a surprisingly strong showing in the second primary, defeating Gandy by over 90,000 votes. In the November general election Winter defeated Republican Gil Carmichael by a vote of 410,620 to 263,703.

A. **KEY TERMS**—Explain the following terms. If necessary, use a dictionary or encyclopedia.

1. incumbent
2. Carroll Gartin
3. per capita income
4. school consolidation
5. separate but equal doctrine
6. Brown Decision, 1954
7. Citizens Council
8. Robert B. Patterson
9. James P. Coleman
10. compulsory education law
11. Resolution of Interposition
12. State Sovereignty Commission
13. Tennessee-Tombigbee Waterway
14. unreconstructed rebel
15. Ross R. Barnett
16. Charles L. Sullivan
17. Paul B. Johnson, Jr.
18. Civil War Centennial
19. white supremacy
20. James Howard Meredith
21. Tougaloo College
22. Lyceum
23. General Charles Billingslea
24. industrial parks
25. Evelyn Gandy
26. long hot summer
27. C.O.F.O.
28. James Chaney
29. Freedom Democratic Party
30. Civil Rights Legislation
31. John Bell Williams
32. William L. Waller
33. Charles Evers
34. reapportionment
35. loyalists and regulars
36. Cliff Finch
37. John C. Stennis
38. James O. Eastland
39. Thad Cochran
40. William F. Winter

B. **MATCHING EXERCISE**

1. Mary D. Cain
2. Brown Decision, 1954
3. Tom P. Brady
4. Robert "Blowtorch" Mason
5. James Howard Meredith
6. Rubel Phillips
7. Fannie Lou Hamer
8. Robert Clark
9. Medgar Evers
10. Gil Carmichael

a. author of *Black Monday*
b. first black admitted to a white school in Mississippi
c. civil rights activist
d. Republican candidate for governor in 1963 and 1967
e. first black elected to state legislature in twentieth century
f. editor, *Summit Sun*
g. slain civil rights leader
h. ruled segregation in public schools unconstitutional
i. helped revive Republican Party in Mississippi
j. unsuccessful candidate for governor in 1959

C. MAKING A TIME LINE—Rearrange the following events in the order in which they took place.

Admission of James H. Meredith to Ole Miss
Assassination of Medgar Evers
Election of black public officials
Election of Cliff Finch
Election of President Jimmy Carter
Election of President John F. Kennedy
Election of Ross Barnett
Election of Thad Cochran to U.S. Senate
Election of William Winter
Long Hot Summer
Merger of Loyalists and Regulars
Passage of major civil rights legislation

After you arrange these events in the correct sequence, study the list. What conclusions can you draw from this sequence of events?

D. WRITING ASSIGNMENT

Suppose you were a journalist covering political and civil rights activity in Mississippi during the 1960's and 1970's. Write brief dispatches on the following topics:

Mississippi's Reaction to the Brown Decision
A Yankee General in the State Capitol
James Howard Meredith
The Ole Miss Riot
Barnett's Plan for Economic Development
Medgar Evers, Murdered in Mississippi
The Long Hot Summer
Mississippi's Reaction to Civil Rights Legislation
Black Officials Elected in Mississippi
The Revival of the Republican Party in Mississippi
William Winter Elected Governor
Republican Elected to U.S. Senate from Mississippi

CHAPTER XIII

Public Affairs in Modern Mississippi

Since World War II Mississippi has undergone enormous changes. If a person had moved away from Mississippi in 1940 and returned to the state today, that person would hardly recognize Mississippi. Many small towns have all but disappeared from the scene. It is very likely that the little one-room segregated school house where that person learned to read and write has been replaced by a new integrated complex called an attendance center. The old dusty, winding, dirt road out to the family homeplace has probably been paved and is dotted along the way with new brick houses. There is probably a factory or two in the little town where the family used to go on Saturday to buy food and clothing and where the children spent the afternoon watching a "moving picture show." The cotton fields are probably planted in soybeans, rice, or wheat. The woods which abounded in wild game have probably been converted into pasture. A person coming back to Mississippi for the first time since World War II might wonder how all these changes came about.

Population Trends

Out-Migration

The most significant population trend in Mississippi during the twentieth century is the large numbers of blacks who migrated out of the state. This Black Exodus was much more important than the exodus that occurred during the 1870's. In the first exodus only about 6,000 blacks left Mississippi but during the second exodus, occurring over a much longer period of time, several times that many blacks moved to northern and western cities in search of jobs and a better way of life. Although beginning as early as 1910, the modern black exodus was accelerated by World War II. The result of this out-migration, as reflected in the following chart, was a net decrease in the percentage of blacks in the state's total population.

Year	White	Black	Percent Black	White
1910	786,111	1,011,003	56.3	43.7
1920	853,962	936,656	52.3	47.7
1930	996,856	1,012,965	50.2	49.7
1940	1,106,327	1,077,409	49.2	50.7
1950	1,188,632	990,282	45.3	54.6
1960	1,257,546	920,595	42.0	57.7
1970	1,393,283	823,629	36.8	62.8
1977 (est)	1,527,100	847,700	35.7	64.3

Out-migration of black Mississippians was influenced by several factors. First of all, mechanization of agriculture displaced many farm workers including both blacks and whites. White farmers and workers could find employment in nearby towns and cities. But the custom of racial segregation made it almost impossible for many black farm workers to find employment in the urban areas where industrial employment was usually open only to whites.

Secondly, many young blacks who wanted an education from an accredited college had to go to schools outside of Mississippi. Prior to the 1960's none of Mississippi's state-supported black colleges were accredited and neither the law school nor the school of medicine were open to blacks. Most of the young college-educated blacks did not return to their native state.

338

And finally, the system of legal segregation placed Mississippi blacks in a status of second class citizenship. Only a few blacks in certain areas of the state were allowed to vote or exercise any of the other rights of citizenship. These conditions were unbearable to many black Mississippians. Because they saw no hope of ending the system in their lifetime, many blacks left the state for other parts of the country where racial discrimination was not sanctioned by law. In 1970 an estimated 800,000 blacks who were born in Mississippi were living outside the state. The majority of these blacks were middle-aged adults who were just entering upon their most productive years.

Out-migration was almost as significant among whites as it was among blacks. In 1970 approximately 650,000 white Mississippians were living outside of their native state. For many years political and business leaders referred to the out-migration of white, college-educated young adults as a "brain drain." These white out-migrants, like their black counterparts, were young, well-educated, and potential leaders. The loss of productivity which Mississippi has sustained because these young black and white people left the state is immeasurable.

Population statistics for the last few years are encouraging, however. The trend toward out-migration has slowed considerably in the 1970's and more young Mississippians are preferring to remain in their native state.

In-Migration

Since its admission to statehood Mississippi's population has been composed primarily of Englishmen, Irishmen, Scots, and Africans. But there have always been small numbers of other ethnic groups living in Mississippi. During the antebellum period a small number of Jews immigrated to Mississippi from Europe. Over the years the Jewish community has remained very small. Other small ethnic groups in Mississippi's population include immigrants from Greece, Lebanon, Syria, Italy, China, by way of California, and Latin America.

Dalmatians — shown here in their native dress — are among several ethnic groups in Mississippi from southeastern Europe.

Migration Within the State

Population shifts within Mississippi have also been very important at various times in the state's history. In the 1830's, you remember, many people moved from south Mississippi into the recently acquired lands in north Mississippi. Another important shift occurred in the post-World War II period. But this time the shift was from north Mississippi to south Mississippi. This migration was caused by the increase of industrial jobs in south Mississippi and the tourist boom on the Gulf Coast.

Industrial Development

Mississippi's rural population has steadily declined since the war and there has been a corresponding increase in the state's urban population. The strongest influences on this trend toward urbanization were the mechanization of farming and the growth of industry in Mississippi.

By 1940 the Balance Agriculture With Industry program had made some progress in expanding Mississippi's industrial production. But the wartime boom is the primary factor in the state's spectacular industrial growth over the last forty years. Every Mississippi governor during the postwar years has given industrial growth a high priority in his administration.

Ingalls

The largest manufacturing establishment in Mississippi is the Ingalls shipyard which came to Mississippi under the BAWI program in 1938. Since that time Ingalls has become part of Litton Industries, a major American corporation. In 1967 the state financed a $130 million construction program to expand the facilities at Ingalls. These new facilities, called the "Shipyard of the Future," are leased to Litton Industries under a BAWI contract.

Factories, Factories, Factories

The success of the Ingalls corporation inspired small towns throughout the state to go on "industry hunting trips" all over the country. Small town mayors, with the assistance of the Agricultural and Industrial Board, actively pursued northern industrialists who made it known that they were interested in establishing small plants in southern states. These hunting trips were remarkably successful. In 1951 forty new plants providing 5,276 new jobs were established. In 1977, over one hundred and twenty new plants were established and provided over 10,000 new jobs. Although there was some opposition to this rapid industrial growth, average per capita income rose sharply during this period. In 1951 the Mississippi average per capita income was only $830, or 50.2 percent of the national average. By 1977 the state's average per capita income had increased to $5,529, or 71 percent of the national average. Most of this increase can be attributed to the number of new factories located in Mississippi's small towns.

Research and Development Center

During the administration of Governor Paul B. Johnson, Jr., the Mississippi legislature created the Research and Development Center. This new agency was created to promote and coordinate the state's economic development. To shield the Research and Development Center from political interference, the legislature placed the agency under the supervision of the Board of Trustees of Institutions of Higher Learning.

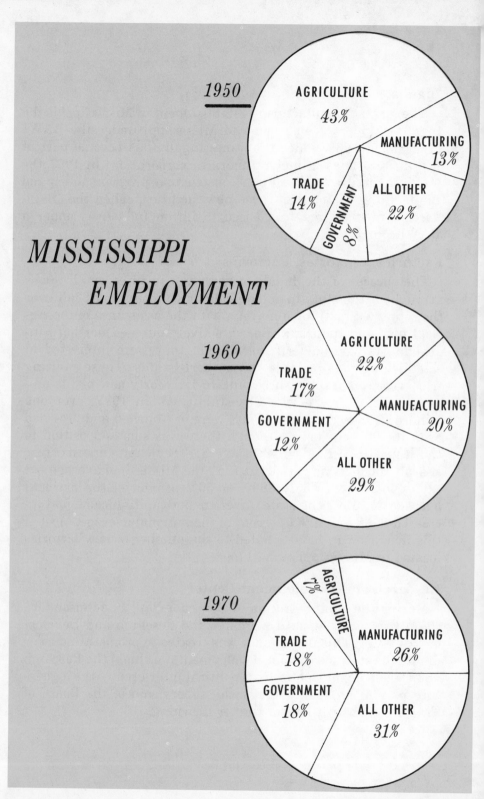

MISSISSIPPI
EMPLOYMENT

1950

AGRICULTURE
43%

MANUFACTURING
13%

TRADE
14%

GOVERNMENT
8%

ALL OTHER
22%

1960

AGRICULTURE
22%

TRADE
17%

GOVERNMENT
12%

MANUFACTURING
20%

ALL OTHER
29%

1970

AGRICULTURE
7%

TRADE
18%

GOVERNMENT
18%

MANUFACTURING
26%

ALL OTHER
31%

Mississippi Economic Council

A statewide organization of industrial, business, agricultural, professional, and educational leaders was established in 1948 to promote general economic development in Mississippi. Since that time the M.E.C. has provided Mississippi with progressive and constructive leadership. The Council endorsed and was largely responsible for Mississippi's workmen's compensation law of 1948. It has sponsored a community development program and has consistently supported reorganization of state and local governments in favor of a more efficient and responsible system. During the stormy 1960's the Mississippi Economic Council was a moderating force. The M.E.C. urged compliance with the civil rights laws as the only reasonable alternative to continued racial violence. Several regional organizations such as the Delta Council have also been instrumental in promoting both agricultural and industrial production in the state.

American Federation of Labor—Congress of Industrial Organizations

Labor organizations have never been very strong in Mississippi. Southern workers, until very recently, have been suspicious of labor unions. Many Southern workers believed that labor unions were affiliated in some way or another with socialism or communism. Southern politicians and newspapers have often accused union leaders of either being communists or sympathettic to the cause of communism. Union leaders claim that the reluctance of Mississippi laborers to join unions has been one of the reasons for low wages and poor working conditions in Mississippi.

After World War II, however, the large increase of industrial jobs caused a gradual change in the state's attitude toward unions. By 1950, the A.F. of L.—C.I.O. had approximately 50,000 members in Mississippi. Within the last twenty years, under the leadership of Claude Ramsey, the AF of L—CIO has grown into a major political and economic force in Mississippi. During the civil rights crisis of the 1960's the AF of L—CIO was also a moderating force which, like the M.E.C., urged its members to accept the changes that were taking place in Mississippi.

Agricultural Changes

After World War II farming in Mississippi ceased to be a small family operation. Small farmers were unable to compete with the large commercial farms which used machines rather than mules. Large machines, even if small farmers could have afforded them, were not practical on small plots of land or on hillside farms. As we have already learned, many of these farmers had to seek employment in nearby towns and cities.

Decline of Cotton

After World War II the development of synthetic fibers like rayon, nylon, and dacron drastically reduced the demand for cotton. Mississippi, however, continued to be one of the three largest cotton producing states in the nation. But cotton was no longer the state's major crop. Cotton was no longer king in Mississippi.

Soybeans

The Mississippi crop which displaced King Cotton was the soybean. This crop can be produced with less care and cultivation than is required by cotton. In addition, there are many more uses for soybeans than there are for cotton which makes soybeans in great demand. In 1972, only 1.6 million acres were planted in cotton as compared to 2.5 million acres in soybeans.

Other Crops

Mississippi farms, especially the small, family-owned type, became highly diversified during the postwar era. Mississippi farmers now produce a variety of row crops. The five major crops are soybeans, cotton, rice, corn, and wheat. Other important crops include barley, oats, hay, and sweet potatoes. Vegetables, fruits, watermelons, and pecans are also important components in Mississippi's agricultural production.

Livestock and Poultry

As many small family farms ceased operation, a large portion of the acreage that had been planted in row crops was converted into pasture land. By the early 1960's, beef cattle had become a major source of income for Mississippi farmers. Many other Mississippi farmers turned to poultry as an alternative to row crops.

Mississippi Farm Bureau Federation

In the 1920's Mississippi farmers experienced a steady decline in farm prices. Since the Grange movement and the Farmers' Alliance were no longer active organizations, farmers became aware of the need for a new organization dedicated to agricultural development. On October 30, 1922, the Mississippi Farm Bureau Federation was organized at Jackson to provide farmers with an organization to promote their economic interests. The Farm Bureau encouraged farmers to establish cooperatives in their communities and urged cotton farmers to join its cotton marketing program. Under this marketing agreement, farmers allowed the Farm Bureau officials to bargain with cotton buyers rather than with individual farmers. Through their control of thousands of bales of cotton, Bureau officials could get a better price than the individual farmers could get.

In addition to the Mississippi Farm Bureau Federation, many other organizations have been established to promote agricultural development. Some of those organizations include the Mississippi Beekeepers Association, Mississippi Cattlemen's Association, Mississippi Pecan Producers' Association, American Dairy Association of Mississippi, Mississippi Poultry Improvement Association, Mississippi Pork Producers Association, Mississippi Rice Growers' Association, and the Mississippi Soybean Association.

4-H Clubs

In 1910 the Mississippi Department of Agriculture sponsored contests in the public schools to recognize and reward young Mississippians for agricultural achievement. Local clubs were organized to conduct the contests. Most of those local clubs were called corn clubs. The first corn club was organized in Holmes County in 1907 by William H. "Corn Club" Smith. This movement quickly spread to other schools and the Corn Clubs eventually developed into the 4-H Clubs.

Scientific Farming

In recent years farming has become a scientific operation. Scientists at Mississippi State University and other research centers have developed new seeds and hybrids which produce greater yields. The results of this research are made available to local farmers through the various scientific journals and through the County Agent who is a part of the Extension Service of Mississippi State University. Almost all farming techniques and methods now in use are the result of years of research and testing. The only thing farmers still have to guess about is the weather.

Transportation

The industrial and agricultural development of Mississippi since World War II has been made possible in part by the expansion of the state's transportation facilities. Farming operations and industrial production require adequate roads, railways, and river facilities to move the raw materials and finished products to the nation's markets. Without these transportation facilities, economic growth and development would be practically impossible.

Highways

In 1916 the state legislature established the Mississippi Highway Commission. Since its creation this three-member commission has supervised and coordinated the state's roadways which include a primary and secondary highway system. The primary network includes the major highways connecting large towns and cities. The secondary system consists of a network of roads crisscrossing Mississippi's rural areas. The highway system includes 10,189 miles of which 9,956 miles are paved. Practically all the unpaved mileage is in the secondary system.

In addition to the state system, there are two other categories of roadways in Mississippi. The largest of these two is the county road system which is financed and maintained by county taxes. These roads are under the jurisdiction of the County Board of Supervisors rather than the state Highway Commission. The

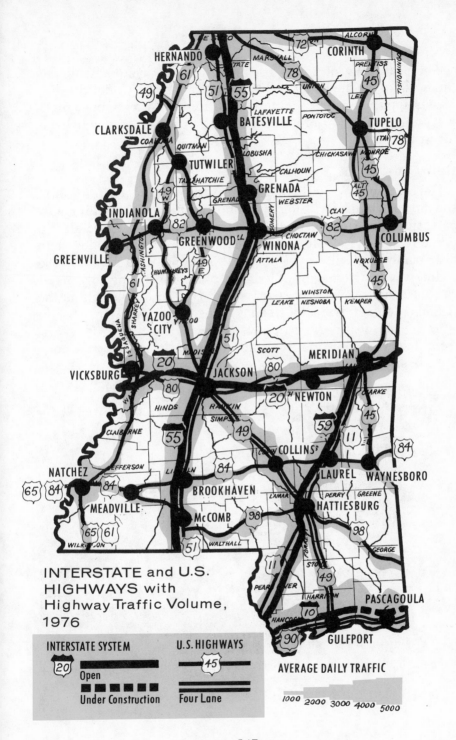

HERNANDO
CORINTH
ALCORN
DE SOTO
72 TIPPAH
MARSHALL
PRENTISS
61
78
UNION
51 55
TISHOMINGO
49
LEE
45
LAFAYETTE
PONTOTOC
BATESVILLE
CLARKSDALE
TUPELO
COAHOMA
QUITMAN
YALOBUSHA
CHICKASAW
MONROE
ITAW
78
TUTWILER
CALHOUN
45
TALLAHATCHIE
ALT
45
49
W
GRENADA
GRENAL
WEBSTER
INDIANOLA
82
CLAY
82
COLUMBUS
GREENWOOD LL
MONTGOMERY
CHOCTAW
WINONA
49
GREENVILLE
ATTALA
NOXUBEE
E
HUMPHREYS
61
WINSTON
45
WASHINGTON
LEAKE
NESHOBA
KEMPER
YAZOO
CITY
ISSAQUENA
SHARKEY
YAZOO
51
SCOTT
MERIDIAN
20
MADISON
80
VICKSBURG
JACKSON
80
20 NEWTON
CLARKE
HINDS
RANKIN
SIMPSON
45
55
49
59
11
CLAIBORNE
84
COLLINS
NATCHEZ
JEFFERSON
COVINGTON
84
65 84
LINCOLN
84
LAUREL
WAYNESBORO
MEADVILLE
BROOKHAVEN
LAMAR
PERRY
GREENE
65 61
McCOMB
98
HATTIESBURG
98
WILKINSON
51
WALTHALL
GEORGE
11
FORREST
STONE
49
PEARL RIVER
PASCAGOULA
HARRISON
10
HANCOCK
90
GULFPORT

INTERSTATE and U.S. HIGHWAYS with Highway Traffic Volume, 1976

INTERSTATE SYSTEM   U.S. HIGHWAYS

20   Open   45
      Under Construction   Four Lane

AVERAGE DAILY TRAFFIC

1000 2000 3000 4000 5000

second category of roads is the interstate system which is financed under the Federal Highway Act of 1956. Under this law Mississippi has been designated 683 miles of these super highways. There are 577 miles of the interstate system now in service in the state.

Railroads

During World War II America's railroads were a vital link in the nation's transportation system. But after the war rail transportation experienced a period of rapid decline, especially in passenger service. More Americans owned automobiles than ever before and air travel in the 1950's and 1960's became the country's favorite means of long distance travel. The only major rail passenger service presently operating in Mississippi is the Illinois Central train between Chicago and New Orleans. In spite of the decline in railway usage in the last forty years, freight service continues to be an important means of transporting Mississippi goods and products to market.

River commerce is still a vital part of Mississippi's economic growth.

Waterways

Although trade on the state's smaller rivers has practically disappeared, the inland ports at Greenville, Vicksburg, and Natchez continue to prosper. Raw materials and manufactured goods are brought to these ports by rail or truck and then shipped to various parts of the country by barges.

The volume of trade at Mississippi's seaports at Pascagoula and Gulfport has also increased as the state's import-export business, especially with Latin America, has increased over the last few years. The intercoastal canal, extending from Texas to Florida, also provides a water route for trade along the Gulf Coast.

Airways

Perhaps the most dramatic influence of World War II on American transportation was the popularization of the airplane. Throughout the war the phrase, "Victory Through Air Power," was frequently quoted by politicians, military leaders and by the American news media. When the war was over thousands of military aircraft were converted to civilian use. The aviation industry became one of the nation's major businesses as cargo and passenger service became the "only way to travel."

To promote and to regulate this new transportation service, the legislature established the Aeronautics Commission in 1946. Since its creation, the Commission has supervised the steady growth of airline service in Mississippi. At the present time there are seventy-five publicly owned airports in Mississippi. Five major airlines provide regularly scheduled air service at ten airports in Mississippi.

Energy Sources

The technological revolution spawned by World War II has placed heavy demands on America's energy resources. Mississippi is helping to meet those demands by increasing its production of oil and natural gas.

349

Oil and Natural Gas

The first commercial oil well in Mississippi was brought in on September 5, 1939, near Tinsley in Yazoo County. Since that time 15,700 wells have been drilled in the state. At the present time there are over 3,000 producing oil wells and 350 gas wells in the state. Mississippi's oil reserves are estimated at 342 million barrels and its natural gas reserves are estimated to be 1.1 trillion cubic feet. Although these reserves may appear large, they are not sufficient to meet America's energy needs of the future.

Atomic Energy

In an effort to conserve our oil and gas reserves and to reduce our dependence upon foreign countries, American scientists and government agencies are seeking new sources of energy. One of the most important and controversial of these new sources is atomic energy.

Grand Gulf Nuclear Power Station, near Port Gibson.

There are two nuclear power plants now under construction in Mississippi. The Grand Gulf Nuclear Power Station near Port Gibson in Claiborne County is being built by the Mississippi Power and Light Company at a cost of $1.9 billion—the largest construction project by an investor-owned corporation in the state's history. The Grand Gulf plant is scheduled for completion in 1984.

The other nuclear plant is being constructed by the Tennessee Valley Authority near Iuka in Tishomingo County. The Yellow Creek Nuclear Power Plant will cost $2.15 billion and will be fully operational by 1986.

The accident at the Three Mile Island Nuclear Plant near Harrisburg, Pennsylvania in 1979 has sparked a nation-wide protest against further construction of nuclear power plants. Opponents of atomic power contend that nuclear energy is an unsafe form of power. They point to the Three Mile Island accident as proof that safety precautions, however thorough they might seem, cannot adequately guard against human errors. Those who support further construction of nuclear power plants contend that atomic energy is America's best alternative to its continued dependence upon foreign oil supplies. They also claim that continued research and the development of more advanced safety techniques can virtually eliminate the margin of human error.

Social Services

The Great Depression of the 1930's demonstrated a need for additional publicly-financed social services to be administered by various government agencies. Although some Americans have opposed the expanding role of government in the private affairs of its citizens, many others have approved of these services which are financed by state and federal funds.

Health and Welfare

Mississippi's first State Board of Health was established in 1877 and has operated continuously since that time. The twelve board members, who are appointed by the governor from the various medical professions, supervise all public health programs administered by county health departments. The State Board of Health is also the licensing agency for physicians and most health care facilities such as nursing homes, child care centers, and ambulance services. Hospitals, dentists, nurses, and chiropractors are licensed by special agencies established for that purpose.

The State Board of Public Welfare, which is also appointed by the governor, provides services to the poor, elderly, and disabled. The Board also cooperates with other state agencies in providing assistance to veterans, parolees, and child care institutions. The county health and welfare departments administer a wide variety of health care services which are made possible from both state and federal sources.

Hospitals

After World War II a major hospital construction program made modern health care facilities available to thousands of Mississippians who had never before enjoyed such care. Many of these hospitals were financed by federal funds under the Hill-Burton Act passed in 1946.

The University Medical Center

One of the major factors in the improvement and expansion of health care in Mississippi was the establishment of the University of Mississippi Medical Center at Jackson in 1950. The Medical Center, which is a branch of the University of Mississippi, includes a School of Dentistry, a School of Medicine, a School of Nursing, a School of Health Related Professions, a Graduate School in the medical sciences, and a teaching hospital. Since its establishment, the Medical Center's faculty and staff have achieved national and international acclaim in several different areas of medical research.

Public Libraries

In 1926 the legislature created the Mississippi Library Commission and authorized the agency to promote the establishment of public libraries throughout the state. The Commission enjoyed only limited success until 1950 when a new system of regional libraries was organized. Since then sixteen regional libraries embracing fifty-two counties have been established. In addition to these regional libraries, twenty-eight county library systems are also in operation. All of the regional offices and most of the county libraries operate bookmobiles or mail services through which books are made available to the general public. Additionally, a statewide telephone and teletype communications system linking practically all public and university libraries provides library users with up-to-date information on the locations of books and other materials.

Education

Public education has been one of Mississippi's greatest challenges in the twentieth century. The school system has been costly and often controversial. But Mississippians have been willing to bear the burden of taxation necessary to sustain the system and in the most difficult circumstances they have supported the continuation of the public school system.

Elementary and Secondary Schools

In the early part of this century political and educational leaders realized that Mississippi could not continue to support the large number of one-room rural schools then in operation. In 1910 a law was passed to combine some of those local schools into larger attendance centers. However, consolidation was very unpopular and little progress was made in reducing the number of school districts. In 1944 there were still 4,846 school districts operating in Mississippi. After World War II the rising costs of public education and the demand for better schools caused state leaders to reorganize the school system. Another factor that contributed to the reorganization plan was the possibility that the federal courts might declare Mississippi's dual system for whites and blacks unconstitutional.

During the second administration of Governor Hugh L. White, 1952-1956, the state initiated a program to consolidate and upgrade Mississippi's public school system. The program was designed first of all, to improve the public education program and secondly, to persuade the federal courts that Mississippi's school facilities were equal for both races. That effort came too late, however, and the Supreme Court ruled that segregation in public schools must be discontinued.

Over the next fifteen years the public school system was the focus of controversy as civil rights leaders and federal officials brought a barrage of suits against the state to desegregate the schools. These suits resulted in a plan called "freedom of choice." Under this plan parents were given the choice of enrolling their children in either the white or black school system. Black parents who chose to send their children to predominantly white schools were subjected to economic and social pressures to withdraw their children. When this pressure was unsuccessful, black parents were sometimes subjected to force and violence.

Because of these efforts to discourage black parents from enrolling their children in white schools, additional suits were filed in the late 1960's. These suits were aimed at the elimination of the dual system entirely. After years of litigation, the Supreme Court ordered the consolidation of the two existing school systems into one integrated system. This order brought a torrent of protest from those whites who opposed integration.

As a direct result of this court order, a large number of white private academies were established in 1969 and 1970. Some of these private schools have ceased operations, but others have survived. The chief reason for the closing of some academies was the high cost of tuition which many Mississippi families were unable to pay during the early 1970's when a national recession caused a slow down in Mississippi's economy. In some cases, the academies were unable to maintain high educational standards and white parents returned their children to the public schools.

As you learned in the previous chapter, about 92% of the enrollment returned to the public schools in the fall of 1970. Within the next few years many others returned when they and their parents realized that the public school system was not in disarray and chaos as opponents of integration had predicted it would be. Mississippi has justifiably received praise from across the nation for the manner in which it worked out a potentially dangerous adjustment in its traditional pattern of racial separation.

Public Junior Colleges

The Mississippi system of junior colleges, which has been copied by several other states, is an outgrowth of the county agricultural high schools. Between 1908 and 1919 fifty-one of these agricultural high schools were established to provide secondary education for boys and girls in the rural areas of the state. In 1922 the state legislature authorized the addition of the first two years of college to the high school curriculum. The first two agricultural high schools to add college level courses were those in Pearl River and Hinds Counties. Within a few years several other agricultural high schools began offering freshman and sophomore courses. After World War II most of the junior colleges discontinued their high school operations and expanded their course offerings in technical and vocational subjects.

The courses offered by junior colleges extend over the full range of the academic and vocational curriculum. Most junior colleges offer courses that are specifically designed to meet the educational and technical needs of the community in which they are located. Because of this close association and cooperation with its community interests, junior colleges are often called community colleges.

Andrews Hall at Perkinston Junior College — the first building at a predominantly white institution to honor a black — was named for Thelma Andrews, a long-time employee of the college.

1 NORTHWEST MISSISSIPPI
  JUNIOR COLLEGE Senatobia
2 COAHOMA JUNIOR COLLEGE
  Clarksdale
3 MISSISSIPPI DELTA
  JUNIOR COLLEGE Moorhead
4 SAINTS JUNIOR COLLEGE
  Lexington
5 HOLMES JUNIOR COLLEGE
  Goodman
6 HINDS JUNIOR COLLEGE
  Raymond
7 UTICA JUNIOR COLLEGE Utica
8 COPIAH-LINCOLN
  JUNIOR COLLEGE Wesson
9 NATCHEZ JUNIOR COLLEGE
  Natchez
10 SOUTHWEST MISSISSIPPI
   JUNIOR COLLEGE Summit
11 NORTHEAST MISSISSIPPI
   JUNIOR COLLEGE Boonville
12 ITAWAMBA JUNIOR COLLEGE
   Fulton
13 WOOD JUNIOR COLLEGE
   Mathiston
14 MARY HOLMES
   JUNIOR COLLEGE West Point
15 EAST MISSISSIPPI
   JUNIOR COLLEGE Scooba
16 MERIDIAN JUNIOR COLLEGE
   Meridian
17 EAST CENTRAL JUNIOR COLLEGE
   Decatur
18 CLARK MEMORIAL
   JUNIOR COLLEGE Newton
19 JONES COUNTY JUNIOR COLLEGE
   Ellisville
20 PRENTISS NORMAL and
   INDUSTRIAL INSTITUTE
   Prentiss
21 PEARL RIVER JUNIOR COLLEGE
   Poplarville
22 MISSISSIPPI GULF COAST
   JUNIOR COLLEGE
   a. Perkinston Campus,
      Perkinston
   b. Jefferson Davis Campus,
      Gulfport
   c. Jackson County Campus,
      Gautier

JUNIOR COLLEGES and
Junior College Districts
● Private   ■ Public
──── District Boundaries
□ Branch of Public Junior College

The Piney Woods Country Life School

In 1913 Dr. Laurence Jones, a graduate of Iowa State University, established The Piney Woods Country Life School near Magee to provide vocational and secondary education for young blacks. This school was similar to the agricultural high schools which had been established for white students. The Piney Woods School gained national recognition in 1954 when Dr. Jones appeared on a network television show called "This Is Your Life." This program featured outstanding Americans who had made significant contributions or achieved some special distinction in politics, entertainment, medicine, or education. The host of the program invited his listeners to send a contribution to Piney Woods in honor of Dr. Jones' lifetime of service to black education. As a result of this suggestion, over two hundred and fifty thousand dollars were sent to a Jackson bank where a special endowment fund had been established for Piney Woods. Dr. Jones, who is the subject of two books and numerous articles, died in 1975. He is buried on the campus where he spent sixty-two years of his life teaching and training young black men and women.

Dr. Walter Washington, President of Alcorn State University — was listed among the one hundred most influential blacks in America by EBONY magazine in 1976.

Institutions of Higher Learning

The eight state universities in Mississippi offer undergraduate and graduate degrees in over one thousand academic areas. All eight of the institutions are accredited and are governed by a thirteen member Board of Trustees. In addi-

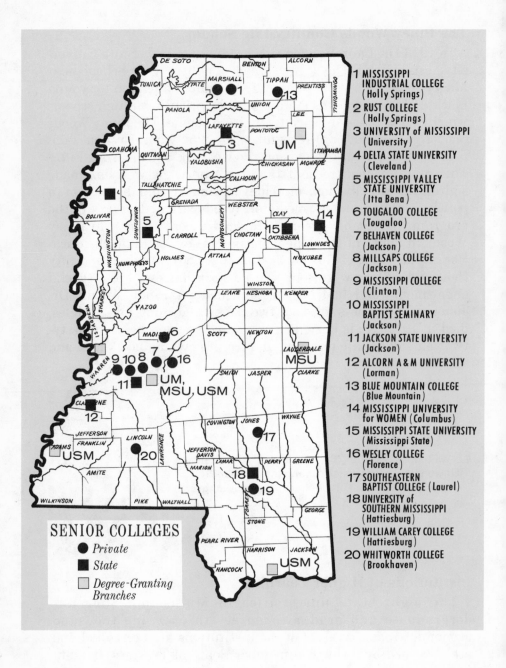

SENIOR COLLEGES
- ● Private
- ■ State
- ☐ Degree-Granting Branches

1 MISSISSIPPI INDUSTRIAL COLLEGE (Holly Springs)
2 RUST COLLEGE (Holly Springs)
3 UNIVERSITY of MISSISSIPPI (University)
4 DELTA STATE UNIVERSITY (Cleveland)
5 MISSISSIPPI VALLEY STATE UNIVERSITY (Itta Bena)
6 TOUGALOO COLLEGE (Tougaloo)
7 BELHAVEN COLLEGE (Jackson)
8 MILLSAPS COLLEGE (Jackson)
9 MISSISSIPPI COLLEGE (Clinton)
10 MISSISSIPPI BAPTIST SEMINARY (Jackson)
11 JACKSON STATE UNIVERSITY (Jackson)
12 ALCORN A & M UNIVERSITY (Lorman)
13 BLUE MOUNTAIN COLLEGE (Blue Mountain)
14 MISSISSIPPI UNIVERSITY for WOMEN (Columbus)
15 MISSISSIPPI STATE UNIVERSITY (Mississippi State)
16 WESLEY COLLEGE (Florence)
17 SOUTHEASTERN BAPTIST COLLEGE (Laurel)
18 UNIVERSITY of SOUTHERN MISSISSIPPI (Hattiesburg)
19 WILLIAM CAREY COLLEGE (Hattiesburg)
20 WHITWORTH COLLEGE (Brookhaven)

tion to the eight state universities and sixteen public junior colleges, there are also five private two-year colleges, eight private four year colleges, six Bible colleges, and two theological seminaries in Mississippi.

College Boom

World War II veterans were given several kinds of financial benefits. This "G-I Bill of Rights," as these benefits were sometimes called, included financial aid and living expenses for veterans enrolled in educational institutions. Because of these benefits, thousands of Mississippians went to college after the war and the state's institutions of higher learning experienced a period of enormous growth and expansion. Most colleges hastily built "Vet Villages" to provide housing for veterans and their families. More classroom buildings, larger faculties and other new facilities were needed to accommodate the increasing enrollments.

The college boom continued into the 1960's when the "war babies," became old enough to go to school. Expanding enrollments were also affected by the fact that more blacks and women were attending college than ever before.

Recreation

Mississippi's rural heritage continues to be a strong influence on the lifestyles and recreational habits of its people. Hunting, fishing, boating, camping, and other outdoor activities are among the most popular forms of leisure in Mississippi. The prosperity which Mississippians have enjoyed since World War II has allowed them to spend more hours away from work and home. The state government operates and maintains a system of state parks which offer a full range of boating and camping facilities. The Mississippi Game and Fish Commission enforces the state's game laws and promotes good conservation practices to insure that Mississippi's wild life is preserved.

Athletic Contests

Before the Civil War young Mississippians engaged in such popular sports as horse-racing, jousting tournaments, shooting contests, and log rolling. Soon after the Civil War two new outdoor sports captured the enthusiasm of Mississippi youths. First, baseball and then soon afterwards, football became the most popular contests of strength and skill in the state. Later, basketball was added. Throughout the twentieth century young men and women have displayed their athletic skills to enthusiastic and devoted fans. Mississippians love contests and these games have become enormously popular in Mississippi schools and colleges. Many educational and civic leaders have attributed the smooth transition from the segregated school system to an integrated system, in part at least, to the popularity of team sports.

How Mississippi is Governed

The constitution under which Mississippi is presently governed was drafted in 1890. That document created a governmental structure closely patterned after the national system. There are three distinct and separate branches of government in Mississippi, each operating under a checks and balance system designed to limit the power exercised by the other branches. The power of government is also distributed among the state, county, district (or beat), and municipal levels. Mississippi's governmental structure and its relationship to the federal government is represented by the following chart.

	Executive	Legislative	Judicial
Federal	President	U. S. Congress	Federal Courts
State	Governor	State Legislature	State Courts
County	Sheriff	Board of Supervisors	County Courts
District	Constable	Supervisor	Justice Court
Municipality	Mayor	City Council/Aldermen	City Courts

Each branch at each level of government has been given jurisdiction over certain matters by the Mississippi Constitution. In the exercise of that jurisdiction many additional boards, agencies, and public offices have been established at the state and local levels.

State Executive Branch

The following officials are elected to four-year terms and constitute the executive branch of the state government.

Governor

Lieutenant Governor	Superintendent of Education
Secretary of State	Treasurer
Attorney General	Auditor
Commissioner of Agriculture	Public Service Commissioners (3)
Commissioner of Insurance	Highway Commissioners (3)

There are also over one hundred agencies, boards, and commissions in the executive branch. Members of those agencies are normally appointed by the governor with the approval of the state senate.

State Legislative Branch

The Mississippi legislature is composed of two houses:

Senate (the upper house)
  52 members elected for four-year terms
  Secretary of the Senate (appointed by Senate)
  12 additional clerks and secretaries
House of Representatives (the lower house)
  122 members elected for four-year terms
  Clerk of the House (appointed by the House)
  9 additional clerks
The State Librarian and legislative Postmaster are appointed by the legislature.

In addition to these officials there are numerous standing and special committees which assist the legislature in research and in the drafting of laws. One of the most important of these standing committees is the Performance Evaluation and Expenditure Review (PEER) Committee which has broad investigative powers.

STATE OF MISSISSIPPI
COMBINED GENERAL AND SPECIAL FUNDS

Total Expenditures - Fiscal Year Ending
June 30, 1977

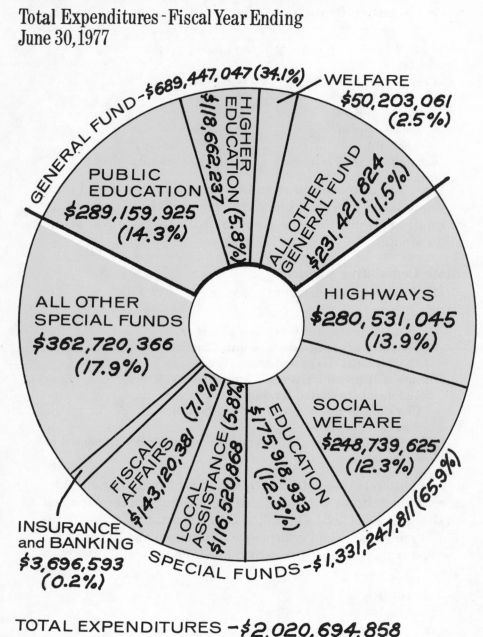

GENERAL FUND - $689,447,047 (34.1%)

WELFARE
$50,203,061
(2.5%)

HIGHER EDUCATION
$118,662,237 (5.8%)

PUBLIC
EDUCATION
$289,159,925
(14.3%)

ALL OTHER
GENERAL FUND
$231,421,824
(11.5%)

ALL OTHER
SPECIAL FUNDS
$362,720,366
(17.9%)

HIGHWAYS
$280,531,045
(13.9%)

FISCAL
AFFAIRS
$143,120,381 (7.1%)

LOCAL
ASSISTANCE (5.8%)
$116,520,868

EDUCATION
$175,918,933
(12.3%)

SOCIAL
WELFARE
$248,739,625
(12.3%)

SPECIAL FUNDS - $1,331,247,811 (65.9%)

INSURANCE
and BANKING
$3,696,593
(0.2%)

TOTAL EXPENDITURES - $2,020,694,858
(100.0%)

State Judicial Branch

Supreme Court Justices
    9 members elected by districts for eight-year terms
    Clerk of the Supreme Court (appointed by Court)
Chancery Courts
    19 Chancellors (judges) elected by districts for four-year terms
Circuit Courts
    19 Circuit Judges elected by districts for four-year terms
District Attorneys
    19 District Attorneys elected by districts for four-year terms

County Executive Branch (All elected for four-year terms)

Sheriff
Tax Collector-Assessor
Superintendent of Education and a 5 member Board of Education
Coroner and Ranger (in some counties)
Surveyor (in some counties)

County Legislative Branch

Board of Supervisors
    5 members elected by districts (beats) for four-year terms
Election Commissioners
    5 members elected by districts (beats) for four-year terms

County Judicial Branch (All elected for four-year terms)

County Judge (in some counties)
Chancery Clerk
Circuit Clerk
County Attorney

District (Beat) Executive Authority

Constables
    elected by districts (beats) for four years
    some large counties have subdivisions within districts (beats)
       and elect a constable for each subdivision

District (Beat) Legislative Authority

Supervisor elected by voters in each district.

District (Beat) Judicial Authority

Justice Court Judge elected by voters in each district.

Municipal organization varies so widely according to the size and type of charter for each town or city that a graphic representation of municipal government is not practical. Each town and city bears a basic, though simplified, resemblance to the structure of state government. There is an executive, legislative, and judicial branch of government in each municipality.

Federal Officials

Mississippi is represented in the United States Congress by two senators elected from the state at large for six-year terms and by five members in the House of Representatives elected by congressional districts for two-year terms. Representation in the senate is equally distributed to all states with each having two seats. The number of seats in the House of Representatives is apportioned every ten years on the basis of each state's population. The total number of seats is fixed at 435 and as population shifts occur states either lose or gain seats in the house. Since 1920 Mississippi has lost three seats in the House because its population increase has not kept pace with the rest of the country.

Mississippi is divided into two federal judicial districts in which judges appointed by the President exercise jurisdiction over cases involving federal law. In each district United States marshals and U. S. attorneys are responsible for the enforcement of federal laws and court orders.

A. KEY TERMS—Explain the following terms. If necessary, use a dictionary or encyclopedia.

1. out-migration
2. "brain drain"
3. in-migration
4. R. & D. Center
5. M.E.C.
6. A.F. of L. & C.I.O.
7. Farm Bureau Federation
8. 4-H Clubs
9. scientific farming
10. County Agent
11. Highway Commission
12. nuclear power
13. State Board of Health
14. State Board of Public Welfare
15. Mississippi Medical Center
16. freedom of choice
17. junior colleges
18. "war babies"
19. checks and balance system
20. Constable
21. Justice Court Judge
22. Attorney General
23. State Superintendent of Education
24. Public Service Commissioners
25. Secretary of State
26. Chancery Courts
27. Circuit Courts
28. legislative branch
29. executive branch
30. judicial branch

B. MATCHING EXERCISE

1. Claude Ramsey
2. soybeans
3. William H. Smith
4. G-I Bill of Rights
5. Board of Supervisors
6. State Senate
7. House of Representatives
8. municipalities
9. Mississippi Supreme Court
10. Lieutenant Governor

a. educational grants to veterans
b. highest court in the state
c. county legislative branch
d. head of A.F. of L. & C.I.O.
e. upper house
f. towns and cities
g. second highest executive office
h. lower house
i. Mississippi's major crop
j. founded first corn club

C. WRITING ASSIGNMENT

1. Find out the names of the state officials who presently hold the following offices:

Governor
Lieutenant Governor
Secretary of State
State Treasurer
State Superintendent of Education
Public Service Commissioner (your district)
Highway Commissioner (your district)
U.S. Senators (two)
U.S. Congressman from your district

2. Find out the names of the county officials who presently hold the following offices:
   Sheriff
   Chancery Clerk
   Circuit Clerk
   Tax Collector
   Board of Supervisors (all five)
   Justice Court Judge (for your beat)
3. If you live in a town or city find out the names of the officials who presently hold the following offices:
   Mayor
   City Council or Aldermen
   Chief of Police
   City Judge

D. INTERVIEW ASSIGNMENT: Either take notes of your interview or, with the permission of the person being interviewed, use a tape recorder.
1. Interview a public official, either state or local. Ask the person to explain the functions of that office and to explain why he or she entered politics.

E. WRITING ASSIGNMENT: Write an epitaph for the following Mississippians.
   Hugh L. White
   Ross Barnett
   James Howard Meredith
   James Chaney, Michael Schwerner, Andrew Goodman
   Fannie Lou Hamer
   James O. Eastland

CHAPTER XIV

Creative and Performing Arts

Some people in other parts of the country think of Mississippi as an economically backward state where illiteracy and racial unrest keeps Mississippi out of touch and out of step with the rest of the nation. This negative image of Mississippi gained wide national acceptance during the hey-day of Vardaman and Bilbo. It is unfortunately true that poverty, illiteracy, and racial violence have sometimes hampered the state's economic and social development in the past. And there is no doubt that some Mississippi politicians have contributed to our state's unfavorable national image.

There is one area however in which Mississippi has achieved national and international distinction. Even though our state has the highest percentage of illiteracy in the nation, Mississippi has produced some of America's greatest writers. Mississippi's literary production since the early 1920's has attracted world attention and is the subject of numerous studies. One scholar described this achievement as follows:

> There is nothing quite like that roster anywhere else in twentieth century American writing . . . The phenomenon of these

writers all coming along at about the same period, all of them natives of a state hitherto not especially noted for its cultural achievements, must inevitably send one searching for an explanation in the life out of which their art evolved.[1]

Since World War II Mississippians have won so many national literary awards that it is difficult to keep up with them. Mississippians have won three Pulitzer Prizes in journalism, two in fiction, one in drama, and one in biography. And one writer, William Faulkner, won two Pulitzer Prizes and the Nobel Prize for literature. To merely list all the awards and achievements of Mississippi's writers would require many pages. At the latest count, approximately 1,800 Mississippians have published books ranging over a wide variety of topics. Since we cannot examine all of these writers, the following discussion will deal only with Mississippi's major literary figures.

Mississippi's Most Noted Authors

Mississippi's four most famous and widely acclaimed writers are William Faulkner, Richard Wright, Eudora Welty and Tennessee Williams.

William Faulkner (1897–1962)

Although he was born in New Albany, Faulkner grew up in Oxford where his father was employed as business manager at the University of Mississippi for several years. Most of Faulkner's novels and short stories are about people who lived in an imaginary town called Jefferson, the county seat of fictional Yoknapatawpha County. Even though these people and places were created by this literary genius, they bear a striking resemblance to real people in real towns not only in Mississippi, but throughout the world. The basic themes that Faulkner writes about are not local but universal—honor and greed, human dignity and depravity, the dissolution of families; class distinction and racial prejudice; love, hate, jealousy and vio-

[1]Louis D. Rubin, Jr., **The Faraway Country, Writers of the Modern South**, pp. 66–67.

John and William Faulkner

lence. These are mankind's deepest and innermost anxieties. The characters in his novels are Mississippians, but the struggles they face are recognizable and shared by men and women everywhere. His writings have been translated into many languages and he is very popular in Europe and Japan.

Faulkner's literary genius has been rewarded by both a Pulitzer Prize and a Nobel Prize. Perhaps the most significant tribute to him as a writer is the fact that William Faulkner has been the subject of more books, articles, and literary studies than any other writer in history except William Shakespeare. Among Faulkner's most important novels are **Sound and the Fury** (1927), **As I Lay Dying** (1930), **Light in August** (1932), **Absalom, Absalom!** (1936) and **The Reivers** (1962).

Richard Wright (1908–1960)

Considered by some literary critics as America's major black novelist, Richard Wright was born at Stanton, twelve miles east of Natchez. His parents were sharecroppers. After the dissolution of his family—his parents separated when he was five—Wright lived with various relatives in Mississippi, Arkansas, and Tennessee.

369

Richard Wright

In 1927 Wright moved to Chicago to escape the racism and degradation he had suffered in his native South. Throughout his youth Wright developed an intense interest in literature and read most of America's major authors. During the depression of the 1930's, he moved to New York and got a job with the Federal Writer's Project. Within a few years Wright's first novel, **Uncle Tom's Children** (1938), was published. The following year he received a Guggenheim Fellowship which made it possible for him to write **Native Son** (1940). This novel was an immediate success. It was a Book-of-the-Month selection and was translated into six languages. In 1945 Wright published an autobiographical novel entitled **Black Boy**. It was also a best seller and established Wright's reputation as America's leading black writer. The basic theme in Wright's early novels was the black man's struggle to maintain human dignity against such great odds as racial prejudice, job discrimination, and political disfranchisement. Wright was an angry man who was bitter and critical of the social and legal injustices blacks experienced in America.

Disenchanted with his native country, Wright and his family moved to France in 1946 where he continued to write. None of his later works, however, equaled the quality and popularity of his earlier novels. On November 28, 1960, Wright died of a heart attack in Paris, France.

Eudora Welty (1909–   )

Mississippi's distinguished woman of letters, Eudora Welty, was born in Jackson, Mississippi. Welty has spent most of her life within Mississippi which is the setting for most of her novels and short stories. Unlike Faulkner's Mississippi, "a place of violent men and desperate struggle," Welty's Mississippi is "a tidy, protected little world" where people live their lives in relative tranquility.

Eudora Welty

This does not mean that Welty does not deal with the struggles and conflicts of the human heart. It only means that Welty treats them in a different way. Her characters are set in more serene circumstances and they respond to the human struggle in a more gentle and less desperate way. But like Faulkner, Welty places great emphasis upon place and family in her novels and short stories.

Welty is a popular lecturer and has held several visiting professorships at major universities in America and England. In addition to numerous other awards for her fiction, Welty received a Pulitzer Prize in 1973 for her novel, **The Optimist's Daughter.**

Tennessee Williams (1910–   )

One of America's most successful playwrights, Tennessee Williams, was born in Columbus and spent much of his childhood visiting his grandparents in Clarksdale. Many of his best plays have Mississippi or Southern settings. His characters speak a language and have manners that clearly reflect the Mississippi influence and background of his early youth. Among his most successful Broadway hits are **A Streetcar Named Desire, The Glass Menagerie**, and **Cat on a Hot Tin Roof.**

A central theme in many of Williams' plays is the deceit and greed of mankind and the certainty of retribution for those weaknesses. In addition to the New York Drama Critic's Award, Williams has also been awarded a Pulitzer Prize.

Other Major Writers

It is difficult to determine precisely who should be included in a list of other major writers and who should be excluded. It is difficult first of all, because good literature is a matter of taste and preference. Some readers who prefer a certain kind of reading material have their favorite authors and others who like a different kind of reading matter have theirs. Secondly, it is difficult to distinguish among Mississippi authors because there are so many writers who have been recognized and rewarded by literary critics. The following list of authors is selected largely on the basis of common agreement among scholars and critics who rank them among Mississippi's most outstanding writers.

Harris Dickson (1868–1952)

Born in Yazoo City, Harris Dickson served for several years as city judge of Vicksburg where he was known for his enforcement of strict and stiff penalties. A versatile writer, Dickson was the most popular Mississippi author from 1900–1925. In addition to romantic novels and short stories about southern belles, Dickson also wrote about various public issues for major national magazines.

Walter Malone (1860–1915)

This DeSoto County poet published ten volumes of poetry. He is probably best known for his poem, **"De Soto,"** which is believed to be the longest poem in the English language except for **"Beowulf"** and **"Farie Queen."** Walter Malone is also the uncle of two famous Mississippi scholars, Kemp and Dumas Malone.

William Alexander Percy

William Alexander Percy (1885–1942)

Although he is best known for his autobiography, **Lanterns On the Levee** (1941), this distinguished Greenville writer also published several volumes of poetry including **In April Once** (1920) and **Sappho In Leukas and Other Poems** (1924).

Stark Young (1881–1963)

The sudden appearance of numerous southern writers in the 1920's and 1930's is called the Southern Renascence. Stark Young of Como is considered one of the most important writers in that Renascence. **So Red the Rose,** which Young published in 1934, is considered one of the three best Civil War novels in American fiction. For many years Stark Young was one of America's foremost literary critics. At various times during his career he wrote for **The Theatre Arts Monthly, The New Republic,** and the **New York Times.**

Harry Harrison Kroll (1888–   )

One of the state's most prolific writers, Kroll published sixteen novels most of which have a Mississippi setting.

Ben Ames Williams (1889–1953)

Born in Macon, Williams' first major novel, **All the Brothers Were Valiant** (1919), dealt with a seafaring family of New England. In later years, Williams wrote several Civil War novels. **House Divided** (1947) ranks with **So Red the Rose** and **Gone With the Wind,** among America's best and most popular Civil War novels. Williams wrote a total of 32 books and edited two.

Cid Ricketts Sumner (1890–1970)

A native of Brookhaven, Sumner wrote several novels about her hometown. Her most successful novel, **Quality,** was the basis for the movie, **Pinky.** She is best known as the author of the Tammy books.

Maxwell Bodenheim (1892–1954)

The author of thirteen novels, nine volumes of poetry, and one book of memoirs, Bodenheim was born in Hermanville. As a young man he was a highly regarded author, but wrote very little during his later life. When he was murdered in Greenwich Village in New York City in 1954, he was hardly remembered as an author.

John Falkner (1901–1963)

Although he is overshadowed by the eminence of his more famous brother, William, John Falkner was a distinguished novelist in his own right. His **Men Working** (1941) and **Dollar Cotton** (1942) rank among Mississippi's finest fiction.

James Street (1903–1954)

One of Mississippi's most widely read authors was James Street of Lumberton. One of his novels, **Tap Roots** (1942), was about the legendary "Free State of Jones" and was made into a popular movie. In his later years Street wrote two religious novels, **The Gauntlet** (1949) and **The High Calling** (1951) dealing with the life of a minister.

Shelby Foote (1916–   )

One of the most prominent of the famous authors from Greenville is Shelby Foote. After publishing several successful novels, Foote devoted the next few years to the writing of his popular and respected three volume history of the Civil War. Foote, who now lives in Memphis, is a popular lecturer at literary conferences and universities.

Thomas Hal Phillips (1922–   )

Between 1950 and 1970, Thomas Hal Phillips of Corinth wrote five novels and several short stories. Phillips received several awards for his writings including a Fulbright and Guggenheim Fellowship and the Eugene F. Saxton Memorial Award. Phillips, who served as Public Service Commissioner in the Northern District from 1960 to 1963, now lives in Hollywood and writes television and movie scripts.

Jonathan Henderson Brooks (1904–1945)

Born in Lexington and educated at Tougaloo College, Jackson State University, and Union Theological Seminary, Brooks dedicated most of his early life to his ministerial duties. Brooks described himself as "a black poet who ploughs the whole day long and burns the midnight oil for a song." In his poetry there is classic beauty and quiet strength. He was a deeply religious man with much of the mystic in him. A collection of Brooks' poems, **The Resurrection and Other Poems,** was published after his death.

Charles Bell (1916–   )

One literary critic has said that Charles Bell of Greenville does for Mississippi in poetry what Faulkner did in novels, Eudora Welty does in short stories, and Tennessee Williams does in drama. Growing up in Greenville, Bell became a close friend and protégé of William Alexander Percy. His poetry has appeared in many national periodicals. In 1953 he published his first book of poems, **Songs of a New America.** Many of these poems deal with moral and philosophical topics and social issues. **Delta Return,** a book of poems about Bell's childhood experiences in the Mississippi Delta, was published in 1956.

David Cohn (1896–1960)

Another of the Greenville authors, David Cohn's books covered a wide range of topics. He wrote about the influence of the automobile on American society, the technological revolution in American agriculture, and the mail-order sales technique of

Sears, Roebuck, and Co. He also wrote a humorous and perceptive account of life in the Delta entitled **Where I Was Born and Raised.** At the time of his death, Cohn left a 700-page autobiography which has not yet been published.

Hodding Carter

Hodding Carter (1907–1972)

Although Hodding Carter was not born in Mississippi, he spent most of his adult life in Greenville where he edited the **Delta Democrat Times.** Carter was an important and influential journalist who frequently criticized Mississippi's tradition of racial discrimination. For his editorials condemning the violence of the Ku Klux Klan, Carter was awarded the Pulitzer Prize for journalism in 1946. In addition to his editorial achievements, Carter also won recognition for his other publications. **The Lower Mississippi** (1942) and **Man and the River,** (1970) are acknowledged as two of the best books about this great river.

Walker Percy (1916–   )

Although born in Alabama, Walker Percy moved to Greenville after his parents died. He grew up in the home of his cousin, William Alexander Percy. Walker Percy earned a medical degree but ill-health prevented his active practice of medicine and he devoted his attention to writing. In 1962 his novel, **The Moviegoer**, won the National Book Award for fiction.

Margaret Walker Alexander

Margaret Walker Alexander (1915–   )

This internationally renowned author was born in Birmingham, Alabama, but spent most of her teaching career at Jackson State University. She has received the Yale Award for Younger Poets, a Ford Fellowship, and a Houghton Mifflin Fellowship. Although she was first recognized and rewarded as a poet, Margaret Walker Alexander is best known for her novel, **Jubilee,** the story of the author's great-grandmother. Alexander recently retired as professor of English and director of the Institute for the study of History, Life and Culture of Black People at Jackson State University.

Ellen Douglas (1921–   )

This seventh-generation Mississippian was writing poetry and sketches at the age of nine. She was born in Natchez but moved to Greenville after her marriage to Kenneth Haxton, Jr. Her novel, **A Family's Affair,** won the Houghton Mifflin Award and was listed as one of the five best novels in 1961 by the **New York Times. Apostles of Light,** which she published in 1973, was nominated for the National Book Award. Her latest novel, **The Rock Cried Out** (1979), has received excellent reviews from literary critics and scholars.

Elizabeth Spencer (1921–   )

Born in Carrollton and educated at Belhaven College and Vanderbilt University, Elizabeth Spencer published her first major novel when she was twenty-seven years old. **Fire in the**

Morning was listed in the **New York Times** book review section as one of the three best novels published in 1948. While serving on the faculty at the University of Mississippi, Spencer published **This Crooked Way,** in 1952. She received a Guggenheim Fellowship in 1953 and spent two years in Italy researching for her novel, **The Light in the Piazza,** published in 1960. The popularity of this novel broadened Spencer's reading audience and almost guaranteed the success of her later novels and short stories. Her most recent novel, **The Voice at the Back Door,** which has a Southern setting and theme, won the Rosenthal Award of the National Institute of Arts and Letters.

Robert Canzonari (1925–   )

This versatile writer of prose, poetry, and non-fiction was born in Clinton. He was educated at Mississippi College and Stanford University and presently is on the faculty of Ohio State University. In 1968 he published **Watch Me Pass,** a book of poetry. During the next two years he published his first novel, **Men With Little Hammers** (1969), an account of life in a small southern college town, and a volume of short stories, **Barbed Wire** (1970). Canzonari, a cousin of Governor Ross Barnett, also wrote a perceptive account of the social and racial struggles in Mississippi during the 1960's entitled **I Do So Politely** (1965).

Willie Morris (1934–   )

A descendent of Cowles Mead, a territorial official, Willie Morris was born in Yazoo City, After graduating from college in Texas Morris moved to New York to pursue a career in journalism. For several years he was editor of **Harper's Magazine,** one of the nation's prestigious journals. While living in New York, Morris wrote a very popular autobiography, **North Toward Home** (1967). After the integration of Mississippi's public school system Morris returned to his hometown to study the conditions of the schools in Yazoo City. The findings of that study were published in 1971 entitled **Yazoo.** This sympathetic and optimistic account of the Yazoo City school system concluded that integration would succeed if adults did not interfere with the young people who could more easily adjust to the new circumstances. Morris has published or edited several other books and during the spring semester of 1980 he was guest lecturer in Southern literature at the University of Mississippi.

Barry Hannah (1943–   )

Mississippi's most recent writer of prominence is Barry Hannah of Clinton. His novel, **Geronimo Rex** (1972), was well-received by critics and the reading public as well. He is professor of English at the University of Alabama and continues to produce fictional works of high calibre. Hannah's collection of short stories, **Airships,** won the 1979 Gold Medal from the American Academy of Arts and Sciences.

Leronne Bennett (1928–   )

One of Mississippi's most prominent and influential black writers is Leronne Bennett, editor of **Ebony Magazine.** Bennett was born in Clarksdale, attended Lanier High School in Jackson, and graduated from Morehouse College in Atlanta, Georgia. In addition to his editorship of **Ebony,** Bennett has published several books concerning the black struggle for legal and social justice in America. Bennett also wrote a biography of Martin Luther King, **What Manner of Man** (1965).

Editors, Journalists, Scholars

In addition to the long list of creative writers of prose and poetry, Mississippi has also produced an impressive array of literary critics, editors, journalists, and scholars. The following discussion includes only the best known of these writers, but others are included in the longer list accompanying the literary map.

Henry Mitchell Brickell (1898–1952)

A native of Senatobia, Brickell is Mississippi's most famous literary critic and is considered by many as one of America's major critics of the twentieth century. Brickell was literary editor of the **New York Evening Post** from 1923 to 1928 and editor of Henry, Holt, and Co. from 1928 to 1933. From 1940 to 1946 Brickell was editor of the O. Henry Memorial Award for outstanding short stories. This award was named in honor of one of America's great short story writers. The O. Henry Award was established by a Mississippian, Blanche Cotton Williams, while he was teaching literature at Columbia University in New York City. In addition to his editorial duties, Brickell also lectured frequently at workshops, seminars, and conferences for young writers.

Turner Catledge (1901–   )

A native of Choctaw County and a graduate of Mississippi State University, Turner Catledge worked his way up in the field of journalism from part-time printer of the **Neshoba Democrat** of Philadelphia, Mississippi, to executive editor and vice-president of the **New York Times.** In his autobiography, **My Life and The Times,** Catledge compared the simple hand-operated press at the Neshoba Democrat with the huge printing machine used at the **New York Times:**

> I'd feed papers through the old press [at the **Neshoba Democrat**] at a rate of about five hundred an hour, then turn them over and put the other side through. I once tried to calculate how long it would take to print our Sunday **New York Times,** with its several hundred pages and circulation of over a million, on the old press. My estimate was about one hundred and sixty-five years.

Other Journalists and Scholars

In addition to the prominent editors already discussed, several others merit special mention. Two Mississippi journalists won Pulitzer Prizes during the 1960's for their editorials dealing with civil rights. Ira Harkey, editor of the **Pascagoula Chronicle,** won the award in 1963, and Hazel Brannon Smith, editor of the **Lexington Advertiser,** received the award in 1964.

One of Mississippi's most widely read authors is Craig Claiborne. In addition to serving as food editor of the **New York**

Times, Claiborne has published several cookbooks and also writes a syndicated column which appears in newspapers throughout the country. Another Mississippian, Dero Saunders of Starkville, edited the popular and influential business journal, **Fortune.**

Among the major scholars who were either born in Mississippi or spent a large part of their academic careers in Mississippi are Kemp Malone, the Chaucer critic, and his brother Dumas Malone, an historian and biographer of Thomas Jefferson. David Donald, a native of Goodman and a graduate of Millsaps College, received a Pulitzer Prize for his biography of Charles Sumner in 1961. P. L. Rainwater, James W. Garner, Thomas Clark, James W. Silver, Glover Moore, and Richard A. McLemore are just a few of the many distinguished historians and scholars Mississippi can claim.

Folklore and Folk Traditions

Mississippi's literary heritage is enriched by the folk tales, legends, ballads, spirituals, riddles, home remedies, recipes, and other oral traditions which have survived down through the years. These stories and traditions are known as folklore. Mississippi's folklore is especially rich and diversified.

Musical Traditions

Some of the old slave spirituals were kept alive and new ones were written by black chain gangs working on railroads, highways, or plantations. Some of the spirituals gave way to the new forms of gospel music which became very popular in both black and white churches.

Another musical tradition which is still popular in Mississippi's rural areas is sacred harp singing. This singing style enabled people who could not read the words of a song to sing the notes of the musical scale. Special song books, which identify the scale through the use of shaped notes, are still being published and are used in sacred harp singing conventions.

B. B. King

The Blues

Against a backdrop of poverty and hopelessness and to the accompaniment of the diddley bow and cane fife, the blues was born in the Mississippi Delta. Black sharecroppers and day laborers put new English words to old African melodies. They sang about their troubles and their hard times and gave birth to the blues. The blues was a musical link to their African heritage. Mississippi's first blues singer to achieve national recognition was William L. C. Broonzy. Born in Scott on June 26, 1893, "Big Bill" Broonzy was one of 21 children. After World War I, Broonzy moved to Chicago and began making records for Paramount Records. He did much to popularize the blues and was a great hit in London and Paris during his world tour following World War II.

Other famous Mississippi blues singers included Robert Johnson, "Son" House, "Mississippi" John Hurt, and W. C. Handy who lived for many years at Clarksdale before moving to Memphis where he made Beale Street famous throughout the world with his "Beale Street Blues."

Chicago also became a center of blues music. But much of the Chicago blues music was about Mississippi and many of the finest musicians were from Mississippi. Some of the famous Chicago blues singers from Mississippi were John Lee Hooker, Muddy Waters, Houlin' Wolf, Bo Diddley, and perhaps the greatest of them all, B. B. King.

Folktales and Legends

The story of the "Free State of Jones" is a good example of how folklore originates. There was some factual basis for the stories that Jones County tried to secede from the Confederacy. But as the story of "The Free State of Jones" was told and retold, the element of truth in the story was gradually overshadowed by the fictional additions that each storyteller added. Another example of folklore is the legend of Sullivan's Hollow. The way some folks tell it, Smith County was the scene of a long-running family feud among the Sullivan clan. Legend has it that large scale bootlegging operations, and wide-spread lawlessness made Sullivan's Hollow unsafe for outsiders in general and revenue agents in particular. But in reality Smith County was probably not any more dangerous than most other rural counties. These folktales and legends are often based on fact. However, the details are expanded by imaginative storytellers who usually add something each time they retell the story. Over the years, a simple story about a brave man can become the saga of a dashing hero.

Among Mississippi's most famous folk heroes are Steamboat Bill and Casey Jones. Steamboat Bill was a riverboat pilot who tried to beat the speed record set by the **Robert E. Lee** in a race from Vicksburg to New Orleans. In his effort to break that record, Steamboat Bill put too much strain on his steam engine and the boiler blew up. According to a popular folk ballad which appeared soon after Steamboat Bill's adventure, a crew member named John Henry, was killed. However, John Henry must have made a miraculous recovery, because he appears later as the hero in several ballads about railroad building in the Delta.

The other folk hero, Casey Jones, died in the famous train wreck at Vaughn on April 30, 1900. Casey was heading South on the Illinois Central line. When he came into Vaughn his train was traveling so fast that he could not stop in time to avoid hitting the rear of a freight train that was pulling off the main line onto a side track. When the collision occurred, Casey Jones was killed and his fireman, a black man named Frank Webb, was injured. Soon after the wreck, Wallace Saunders, a worker at the Illinois Central station in Canton who knew both

Jones and Webb, composed a ballad about Casey, his fireman, and the fatal collision. The ballad was sung throughout America and Casey Jones became a national folk hero.

Lamar Fontaine—Super Spy or Super Liar

When Lamar Fontaine was invited to speak before the Mississippi House of Representatives, a local newspaper called him "Mississippi's greatest living celebrity." Fontaine's fame was originally established by his daring exploits as a Confederate spy who slipped through General Grant's lines to take percussion caps to the Confederate soldiers who were under seige in Vicksburg. After the war, Fontaine wrote a book about his adventures. In addition to being a Confederate spy, he claimed that he had traveled over a thousand miles and had lived for some time with an Indian tribe before he was ten years old. By the time he was thirty, he claimed that he had (1) spent a winter in Greenland where the temperature dropped to 90° below zero; (2) crossed the Sahara desert where he experienced daytime temperatures of 170°; (3) fought in the Crimean War and had been decorated for bravery by the Czar of Russia; (4) lived in the Himalayas Mountains of India and was made a Buddhist priest; (5) walked along the Great Wall of China for a distance of 250 miles; (6) served with Commodore Matthew Perry when Japan opened its doors to western trade; (7) climbed the tallest pyramid in Egypt; (8) camped at Mt. Sinai; (9) bathed in the Dead Sea; (10) walked the streets of Jerusalem; and, (11) explored the ruins of the ancient Incas in South America.

When the Civil War began, Fontaine volunteered his services and joined the Mississippi Rifles at Jackson. Although the early exploits claimed by Fontaine cannot be verified, his role as a Confederate spy is factual. For his valuable service to the Confederacy, he was awarded the Confederate States of America Congressional Medal of Honor by the Sons of Confederate Veterans. Although this honor was deserving, it does not settle the basic question about Fontaine—was he a super spy or a super liar. Maybe he was both.

Collection and Preservation of Folklore

The technological revolution caused by World War II has brought radio, television, telephones, and other communication forms to the most remote areas of the South and Mississippi. Illiteracy is being reduced and fewer people now depend upon oral traditions than ever before. Already, much of Mississippi's folklore has been lost. But, because of the foresight of several collectors and the continuing work carried on by the Mississippi Folklore Society, much of Mississippi's folklore has been preserved. The pioneers in this work were John Avery Lomax (1867–1948), who is considered by many as America's foremost folklorist, and Arthur Palmer Hudson (1892–1978). Hudson and Lomax, and his son Alan Lomax, saved thousands of songs, ballads, anecdotes, legends, and folktales from obscurity. The Mississippi Folklore Society, originally established in 1927 by Arthur Palmer Hudson, was revived under the leadership of George Boswell and Ovid Vickers in 1966. Since 1967 the Society has published a journal, **Mississippi Folklore Register,** which contains articles on folklore and folk culture.

Most of the state colleges and universities have established some kind of center or museum for the collection and display of Mississippi's cultural artifacts. Perhaps through a combined effort among local historical societies, academic institutions, and public schools we can preserve the rich treasures of our cultural heritage. The Mississippi Department of Archives and History has an historic preservation department which coordinates this kind of work. Also, federal funds are sometimes available for the collection and preservation of folklore, artifacts, and historic bulidings.

Creative Arts

Although Mississippi artists and performers have not achieved the prominence of the state's literary figures, they have brought fame to themselves and to our state.

Art Festivals

In 1911 the Mississippi Art Association arranged the first public exhibition of Mississippi artists at the annual State Fair.

Since that time art exhibits have become very popular in Mississippi and the state's artists, as well as world famous artists, have exhibited their works throughout the state. Many local art festivals and exhibits are now held annually in cities, at universities, and even in small towns. Art festivals and craft shows are also held in conjunction with the opening of antebellum homes in those towns that sponsor annual pilgrimages.

In 1965 the United States Congress created the National Endowment for the Arts and made federal funds available to promote the development of art in America. The Mississippi Arts Commission distributes these funds to artists and art organizations throughout the state. Under the leadership of this Commission, art extravaganzas are held each year in Mississippi.

Allison's Wells Art Colony

Much of the credit for Mississippi's recent artistic achievement can be traced to the art colony established at Allison's Wells resort hotel near Canton. John and Hosford Fontaine who owned the hotel, Marie Hull, Ralph Hudson, chairman of the art department at Mississippi State College for Women, Karl and Mildred Wolfe, and other Mississippi artists organized this art colony in 1948. Until the hotel burned in 1962, Mississippi artists met each summer for a workshop conducted by internationally famous artists who discussed artistic techniques and styles. After 1962, the art colony was first moved to Stafford Springs, near Meridian, and then later to Utica where it is continued under the name of Mississippi Art Workshops.

Mississippi Arts Center/Russell C. Davis Planetarium

In 1927 Thomas Gale donated his home on North State Street to the city of Jackson to be used as a Municipal Art Gallery and to provide headquarters for the Mississippi Art Association. The M.A.A. still maintains a collection at the Gallery and sponsors several exhibits there each year. However, in 1977 a new art gallery and planetarium were built on Pascagoula Street. This spacious new facility is the home of the Jackson Ballet,

OPERA/SOUTH, Mississippi Opera Association, Jackson Symphony Orchestra, and the Mississippi Art Association.

In addition to these galleries in Jackson, many other galleries and museums of art are located in Mississippi cities and at the state's colleges and universities.

Theora Hamblett

One of Mississippi's best known painters of recent years is Theora Hamblett of Oxford. Ms. Hamblett is the only Mississippi painter whose works are exhibited in the Museum of Modern Art in New York. This remarkable artist did not begin painting until she was sixty years old. Her paintings were done in an artistic style known as primitive art. Although Theora Hamblett's active career was relatively short, she produced a significant number of paintings. The ideas and themes for her paintings came to her in dreams or visions.

Marie Hull with one of her students, Malcom Norwood.

Marie Hull

Known for her landscapes and still life, Marie Hull is probably Mississippi's most prolific and influential painter. She is acknowledged as the "dean" of Mississippi artists. Her active artistic career has spanned more than seventy years and she continues to paint at the age of ninety-two. During most of her career, Marie Hull gave private lessons to young artists in her home for the sum of $2.00 a lesson.

387

Karl and Mildred Wolfe

Karl and Mildred Wolfe

Few people have done more to make art a part of life in Mississippi than Karl and Mildred Wolfe. Not only were they instrumental in establishing the art colony at Allisons Wells, they have contributed over the years some of Mississippi's finest art. In addition to painting, they also produce sculpture and stained glass.

Walter Anderson

Before his death in 1965, Walter Anderson of Ocean Springs, had received little attention as an artist. After he died, however, his family discovered over 7,000 water colors which Anderson had painted but had kept from public view. The discovery of these paintings, in addition to the thousands of ink drawings, murals, and illustrations, have established Anderson as one of Mississippi's most accomplished artists and certainly one of the state's most prolific painters.

Other Artists

Among the state's other accomplished artists are William Hollingsworth, whose promising career was ended by his death in 1944; Andrew Bucci and Caroline Compton of Vicksburg; Marshall Bouldin III, the Delta artist whose portraits have been highly acclaimed; William Steene of Ocean Springs; Homer Casteel, Jr. and Fred Mitchell of Meridian; Malcom Norwood, Lallah Perry, and Mary Anne Ross of Cleveland; Millicent Howell of Philadelphia, Sam Gore of Clinton, Bill Dunlap, a member of the art faculty at Memphis State University; Glennray Tutor and Jere Allen of Oxford; and the "Summit Three," Bess Dawson, Ruth Holmes, and Halcyone Barnes of Summit who usually exhibit their works together.

Sculpture and Ceramics

The list of Mississippi artists who work in art forms other than painting has been growing in recent years. Among the state's best known sculptors are Joseph Barras of Jackson, Richard Boathe of Bay St. Louis, and Leon Koury of Greenville who is best known for his busts of William Faulkner and Hodding Carter. Other highly regarded sculptors include Walter Anderson of Ocean Springs, Fay Jones of Pass Christian, Katherine Speed of Jackson, James Seawright, and William Anderson who was on the faculty of Alcorn State University for several years.

Ceramics is one of the most popular and fastest-growing art forms in Mississippi. Lee and Pup McCarty of Merigold have demonstrated the artistic beauty and grace which can be achieved in this art form. George Alsup and Joe Woodward have also produced outstanding ceramic pieces and are among the state's best known ceramic artists.

Performing Arts

A list of Mississippi's performing artists, especially in the field of music, reads like a "Who's Who" in the world of entertainment. The Mississippi performers are noteworthy not only because of their number, but also because of the variety of musical fields in which they have won distinction.

The King

Elvis Presley, the man who changed the sound, the style, and the beat of American music, was born in Tupelo. Before he hit the big-time with his appearance on the Ed Sullivan television program, Elvis played in high school gyms and night clubs throughout north Mississippi. His death in 1977 ended one of the most fabulous and successful careers in the history of entertainment.

The Father of Hillbilly Music

One of the most popular musical styles in America is country and western which was known in its early years as "hillbilly music." The man who did more to popularize this musical style than any other performer was Jimmy Rodgers, the "Singing Brakeman" of Meridian. His songs, which were very popular during the depression years of the 1930's, were about railroads, poverty, and broken hearts. He had enormous influence on both country and western musicians as well as blues performers. His highest tribute came in 1961, when he became the first person to be inducted into the Country Music Hall of Fame.

Charley Pride

The most popular country and western black artist in America today is Charley Pride who was born and reared in Sledge, Mississippi.

William Grant Still

Composers

Mississippi has produced two nationally acclaimed composers. William Grant Still, who was born on a plantation near Woodville, was one of America's premier black composers. In 1933, he wrote "Afro-American Symphony," the first major composition by an American black to be played by a white orchestra before a white audience. In addition to this and other symphonies, Still also composed several opera and ballets. In 1936 he conducted the Los Angeles Philharmonic Orchestra in concert at the Hollywood Bowl.

Mississippi's other notable composer was Lehman Engel of Jackson. Engel composed and conducted the musical scores for many Broadway hits including **A Streetcar Named Desire** and **Wonderful Town.** In 1957 he wrote **Playing and Producing a Musical Show,** a guide for local theatre groups.

Leontyne Price —:returned to her native state in 1980 to sing the national anthem at Governor William Winter's inauguration.

Leontyne Price

In her debut with the Metropolitan Opera Company, in which she starred as Leonora in "Il Trovatore," Leontyne Price received a forty-two minute ovation. This great prima donna, who was born and reared in Laurel, has been acclaimed in the United States and Europe as a star of the first magnitude. Perhaps the highest of many honors bestowed upon Ms. Price was her selection to open the new Metropolitan Opera in 1966 at Lincoln Center in New York. She sang the lead role in "Anthony and Cleopatra," an opera composed especially for her by Samuel Barber.

Jackson Symphony Orchestra

Since its organization in 1944, the Jackson Symphony Orchestra has provided Mississippi music lovers with outstanding performances combining both local and nationally known musicians. Under the leadership of Louis Dalvit, the Jackson Symphony has achieved Metropolitan status, the highest rank accorded to local symphony groups.

Mississippi Opera Guild

Originally established under the name of Jackson Opera Guild in 1945, the Mississippi Opera Guild was one of only twelve such organizations in the United States at the time of its formation. The first opera produced under the sponsorship of the Guild was performed in the Bailey Junior High School auditorium. The purpose of the Guild is to serve as a support group for the Mississippi Opera Association in the promotion and production of opera performances in Mississippi.

OPERA/SOUTH

In 1971 OPERA/SOUTH, sponsored by the traditionally black colleges and the Mississippi Inter-Collegiate Opera Guild, was established in Jackson. The purposes of OPERA/SOUTH was to bridge the gap between the classroom and the stage by allowing students to work in a professional opera company. In addition, OPERA/SOUTH would provide young Americans, and particularly blacks, an opportunity to develop their professional skills and it would attract new audiences who had never attended opera performances before. Since its founding, performances at OPERA/SOUTH have been reviewed and acclaimed by newspapers, magazines, and professional journals throughout America and Europe.

Jackson Ballet Guild

The Jackson Ballet Guild, founded in 1964, is the supportive arm of the Jackson Ballet and the Jackson School of Ballet. Its purpose is to promote the development of a professional company which will provide classical ballet instruction for young Mississippi dancers. In the spring and summer of 1979 Jackson was briefly the ballet capital of the world. In addition to the appearance of Mikhail Baryshnikov, one of the world's great dancers, an international ballet competition attracted young dancers from all over the world to Jackson.

Other Performing Artists

Among the many Mississippians who achieved fame as singers, musicians, and actors are John Alexander and Andrew Gainey of the Metropolitan Opera Company; Bud Scott, a jazz musician from Natchez who played for Presidents William McKinley, Theodore Roosevelt, and William Howard Taft; Bobby Gentry, who composed and sang **"Ode to Billy Joe"**; the distinguished actors, Dana Andrews, Stella Stevens, and James Earl Jones, who portrayed Alex Haley in **"Roots,"** the most popular television program in history.

Some Mississippi writers, artists, and entertainers have not been mentioned in this chapter simply because there are too many to be covered in a general discussion of the creative and performing arts. This discussion should, however, make you aware of the enormous contribution Mississippians have made to the cultural enrichment of our nation.

A. KEY TERMS—Explain the following terms. If necessary, use a dictionary or encyclopedia.

1. Pulitzer Prize
2. Nobel Prize
3. novel
4. short story
5. Yoknapatawpha County
6. playwright
7. folklore
8. the Blues
9. B. B. King
10. "Big Bill" Broonzy
11. W. C. Handy
12. "Free State of Jones"
13. Sullivan's Hollow
14. Casey Jones
15. Arthur Palmer Hudson
16. Allison's Wells Art Colony
17. Mississippi Arts Center
18. Theora Hamblet
19. Marie Hull
20. Karl and Mildred Wolfe
21 sculpture
22. ceramics
23. Walter Anderson
24. OPERA/SOUTH

B. MATCHING AUTHORS WITH THEIR WORKS

1. William Faulkner
2. Richard Wright
3. Eudora Welty
4. Tennessee Williams
5. William Alexander Percy
6. Stark Young
7. Cid Ricketts Sumner
8. James Street
9. Shelby Foote
10. David Cohn
11. Hodding Carter
12. Margaret Walker Alexander
13. Ellen Douglas
14. Elizabeth Spencer
15. Robert Canzonari
16. Willie Morris
17. Barry Hannah
18. Leronne Bennett
19. Turner Catledge
20. Walker Percy

a. *The Glass Menagerie*
b. *So Red the Rose*
c. *Tap Roots*
d. *Absalom, Absalom!*
e. *The Civil War*
f. *Where I Was Born and Raised*
g. *The Optimist's Daughter*
h. *Quality*
i. *Lanterns on the Levee*
j. *Black Bay*
k. *Jubilee*
l. *I Do So Politely*
m. *The Lower Mississippi*
n. *Geronimo Rex*
o. *Apostles of Light*
p. *The Voice at the Back Door*
q. *What Manner of Man*
r. *My Life and the Times*
s. *North Toward Home*
t. *The Moviegoer*

C. MATCH THE FOLLOWING:

1. Elvis Presley	a.	"Afro-American Symphony" '
2. Jimmie Rodgers	b.	wrote music for *A Streetcar*
3. Charley Pride		*Named Desire*
4. William Grant Still	c.	Metropolitan Opera Star
5. Lehman Engel	d.	wrote "Ode to Billy Joe"
6. Leontyne Price	e.	Father of Hillbilly music
7. Bobby Gentry	f.	famous black country recording star
	g.	The King

D. WRITING ASSIGNMENT

1. Find out if your community has ever been the setting for a short story, or book, or movie. If so write a brief report about the author and the story.
2. Is there a famous writer, artist, or performer from your community? If so, write a brief report about the local celebrity.
3. Explain why you think Mississippi has produced so many great and famous writers.

GOVERNORS OF MISSISSIPPI
Mississippi Territory, 1798–1817

Winthrop Sargent — May 7, 1798 to May 25, 1801.
William C. C. Claiborne — May 26, 1801 to March 1, 1805.
Robert Williams — March 1, 1805 to March 7, 1809.
David Holmes — March 7, 1809 to December 10, 1817.

STATE OF MISSISSIPPI SINCE 1817

1. David Holmes
   Dec. 10, 1817 to Jan. 5, 1820
2. George Poindexter
   Jan. 5, 1820 to Jan. 7, 1822
3. Walter Leake
   Jan. 7, 1822 to Nov. 17, 1825
4. Gerard C. Brandon
   Nov. 17, 1825 to Jan. 7, 1826
5. David Holmes
   Jan. 7, 1826 to July 25, 1826
6. Gerard C. Brandon
   July 25, 1826 to Jan. 9, 1832
7. Abram M. Scott
   Jan. 9, 1832 to June 12, 1833
8. Charles Lynch
   June 12, 1833 to Nov. 20, 1833
9. Hiram C. Runnels
   Nov. 20, 1833 to Nov. 20, 1835
10. John A. Quitman
    Dec. 3, 1835 to Jan. 7, 1836
11. Charles Lynch
    Jan. 7, 1836 to Jan. 8, 1838
12. Alexander G. McNutt
    Jan. 8, 1838 to Jan. 10, 1842
13. Tilghman M. Tucker
    Jan. 10, 1842 to Jan. 10, 1844
14. Albert C. Brown
    Jan. 10, 1844 to Jan. 10, 1848
15. Joseph M. Matthews
    Jan. 10, 1848 to Jan. 10, 1850
16. John A. Quitman
    Jan. 10, 1850 to Feb. 3, 1851
17. John I. Guion
    Feb. 3, 1851 to Nov. 4, 1851

18. James Whitfield
    Nov. 24, 1851 to Jan. 10, 1852
19. Henry S. Foote
    Jan. 10, 1852 to Jan. 5, 1854
20. John J. Pettus
    Jan. 5, 1854 to Jan. 10, 1854
21. John J. McRae
    Jan. 10, 1854 to Nov. 16, 1857
22. William McWillie
    Nov. 16, 1857 to Nov. 21, 1859
23. John J. Pettus
    Nov. 21, 1859 to Nov. 16, 1863
24. Charles Clark
    Nov. 16, 1863 to May 22, 1865
25. William L. Sharkey
    June 16, 1865 to Oct. 16, 1865
26. Benjamin G. Humphreys
    Oct. 16, 1865 to June 15, 1868
27. Adelbert Ames
    June 15, 1868 to March 10, 1870
28. James L. Alcorn
    March 10, 1870 to Nov. 30, 1871
29. Ridgley C. Powers
    Nov. 30, 1871 to Jan. 4, 1874
30. Adelbert Ames
    Jan. 4, 1874 to March 29, 1876
31. John M. Stone
    March 29, 1876 to Jan. 29, 1882
32. Robert Lowry
    Jan. 29, 1882 to Jan. 13, 1890
33. John M. Stone
    Jan. 13, 1890 to Jan. 20, 1896

34. Anselm J. McLaurin
    Jan. 20, 1896 to Jan. 16, 1900
35. Andrew H. Longino
    Jan. 16, 1900 to Jan. 19, 1904
36. James Kimble Vardaman
    Jan. 19, 1904 to Jan. 21, 1908
37. Edmund Favor Noel
    Jan. 21, 1908 to Jan. 16, 1912
38. Earl LeRoy Brewer
    Jan. 16, 1912 to Jan. 18, 1916
39. Theodore Gilmore Bilbo
    Jan. 18, 1916 to Jan. 20, 1920
40. Lee Maurice Russell
    Jan. 20, 1920 to Jan. 22, 1924
41. Henry Lewis Whitfield
    Jan. 22, 1924 to March 18, 1927
42. Dennis Murphree
    March 18, 1927 to Jan. 17, 1928
43. Theodore Gilmore Bilbo
    Jan. 17, 1928 to Jan. 19, 1932
44. Martin Sennett Conner
    Jan. 19, 1932 to Jan. 21, 1936
45. Hugh L. White
    Jan. 21, 1936 to Jan. 16, 1940

46. Paul B. Johnson, Sr.
    Jan. 16, 1940 to Dec. 26, 1943
47. Dennis Murphree
    Dec. 26, 1943 to Jan. 18, 1944
48. Thomas L. Bailey
    Jan. 18, 1944 to Nov. 2. 1946
49. Fielding L. Wright
    Nov. 2, 1946 to Jan. 22, 1948
50. Fielding L. Wright
    Jan. 22, 1948 to Jan. 22, 1952
51. Hugh L. White
    Jan. 22, 1952 to Jan. 17, 1956
52. J. P. Coleman
    Jan. 17, 1956 to Jan. 19, 1960
53. Ross R. Barnett
    Jan. 19, 1960 to Jan. 19, 1964
54. Paul B. Johnson, Jr.
    Jan. 21, 1964 to Jan. 16, 1968
55. John Bell Williams
    Jan. 16, 1968 to Jan. 18, 1972
56. William Lowe Waller
    Jan. 18, 1972 to Jan. 20, 1976
57. Cliff Finch
    Jan. 20, 1976 to Jan. 22, 1980
58. William Winter
    Jan. 22, 1980—

Acknowledgements

There are many people who were very helpful at various stages in the preparation of this textbook and I wish to acknowledge their assistance. Dr. Janet Ford, Department of Sociology and Anthropology, University of Mississippi, read the chapter on Mississippi Indians; Dr. Cleveland Donald, Director of Black Studies at the University of Mississippi, read the section on slavery; Penny Haws, Chairperson of the Department of English and David Chandler, Social Studies teacher, at Oxford Junior High School read the manuscript in its early draft; John Perry Sansing read the chapters on recent Mississippi history; Mr. Conan Doyle Hawkins and Lucie Bridgforth read the entire manuscript. All of these people made valuable suggestions to improve the textbook. I wish to thank Dianne Ferguson and Betty Stubblefield, my student secretaries, who typed most of the manuscript and Betty Galloway who also typed portions of the manuscript.

The staff of the Mississippi Department of Archives and History, especially Jo Ann Bomar, were of great assistance in the selection of photographs which appear on pages, 20, 56, 62, 63, 72, 83, 97, 107, 114, 122, 130, 131, 133, 147, 163, 189, 191, 201, 210, 216, 218, 220, 230, 233, 236, 251, 256, 258, 259, 261, 268, 270, 277, 278, 280, 286, 289, 291, 295, 300, 308, 310, 320, 334, 340, 348, 357, 369, 371, 373, 376, 377, 382, 387, 388, and 390.

I would also like to acknowledge the following photographic credits: Melba and Chip Bowman, 17; Library of Congress, 34, 184; Smithsonian Institution, 36, 39, 40, 45, 52; Illinois State Historical Society, 61; Franklin L. Riley, *School History of Mississippi*, 95, 103, 154, 213; Charles Sydnor and Claude Bennett, *Mississippi History,* 99; William Hogan and Edwin Davis, *William Johnson's Natchez* (LSU Press, 1951), 161; Mississippi State Highway Department, 239; Professor Russell Barrett, 315; Dr. Clyde Strickland, 356; Mrs. H.D. Worthy, 147; the Mississippi Secretary of State, 22; Constance Webb, *Richard Wright, A Biography* (Putnam, 1968), 370; the Mississippi Research and Development Center, 25, 27, 347, 358; Bob Pickett, for the cover photograph; and Ms. Jane Baker, 348.

For their assistance in various other ways, I wish to thank Dr. Frederick Laurenzo, Paul Burch, Gene Threadgill, Dr. John Guice, Holt McMullen, Nicey Sullivan Lewis, Michael Logue, Dr. Claude Fike, Chancellor Porter L. Fortune, Jr., Dr. Jack Gunn, Dr. John E. Gonzales, Dr. Martha Bigelow, and Dr. and Mrs. Verner S. Holmes, Sr.

I would like to express my appreciation to Mr. W.E. Rosenfelt, Editor-in-Chief of T.S. Denison and Co. for his encouragement and guidance. Without him and his support this book could not have become a reality.

David G. Sansing

Index

(Preceding the page number, c stands for chart, m stands for map, and p stands for photo or drawing.)

401

Johnson, Paul B., Jr., 319-321,
(p 320)
Johnson, Paul B., Sr., 298
Johnson, William, 161, (p 161)
Johnston, Albert Sidney, 174
Johnston, Joseph E., 182, 184, 186,
189
Joliet, Louis, 59-60
Jones, Laurence, 357, (p 268)
Judicial branch, 363
Junior colleges, 355-356, (p 355,
m 356)

—K—

Kansas-Nebraska Bill, 166
Kearney, Belle, 276, (p 277)
Keelboats, 98-99, (p 100)
Kentucky Arks, 85, 98
Kentucky Triangle, 85-86, (m 86)
King, B.B., 382, (p 382)
Knight, Newton, 192
Know Mississippi Better train, 279
Koroa Indians, 48
Kroll, Harry Harrison, 373
Ku Klux Klan, 212-213, 275, 303,
322-323

—L—

Labor unions, 303, 343
Lamar, L.Q.C., 228-231, (p 230)
Land claims, 75, 80, 87-88, (m 76)
LaSalle, 60-61, (p 61)
Law, John, 64-65
Lee, Robert E., 168, 185, 189
Legislative branch, 361
Libraries, 352-353
Lincoln, Abraham, 168-169, 197
Livestock, 35, 74, 104, 290, 344-345
Loess Bluffs, 23
Long Hot Summer, 321-323
Longino, Andrew H., 256-260
Loring, William W., 179, 183
Louisiana Purchase, 88-89
Lowry, Robert, 231
Lynch, John Roy, 221, (p 223)

—M—

Malone, Walter, 372
Marquette, Father Jacque, 59-60
Marschalk, Andrew, 106
Mason, Sam, 85
McLaurin, Anselm J., 231-232,
265-266
McLaurin Clan, 232
McLernard, John A., 178, 180
Meredith, James Howard, 304,
315-318, (p 315)
Military installations, 301
Mingos, 39-40
Mississippi: climate, 15; location,
(m 13, 14); size, 5
Mississippi Agricultural and
Mechanical College, see
Mississippi State University
Mississippi and the Mob, 275
Mississippi Arts Center, 386-387
Mississippi Bubble, 64-65, 117-119
Mississippi Colonization Society,
160
Mississippi Company, 64-65
Mississippi Economic Council, 343
Mississippi Opera Guild, 392
Mississippi Plan, 218-219
Mississippi River, 58-62, 85-86
Mississippi State College for
Women, see Mississippi
University for Women
Mississippi State University,
235-236
Mississippi Triumvirate, 229-231,
(p 230)
Mississippi University for
Women, 237
Missouri Compromise of 1820, 126
Montgomery, Isaiah T., 250,
(p 251)
Morris, Willie, 378-379
Municipal government, 364
Murphree, Dennis, 279, 298
Music, 381-382, 389-393

—N—

Nanih Waiya, 43, 53

403

404